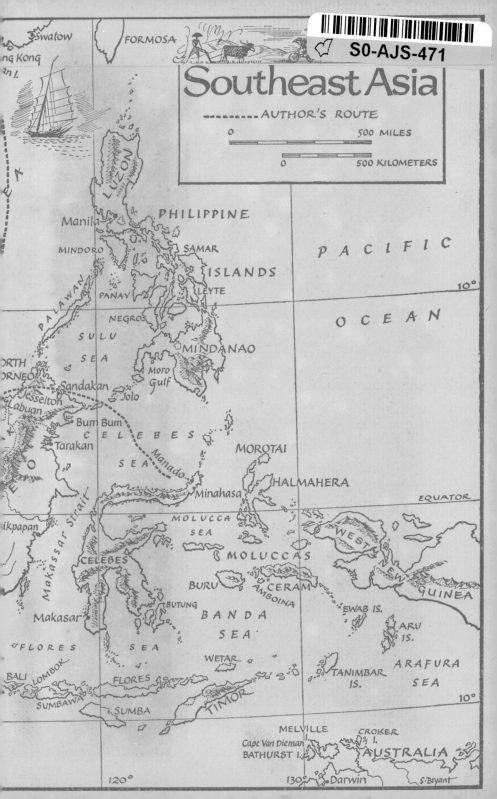

Birds' Nests
in Their Beards

Books by
William Stevenson

The Yellow Wind

Birds' Nests in Their Beards

Birds' Nests
in Their Beards

WILLIAM STEVENSON

illustrated with photographs
by the author

HOUGHTON MIFFLIN COMPANY BOSTON

The Riverside Press Cambridge

1964

First printing

Preface

AFTER SIX YEARS in Hong Kong my family sailed with me to
India. We occupied all the cabins of a small freighter which,
being on its maiden voyage, performed some last-minute speed
trials outside the harbor. For several hours it churned around
the colony. We were in happy despair, unable to escape from
the ship's rails, and yet tortured by repeated views of landmarks
reviving so many memories. There, we said, was the hospital
where Sally, our youngest, was born. There was the fishing
fleet, where our own junk still rocked at its moorings. The
children raced up and down the hot metal deck pointing out the
dear familiar landmarks.

And then Hong Kong lay behind us. My unlucky brush with
the rebels against Sukarno of Indonesia had reached its unfore-
seen climax. We had shed our oriental lives. Or so we told
each other.

Nothing was further from the truth. That night we skirted
the edges of Typhoon Alice. The captain kept us talking in the
lounge until midnight. By then the little ship was tossing wildly,
and as we fought a way back to our quarters we paused to
check the children.

In Sally's cabin the porthole was open and the crib was bare.
I ran out yelling something inappropriate like "Stop the ship!"
Seamen have a way of moving fast; and soon all pandemonium

had broken loose. The captain, a tubby Norwegian with a grand passion for liar's dice and pickled herring, flooded the sea-washed decks with light. Probably a siren wailed. And then, up from the heat of the galley, came the ship's cook to ask in his self-effacing Chinese way if the vessel perhaps was sinking. Asleep in his arms was Sally.

"Why," roared the captain when his sanity had been restored, "did you take the baby below?"

"Baby cry," said the cook. "So I sing baby bye-bye." It was of course a perfectly valid explanation if you happened to be Chinese.

The Orient pursued us to Calcutta, where the Chinese shipping agent came aboard bearing a telegram as if it were a wreath. "Very bad news, missy," he said, handing it to my wife.

"You read it," said Glenys. "It's bound to be something awful like you've been fired."

We had both forgotten that after weathering the storm we radioed Hong Kong asking the fate of the family renting our house. It stood on top of the local mountain, exposed to all winds. I had failed to instruct the new tenants on how to batten it down against typhoons and my conscience had been heavy, at least for a time.

Now I tore open the thin orange envelope and uncreased the gummy message. HOUSE STILL STANDING it said. ALL OCCUPANTS DEAD — I pawed frantically at the smudged last line — FROM EXHAUSTION.

We read it over several times, giggling. The Chinese agent left us cackling like hysterical hens. No doubt the legend was born then that Occidentals always titter in the face of tragedy.

Writing this now in the heart of Africa, I am reminded that the time has gone when you sailed or flew out of one life into another. I have just left a conference of delegates from 64 Afro-

Asian countries dominated by the fact that outside Russia and China the biggest communist party in the world is Indonesian; and that whenever Djakarta sides with Peking the balance of communist power (in terms of sheer weight of numbers) shifts to Asia.

At this point the reader may ask if this is a personal story or a book about politics. The two should not be mixed unless the author commands an authority I lack. I am mixing them, however, because of the unusual events herein described. This is one occasion when a reporter who would prefer anonymity feels obliged to say: "A very odd thing happened to me. I can't explain all of it but just listen a moment —"

This is the story of another Cuba that is likely to negate those sacrifices made during the Asian brushfire wars of the 1950's and early 1960's by the French in Indochina, by the British Commonwealth in Malaya, by Americans in South Vietnam and by all of us in Korea.

This Asian Cuba followed a pattern. First there was poverty and backwardness, for which the West was blamed. Then came a national hero to throw out the alien oppressors. He became the symbol of patriotism so that anyone opposing him was at once a traitor. Thus when the West came to the aid of these "unpatriotic" opponents it allied itself in effect with traitorous forces. Meanwhile the national hero, outraged by this western interference, turned to the Soviet bloc for help in crushing the rebels and by degrees became a political and economic prisoner. Everyone is now familiar with this sequence of events in Cuba. After all, it happened almost within shelling range of Florida.

Indonesia is no less grave a development, but harder to comprehend because it lies so far from us. In many minds it is still a lotus land ruled by Tintiya the Unthinkable and Solitary and

Original God. To many kindly and well-meaning souls it is a former colony, cruelly oppressed for three centuries, now groping for self-discovery as a nation. Few of us can believe that modern Indonesia has its own imperialist aims, disguised by a pretended urge to "liberate" nearby lands, inflamed by communist slogans and fed by our own irresolution — the irresolution that allowed Britain to initiate a military operation in Suez and fail to complete it; that permitted the United States to begin an invasion of Cuba and then withdraw vital air cover. It is associated with a doctrinaire conviction that all white imperialism is wicked and that all Afro-Asian nationalists are inspired lovers of freedom.

It is not necessary to argue that having started an invasion of Egypt, the British should have conquered regardless; that having incited an attack on Cuba, the United States should have won victory at all costs; or that having egged on the rebels of Indonesia, both these old western allies ought to have backed to the hilt an inefficient band of revolutionaries who on at least five occasions hurled death and destruction at Sukarno — and missed.

The reader is only invited to judge if the West should have encouraged the revolution against Sukarno; and if, having meddled clumsily in that unhappy affair, we made ourselves contemptible by competing with Russia to win back Sukarno's favor. No fair judgment can be made on the basis of cold facts alone or of a detached recital of events. It was different when our interference in the affairs of an Asian state was backed up by force. Today force is not by itself enough. The United States Seventh Fleet is the most powerful in history and yet it has not prevented Sukarno from enlarging his Indonesian empire to include west New Guinea. That victory was won in the United Nations.

And so I have tried to give a personal view of human beings as well as their statistical background; a view pretending to no authority but honestly held after what I hope may seem to have been some amusing adventures.

Between 1950 and 1960 Indonesia was part of my journalistic parish. I covered it by frequent travels from Hong Kong, keeping notes on the rebellions that flickered among its eight thousand big and small islands between continental Asia and Australia.

The story begins with the first Afro-Asian conference held in Indonesia in 1955, when my notes record the first indication of an organized militant opposition to Sukarno. It ends eight years later here at the Moshi conference in Africa. Sukarno and his Peking allies have won a kind of moral sanction from Afro-Asians to open a new guerrilla front in Southeast Asia. The guerrillas, trained and equipped in Indonesia, and directed by the Indonesian communist party, staged an uprising at the end of 1962 in a part of British Borneo. Although the revolt was suppressed it revealed a new North Borneo National Army, which is sworn to free this territory for Sukarno. The army was formed to delay and reshape the bold project for a State of Malaysia that would stretch from Malaya through Singapore to Borneo and thus provide a prosperous buffer between communist China and Sukarno's expanding republic. The new Federation came to life, despite communist opposition, in the late summer of 1963.

These notebooks of mine travel full circle, tracing a large-scale revolution which at one time used (uninvited) bases on British territory to threaten Sukarno's empire and which has now, as it were, reversed itself. They reflect the earlier imbecility of dismissing Indonesian military ambitions as a joke. Here for example is Sukarno telling me: "The peoples of Afro-Asia are more than half the human race. We can mobilize that strength and tell the whites never to bully us again." Beside this quotation I scrawled some scoffing remark. . . .

Today the Republic of Indonesia commands the biggest navy

in the Indian Ocean. It includes one of Russia's most modern Sverdlov-class cruisers, so complex a warship that British and American experts were sure Indonesians could never man it. The republic fields the fifth largest army in the world, the third largest communist party, and a growing air force whose modern Russian-designed jets are flown by young Indonesians trained on communist bases in defiance of western sneers ("Of course these chaps aren't mechanically minded enough to operate sophisticated weapons").

Sukarno can now avenge himself for the humiliations, fancied or real, inflicted on him during the western-supported revolution. Our memories, however, are short; and if he should reach out for the Australian half of New Guinea, attack Portuguese Timor, or make a fresh bid to kill British interests in Malaysia most of us, I expect, will have forgotten why. Already there is western chagrin and ire at the way Sukarno has inherited Dutch colonial rule over 700,000 primitive Papuans, by mixing diplomatic negotiations in the United Nations with a military invasion of west New Guinea, a piece of real estate as big as California.

Is simple revenge the motive for Sukarno's actions today? Since no detached historical review provides a complete answer, nor does one reporter's subjective recollections, I have used research and notes. The sources of this research are given in a bibliography at the end of this book. The notes have been augmented by the memory of conversations and the assistance of Indonesian friends. To identify the friends would be unfair at this time and so this must be my acknowledgment of their invaluable help. They will forgive me, I know, for reconstructing conversations so as to convey the meaning and facts as concisely as possible. My thanks go as well to the *Globe & Mail* of Canada for allowing me so much time to explore a story that yielded few headlines.

I have identified people where discretion allows. Doctor

Sumitro, the professional revolutionary whose idealism was ill-advisedly harnessed to the commercial ambitions of gun-runners; Stephen Garry Bowers, the water-boatman of Borneo who twanged his guitar for Sulu pirates; Police Chief Fairfoul, the Scots guardian of Sandakan's elastic laws; Mister Willi, a rebel courier bobbing up at every rebel rendezvous; and high above this bizarre lot, President Sukarno flitting like some rare tropical bird from one exotic oasis to another.

The airman who worked on bombers attacking Indonesian ports must remain, it will be readily seen, anonymous. Emiria Sounassa, "queen" of west New Guinea, gave me permission to discuss her plight. This talented and wise lady lightened my journeys with such jovial aphorisms as "My husband the sultan and I are both primitive — our palace is in the trees."

Jana deserves her privacy. With the grace and ferocity of a leopard she stalked her prey in the fur-lined jungles of Europe, no less sure of herself than if she were diving naked for pearls in the Java Sea. Like Kipling's cat she walked alone, and all places were the same to her.

There were pirates too numerous to mention by name, as they say in the theater reviews. One of my children, reading this, says that this is the least credible portion of my tale. But I am rescued by a news dispatch dated February 12, 1963, recording that ten pirates are believed drowned and three have been captured after Her Britannic Majesty's destroyer *Barossa* boarded a pirate vessel during the night off Sandakan.

Sandakan. This is where most of my characters assembled at one time or another; a British outpost of empire, a little Borneo town living still in its piratical past, doing a roaring trade in guns and gold, and sheltering those who conspired against the neighboring Indonesian giant.

Inevitably this book implies criticism, and so a final word about myself. I write as an English-born Canadian who has worked and studied happily in the United States. When I write of mistakes "we" made, my viewpoint is an Atlantic one. If the Central Intelligence Agency or American gun-runners seem from this narrative to be blameworthy, none of us in the Commonwealth can afford to gloat. Nor should Americans chuckle at British complacency while Sukarno lit fuses under the Borneo powder-keg.

Such blunders are part of the penalty we pay for being democracies. Indonesia confronts us with a dilemma of our times. Do we interfere decisively in a foreign situation of potential danger to ourselves, using methods of which officially we disapprove? Or do we play the game in accordance with our own rules, knowing that an unsporting enemy will exploit a sense of fair play?

Tocqueville tells us the problem is not new:

> Foreign politics demand scarcely any of those qualities which are peculiar to democracy; they require, on the contrary, that perfect use of almost all those in which it is deficient. . . . A democracy can only with great difficulty regulate the details of an important undertaking, persevere in a fixed design, and work out its execution in spite of serious obstacles. It cannot combine its measures with secrecy or await their consequences with patience.

WILLIAM STEVENSON

Moshi, Tanganyika
February, 1963

Contents

Contents

Illustrations

following page 142

British customs checks smuggled copra from Indonesian
rebel areas after it is landed at Sandakan.

A low-lying and very fast smuggling *kumpit* unloading its
contraband under the flag of the British marine police.

Skipper of a blockade-runner.

Rebel supply vessels.

Air travel in Borneo is informal.

The home of Emiria Sounassa, "Queen" of west New Guinea,
on the outskirts of Djakarta.

MF 275, the rebel blockade-runner.

"Mister Willi," the rebel courier, and author aboard
the blockade-runner.

Captain Ling and his navigator.

A Bugi rebel sailor.

Birds' Nests
in Their Beards

I

The Sweet Smell of Conspiracy

SIX DEGREES above the equator and perched on the eastern shoulder of British Borneo lies the town called Sandakan, which is famed for its birds' nests and cutch. The birds' nests are sold wherever in the world there are Chinese to drink them as soup. The cutch, which is used to tan leather, comes from the mangrove bark of nearby swamps.

Sandakan is conveniently placed for the conduct of its chief industries of smuggling and piracy. It lies under British protection, but it is near to the Indonesian part of Borneo called Kalimantan. When I first went there its lax trading laws attracted, like bees to honey, swarms of small sailing vessels from those parts of Indonesia where President Sukarno's authority descended with a soft languorous touch rather than with the crack of a whip.

The secret presence of anti-Sukarno rebels was never, by common consent, mentioned. Nor, for that matter, was it considered "the proper thing" to discuss the activities of Sukarno's agents. Of paramount importance was the undeniable fact that both sides brought money into this stranded colonial outpost.

The bearded rebels conducted a widespread military campaign against Indonesia's "guided democracy." As late as 1962 they had tried yet again to blow up the president, at a time when their saboteurs were sticking plastic explosives to communist-supplied ships and planes and their guerrillas were skirmishing with the loyalist army.

Sandakan was only one of several foreign bases employed by the rebels when fighting began. What distinguished this little town from others was a slump in its traditional trades. The piracy had fallen off, and smuggling luxury goods to the neighboring Philippines was becoming hazardous. There were some 15,000 Malays and Chinese eking out a perilous living, with a fair sprinkling of Australians and Englishmen, and few of them were opposed to free enterprise. Only their interpretation of the word "free" was more than usually generous. Then came the revolution.

The town responded magnificently with the trigger-quick reactions learned from a buccaneering past. Years ago the harbor had sheltered many a fleet of heavily armed marauders, sometimes as many as 200 sail, cruising these waters and terrorizing merchantmen as far away as the Bay of Bengal. Then more respectable pirates moved in. The harbor became an anchorage for Her Majesty Queen Victoria's men-o'-war. Adventurers and dreamers like James Brooke, the first White Rajah, built wooden houses on teakwood stilts in the perfumed swamps of Sandakan Bay. Behind the façade they conducted a lively trade in guns.

Little today has changed. The wooden houses still keep an air of dignity and reserve. Hats and gloves must be worn by ladies at the Queen's Birthday Parade. There is cricket on Sunday mornings. Each year comes a Christmas Message from the governor. The colony's annual report is chiefly concerned with the state of the timber trade and mentions in passing the inexplicable disappearance of a Shell oil tanker or a piratical raid in which "the culprits took to their heels in the direction of Indonesia."

Even the budget gracefully conceals the sources of prosperity.

"The barter trade" provides the citizenry with its means of livelihood. If you look more closely, you may notice what a remarkably large income is derived from the re-export of raw materials (a disarming euphemism for goods smuggled out of Indonesian rebel areas). There is a handsome yield from taxes levied by customs on such goods; nearly $10 million in 1960 for example out of total revenues of almost $20 million.

There is nothing in the official records, visible at least to the naked and untutored eye, to show by what unorthodox means Sandakan recovered from the slaughter of 1945, when defeated troops of Japan's thirty-second Southern Army razed the town and machine-gunned its fleeing inhabitants. Nothing marks the spot where men claiming to represent the United States Central Intelligence Agency disappeared, or were kidnapped, or at any rate played their awkward part in a discreditable western performance. The intrigues that swirled around Sandakan achieved the fury of a tropic storm, but without the thunder. When they again reached a climax the winds were all blowing in an entirely different direction. What began as an anticommunist crusade ended in a guerrilla war against Britain.

I flew to Sandakan in 1958 after seeing an advertisement in the *South China Morning Post*. This is a formidable newspaper crammed with official news, rather like an oriental Court Circular, and it appears daily in Hong Kong.

The advertisement said:

EDIBLE BIRDS' NESTS

Tenders are invited
for the sale of
Birds' Nests, either
Black or White.
Particulars from
Forestry Conservator,
Sandakan, N. Borneo.

How, I wondered, did you sell birds' nests? Stick a bamboo pole through them and wander from house to house like a Belgian onion seller? Were black nests better than white ones? Who collected them and why?

A few inquiries revealed that a profitable and lively trade in birds' nests was being conducted between a dwindling number of suppliers and an expanding market. The best nests had come from parts of China and North Vietnam now under communist rule. Red China had stopped the export of birds' nests, presumably to annoy the gourmets on Formosa. Worse still, the State Purchasing Agency in Peking was madly buying up birds' nests from foreign sources. As one threadbare Nationalist Chinese general expressed it: "They can't bombard us into surrender so they're trying to starve us out."

From as far afield as the old Annamite palace at Hué, the imperial kitchens in Tokyo, and an emigré Yunnanese restaurant beside the railroad tracks in downtown Taipeh, the information rolled in. All of it pointed to Sandakan as the salvation of non-communist connoisseurs of birds' nest soup. Clearly this was enough to warrant a journalistic expedition. But Borneo was a thousand miles south of Hong Kong and I would need to collect some other assignments to justify the travel expenses alone.

The trouble was that Borneo did not interest the outside world. The Canadian Broadcasting Corporation, whose correspondent in the Far East I had been for some time, thought the women's programs could use something on nests and how to cook them. But Borneo itself? Well, wild men came from there but they weren't terribly interesting politically.

There is a certain cosiness to life in Asia. People are far less provincial in their mental habits, perhaps because there is so much traffic between the big centers. Flying is much more routine, for example, and birds of passage are constantly zooming into Hong Kong or Singapore with twigs of gossip from Bangkok or Tokyo. A person can make himself quickly up to date on scandals as far afield even as Peking.

Somehow Borneo had kept off this grapevine. Nobody had much to say about the island, one of the world's greatest, five times the size of England and Wales together. In all the post-war years of wars and riots east of Suez, nothing had ever happened in Borneo to merit the world's attention. It was simply a big lump of mountains and jungle where, I thought, nothing ever would happen. Still there were a few hints of coming trouble. China had suddenly and ominously discovered historical links with the island. Other overpopulated neighbors were eying it hungrily too. In the end I justified a visit on the grounds that I needed background on this territory. Its sprawling empty jungles must some day draw the desperate Asian giants greedily seeking more living space for their fecund millions.

I flew as far as Labuan in a Cathay Pacific Electra. It was the airline's local milkrun, a four-hour flight over the flat blue calm of the South China Sea. We landed and I braced myself for the normal irritations of airport formalities. But Labuan was more like a small provincial railway station in England, a sort of Asian whistle-stop. Here were no leathery men with stens slung across their shoulders, thrusting their fingers like bony antennae into your bags bloated with dirty laundry. Only a barrel-chested furry Yorkshireman named Raby guarded the gates. He played the roles of immigration officer, director of customs and fire chief, and he was obviously delighted that anyone should visit his island.

Labuan was a free port, six miles off the northwest coast of Borneo, and it had a Victorian fustiness about it which was totally misleading. But this I had yet to discover. On the first visit, it struck me as the most stagnant of backwaters. Even buying an onward ticket to Sandakan was like catching the local commuter's special — a kind of oriental Titfield Thunderbolt. You had to tap on a wooden shutter and eventually it was lifted by a man in a striped shirt and suspenders who was clearly surprised that you should wish to travel away from here at all. There were blazing flame-of-the-forest trees around the airstrip and gorgeous rhododendrons behind the hangars. Someone who looked astonishingly like an English stationmaster was examining the flowerbeds. And, unbelievably, there was the name of the station spelled out in the flaming red colors of dwarf phlox, rooted in a field of sweet alyssum whose white flowers are known wherever Englishmen go out in the noonday sun as madwort.

The plane to Sandakan was just as disarming. It was an old biplane with struts and wires between the wings and two tiny cowled motors that bubbled and squeaked like steam kettles. Five of us got in, squatting in bucket seats behind the pilot, a big Australian with headphones cozied in outside earmuffs. He looked archaic but professional, a Buddha-like shape looming above us at the top of the steeply sloping fuselage floor, linked by mysterious wires and tubes to his vibrating machine.

We flew slowly above the seas of green jungle, buffeted by hot winds. I opened a copy of the *North Borneo News and Sabah Times* and read that Mr. Justice Rogers in his six-seater railcar had collided with a boulder at Mile 73 outside the capital of Jesselton. The headline across the top of the back page announced BRUNEI BILL, ANN CLAPHAM UP, SLAMS BIG FIELD, which turned out to be a horse race. "There was some dismay at the start," the *Times* noted, "when two riders were found in an awkward position, facing the wrong way."

I peeked through the shuddering window, or perhaps porthole is a more descriptive word, and tried to imagine what kind of Europeans lived in the tiny settlements fringing this unexplored land. In the whole of Borneo there were only three million people. In the British territories, comparable in size to all of Ireland, there were fewer than half a million. The hinterland was a tangle of hills and mountains. Even Mr. Justice Rogers on his railcar could not have traveled far into them. There were only 116 miles of railway in the entire country.

We floated onto the grass airfield at Sandakan and I took a small taxi into town, driving along a smooth winding road through rubber plantations and sleepy thatch-roofed villages. The town had a remarkably prosperous air about it, for no obvious reason. The Sulu Sea stretched away below us, innocent of the smoke smudges that stain the waters of busier ports. The harbor was a silver mirror, unblemished by iron ships. The concrete buildings clustered along the main waterfront were functional in design and spankingly new. The rest of the town stretched voluptuously into the folds of the green hills, or straggled along the salt marshes in a series of wooden settlements like sun-bleached flotsam left by the tide.

There was a sweet stale smell that clung to the crooked sloping streets and filtered back into the rain forests. The smell had a sickly familiarity and would have provided the clue to Sandakan's affluence, if I had recognized it.

I stayed in a cheap Chinese hotel — Sun Kwong Lung's, "made of permanent materials" — opposite the Jolly Movie House. Notices on the bedroom walls warned the unwary traveler against Indonesian navy patrols off Bum Bum. I wondered why anyone should care.

The local guidebook informed me that birds' nests were an important item of trade. "They are excellent," it said, "as an aphrodisiac, having special properties that make men . . . men, and all women divine." An advertiser recommended, as a simple alternative, Doctor Yapp's Masculine Pills for Lasting Strength and Happiness. There was a testimonial from a distinguished British peer (at least his name was on it): "After a short course of your pills, I am fully restored to vigor and my wife, the Lady ——, is now pregnant."

Was this the secret of Sandakan's prosperity? All over Asia, perhaps, there were rich old men eagerly awaiting fresh consignments of birds' nests and Doctor Yapp's invigorating pills. Were nests and pills sent out in plain wrappers? I stood at my tiny bedroom window, looking down into the paved streets crowded with Chinese and Malays, trying to read a guilty knowledge on their faces. They all looked quite normal and virtuous, if not virginal.

I went along to the biggest dealer in birds' nests, Mr. Thaihong Hang. The warehouse was musty and dark inside. It was jammed with coiled ropes, pots and pans, canned fish, dried herrings, kerosene stoves, nets, celluloid ducks, fountain pens and columns of toilet rolls. Suspended from the high rafters, cupped one inside another and strung together, were the birds' nests. Several Chinese sat before a blackboard, listening to a swarthy dark-skinned man in battledress who stopped abruptly as I stumbled through the gloom. Chairs were hurriedly scraped back. The audience dissolved like dying wisps of ectoplasm.

"Thai-hong?" I asked. "Is he here?"

The man in battledress said roughly, "I am Mister Willi. You deal with me."

So quite unsuspectingly I asked about the birds' nests.

Looking back, one sees how lunatic the following two days were. Mister Willi was a squat, bullnecked Indonesian rebel whose comrades were fighting on the island of Celebes about 400 miles away. Unknowingly I had interrupted his instructions to ships' masters waiting to sneak past patrolling Indonesian warships with supplies for the beleaguered garrisons.

Mister Willi for his part listened with polite disbelief while

I explained my journalistic interest in birds' nests. He found it hard to believe that I had come all this way on such an errand and expected that I would eventually get around to the true purpose of my visit. The situation was very oriental, Mister Willi promising to get in touch with me next day.

He did, through Jana. She turned up soon after breakfast, a graceful woman whose age was hard to judge, but whose hard-muscled body fitted well in a bright yellow blouse and black skirt. She was dressed less for a fashion show than for a trek in the jungle. This, I quickly discovered, was exactly what she had in mind — a trip by boat across Sandakan Bay and a hard nine-mile walk through jungle to the Guomontang Caves. It was in these caves that the edible nests were "cultivated." Jana said the expedition was all laid on. We were to meet Mister Willi near one of the slipways. She carried an army haversack and seemed alarmingly brisk and efficient.

In my innocence I was delighted that Mister Willi had gone to so much trouble. It was not altogether surprising. There is a natural friendliness and courtesy in the quiet corners of the East, where the stranger is made welcome and people will go to remarkable lengths to be kind. As we walked down to where Mister Willi waited with the boat, I asked Jana about him.

"We are both Christians from Celebes," she said, brusquely shutting off further questions. The fact that she came from Celebes explained her tawny skin and lithe figure, but I could not understand her reference to being a Christian. It seemed irrelevant to her work for Thai-hong Hang, import-export merchant of Sandakan. Much later I realized that in Celebes it was an important distinction.

The day passed pleasantly enough. The caves were deep inside a hill, at the end of dark echoing tunnels. In the lower cave were the black nests made of feathers bonded with the saliva of swiftlets. These were cheaper because they had to be sent to Hong Kong for cleaning. The more expensive white nests were in an upper cave. These were made of pure mucin that hardened on exposure. The white nests were almost immediately edible. You softened them in hot water and later boiled them in a meat broth for five hours. Then the meat was removed and the mixture left to simmer for two more hours. The nests were selling in Singapore for $280 a pound.

There were thousands of bats in the cave, their soft wings fanning the stagnant air in our faces while we moved blindly over the icy rock. A match spluttered as Mister Willi lit a candle and stuck it on a damp boulder.

"Sometimes half a million nests are taken from here in one year," said Jana. "It is very sad." I could barely see her face in the tiny yellow glow from the dancing candle flame. "The men come here three times in the year. They have ladders hanging from the walls, waiting. The ladders are made from cane and they rot easily. It is dangerous work and the men must work quickly. They tip the nests like this, one after another. Soon the ground is covered in broken eggs and dying chicks." She was crouching beside the candle, her eyes large and luminous. "Sometimes the ladders break and the men are killed," she said with something like relish in her voice. Mister Willi shifted uneasily. "Let us eat," he said. Jana unbuttoned the haversack and pulled out sandwiches and a coffee flask. "It makes a bloody mess when the men get killed," she said.

We left the caves at sunset just as the bats flew out and the swiftlets swarmed in, forming two black columns that smudged the orange sky.

Back at the hotel I was amused to find that my bags had been examined. Nothing was missing. It was a typically noisy Chinese hotel. You could hear the endless broadcast of a Cantonese opera through the paper-thin walls, and the clatter of mah-jongg tiles. With so much commotion anyone could have slipped into my room. But when you ruled out theft, it was hard to think why anyone should.

I decided to take a stroll outside. In the hotel corridors, late-arriving travelers were already dossing down on temporary cots shrouded in mosquito nets. I walked through the bar-restaurant, which provided the only exit to the street. It was open on one side so that you could sit and drink beer with your noodles and watch the passing parade. The calendars on the wall portrayed Chinese actresses with grotesque bosoms. A jute box wailed. Two girls chattered over the top of a transistor radio. The Cantonese opera played on, and on . . .

There was the vaguely familiar odor again. Opium? No. The sickly-sweet smell came from a wooden jetty beyond the movie house. I walked over. The jetty extended beyond the street lights, vanishing into a darkness that rustled with secret harbor noises. There was a small ketch tied up alongside the distant wharf. Light streamed from its wheelhouse, splashing the sides of a concrete wall. The shadows of men were flung against the wall; shadows that moved in two directions: tall and straight toward the ketch, bent and humpbacked coming back. When I was near enough to hear the ship's generators, I saw that the men were unloading heavy sacks.

A voice beside me said: "Would you join me in a drink?" I turned around, startled. It was Mister Willi. He was wearing a beret and looked rakish and continental.

"That's very kind of you. I was —"

"Taking a breath of air?"

"Yes."

"Then you must have a *gin-pahit* with me." Skillfully, he steered me back to Sun Kwong Lung's. "I hope you were not

disappointed today?" He had taken me to a corner of the restaurant and sat regarding me with mournful eyes from across the
marbled surface of a small table. Behind him on the peeling
yellow walls, the pale pinkish geckoes tut-tutted away like tiny
disapproving dragons.

"No. I thought it was a very useful day. In fact I think I
can take the plane out tomorrow with a clear conscience. I've
got all I need."

He seemed dismayed. "But you have hardly seen Sandakan.
Is it so very small, you can only spend one day in it?"

"Well — it's not exactly the Berlin crisis, is it?" I smiled,
anxious not to hurt his feelings, hurrying on. "I'd love to spend
longer but my newspaper —"

"You really are a newspaperman." He said this as if there had
been a doubt which was now cleared up. He ordered another
drink. "We thought you might have some other business with
us." And then he told me about the Pemerintah Revolusioner
Republik Indonesia — the PRRI.

When he had finished, I said, "Should you be telling me all
this?"

"Yes. We know a good deal more about you than we did
when you first came to us yesterday. We need to tell the outside world about our struggle. We can only do this through
trusted journalists."

I was vague about the whole thing. Everyone knew, of course,
that regional military commanders in Indonesia were up in arms
against President Sukarno. A revolutionary government had
been proclaimed with prominent men in the rebel cabinet. From
the way Mister Willi talked, a guerrilla war was getting underway to destroy a procommunist regime. But I was far from
convinced that Sukarno was taking the republic toward communism. And there was something glib in the way Mister Willi
rattled off his story. He looked too sleek and fleshy for a man

suffering for a cause. He smoked an expensive brand of American cigarette and his hungry eyes followed the sensuous movements of the little prostitutes parading their haunted, chalk-white Chinese faces under the naked ceiling lights, walking back and forth between the tables, rattling bangles and conscious of Mister Willi's eyes rolling in his head.

"What are your people doing here in Sandakan?" I asked him.

His hand flickered up to his face, and he stroked his tiny clipped mustache with slender nervous fingers. "It is a base. To finance the revolution, we have to sell raw materials to the outside world. From here we keep in touch with the rebel areas. I cannot tell you more."

"Yet you wanted me to stay longer here?"

"Yes." He hesitated. "Some important people were coming. You would have met them. They would be able to speak to you more freely."

I said again that it was necessary to leave next day. I expressed a polite interest in his revolution.

"Then you would, perhaps, be willing to go to Celebes? In one of our vessels?" He searched my face hopefully.

"And probably lose my head? No thank you." I prepared to go. Mister Willi put a restraining hand on my arm.

"Could you find time to see Doctor Sumitro?"

There was a small silence broken by the tut-tutting of the geckoes. I had never heard of Doctor Sumitro but the name intrigued me.

"Yes. Okay. I'll see him. But where? And when?"

Mister Willi's face wrinkled with relief. He took off his beret and laid it upside down between us. I recognized it as an old British Army commando's hat. "He will see you in Singapore," said Mister Willi. "Next week."

We sat talking late into the night after that, Mister Willi

blunting my growing curiosity with irrelevant chatter. I tottered off to the airstrip soon after dawn. There was a fresh breeze blowing off the sea and small sailing craft scudded across the harbor. As we circled slowly for altitude I speculated about the cargoes in the little boats below us. Sandakan did not look half so innocent now. In fact the more I looked down upon it, the more the town began to assume a positively sinister aspect. I decided it was the effect of too many *gin-pahits*. Still, one thing was fixed in my memory: the curious haunting quality of that sickly-sweet smell. And I found myself wondering what other business Mister Willi had supposed I might have with the man who sold birds' nests.

2

Island of Noisome Vapors

IF MISTER WILLI, from his remote outpost in British Borneo, could arrange a meeting with Doctor Sumitro of the Indonesian revolutionary government within twenty-four hours of accidentally bumping into me, the rebels must be well organized. Some inquiries in the colony's capital of Jesselton seemed to be indicated, if only to find out more about this seemingly soporific corner of the globe.

On the Jesselton plane was an assistant public prosecutor, a Chinese lady named Miss Li. She had just conducted her first murder trial. "I felt terrible when we all had to stand up in the court while the judge pronounced sentence of death," she said, her gold-rimmed spectacles flashing. "Now I've got another case coming up. Sixteen Indonesians charged with murder. A racial thing. We'll have to fly thirty witnesses to the hearing. It'll cost Government something like 30,000 pounds to give them a fair trial. And the poor fellows don't even understand what we're doing for them."

She supposed that although ten thousand Indonesians a year crossed the border into the colony, mostly by sea, racial conflict was not a tremendous problem. "Look at me. I'm Chinese. My forefathers came here from central China. There was a time when Borneo came within the Chinese empire overseas . . . Nan Yang. Now it's just part of the melting pot."

Was it normal for a woman — a Chinese — to hold such a responsible position as hers? She shrugged. "The British have been working like mad to help us stand on our own feet. Training people like me, finding us jobs. I studied law in London." She giggled. "And then I fell under an Irishman's influence. Brendan Behan. The playwright. No, I never met him but I've never forgotten something he wrote." She quoted: "I respect kindness to human beings first of all, and kindness to animals. I don't respect the law; I have a total irreverence for anything connected with society except that which makes the road safer, the beer stronger, the food cheaper and old men and women warmer in the winter, and happier in the summer."

She glanced out at the steaming carpet of jungle beneath us. "Isn't that terrible — preaching disrespect of the law? But I often think of it. Especially if I seem to be forgetting that the people in the dock are only human, like ourselves," said Miss Li.

The law courts of London had left their imprint on Miss Li, just as her forebears had left their mark on Borneo centuries earlier. We talked of Chinese explorers. "Yes," she said, "I've seen Chinese beads dug up near the mouth of the Sarawak River that were three thousand years old. There are Chinese coins in the museum dating back to 200 B.C., brought here by Cantonese merchants."

Did this mean that China might someday revive its traditional interest in the island? The new communist regime in Peking had claimed so many bits of adjacent territory. Miss Li shot me a quick appraising look. "I would think," she said carefully, "that it might become a race between Indonesia and Peking." Later, in Jesselton, I asked her about the rebels. "I wouldn't trust any of them," she said firmly. "They could switch sides without turning a hair."

The capital had the unreal flavor of a European community

imposed upon a gaudier tropical landscape. Thirty years before, a British district officer named Oscar Cook had noted that "life for the white people runs along more or less accepted European lines. There are always tennis, bridge and poker; there is the Club to be visited daily; there is the routine of 'calling' and tea-parties. It is different in a rural district where the officer is generally alone in hourly contact with natives. Sometimes for months he may not meet another white man nor hear English spoken. The place creeps into his being and he learns the native superstitions and thinks and feels from their point of view."

Times had changed little. There were the few solitary Englishmen steeped in local lore and there were the Club-men and their wives. Two distinct groups. The wives, on the whole, seemed intent upon preserving an Edwardian pattern of existence. One was tempted to wonder if the news had yet reached them of the Bolshevik uprising in Russia.

A lot of harsher things have been said about the wives of the empire-builders; that they were insufferable snobs; that they created the color bars and destroyed the good will and happy race relations built by their men. The women in this category, however, are the most readily perceived by itinerant novelists, who generally favor this view. The women who helped run the rubber plantations and the estates, naturally, are seldom seen. They are brusque and masculine, and they have had to raise families and manage affairs while their men were absent chasing bandits or fighting wars. They are not the type to decorate the cocktail bars.

Miss Li was not exactly a pioneer. But she had the qualities of the frontierswoman with the same passionate loyalty to simple ideals that, in her case, crystallized around the Union Jack. She wanted me to appreciate just what Britain and the West would lose if Borneo fell into the wrong hands.

She dug up the first detailed account of the island, written in the seventeenth century by the English seafarer Captain Daniel Beekman: "Borneo lies on the North of Java and on the East of Sumatra, and off the Peninsula of Malacca . . . in length 700 miles, in breadth 480, and in circuit about 2000. It is counted the biggest Island, not only in the Indian Sea, but in the whole World, except perhaps California [*sic*] in the South Sea."

Captain Beekman did not know about the bigger island further eastward of New Guinea, his measurements were not very accurate, and his knowledge of other parts of the world was sketchy. But his description of the scenery is still valid: "The Country looks like a Forest, being full of prodigious tall Trees, between which is nothing but vast swamps of Mud. At high Water you may sail in a great way among these Trees in several places, but at low Water it is all Mud, upon which the Sun (especially in the Equinox) darting his scorching Beams perpendicularly, raises noisome Vapours, Fogs, etc. which afterwards turn into most violent Showers."

Miss Li had a friend, an elderly Welshman, who wanted me to get the full flavor of the noisome vapors by exploring around Jesselton. I had some time to kill awaiting editorial reaction to my request to meet Doctor Sumitro in Singapore, and I spent some informative hours in the company of this man whose mind skipped and danced around the notion that Borneo ought to be incorporated within a new Commonwealth in which the United States would be a partner.

"Can't you see it?" he kept asking. "We'd have the fresh stimulation of American ideas. You Canadians would play the diplomatic role because everyone trusts you. And the British would continue withdrawing from their colonies without having to hand them over to Russia and China." He quoted the case of Borneo. Once the British vacated their part, it would be grabbed by others. "Probably by the Philippines," said my

Welshman. "Now if America brought the Philippines into association with us, there'd be no fighting *there*. And nobody else'd dare move in."

There was no question that Borneo must seem a tempting prize. Its huge kidney shape was strategically placed across the equator, with a heavily indented coastline of 3000 miles offering any number of small beachheads for compact amphibious forces. The larger Indonesian part was washed by the Java and Celebes Seas, south and east. Along the west coast and northern tip were the three British territories of North Borneo, Sarawak and the oil-rich Delaware-size sultanate of Brunei.

Some plan to bring British Borneo safely into alliance with trustworthy friends was clearly a responsibility that the colonial power owed to the Dyaks who now formed only about one-third of the population. The great island was still theirs. The name Dyak had been applied indiscriminately by the Dutch to all non-Moslem natives, and they had been divided ever since into two groups — the Land Dyaks and the Sea Dyaks. The former lived mostly on dry land. They were armed with seven-foot blowguns and lances and they seldom wore much else than loincloths of beaten bark and sometimes headdresses of magnificent hornbill plumes. One old chieftain showed me the only piece of mechanism his people had: a tinderbox with a piston by which he compressed air to blow up sparks from a piece of smoldering tow. With this he could set fire to the impenetrable vegetation, clearing soil for cultivation.

The Sea Dyaks were in general fearful of the sea, and lived on the rivers. These great waterways have always been the sole means of inland communication. This is more clearly understandable from the air, when it becomes apparent that although the hills and mountains of Borneo are not high, they present an irregular confusion of ranges and deep winding valleys.

Few of the rivers were navigable beyond the first hundred

miles, and any other form of travel was exhausting. You could hack your way inland from the windless sweltering coastal swamps but it was a gloomy and killing experience. Men blazed a trail with the all-purpose *parang*, used both as a tool and a weapon. Above them, admitting little air and less sunlight, stretched a roof of jungle vegetation suspended on trees rising as much as 200 feet. Trapped between a suffocating mattress below and an oppressive upper story of jungle, your optimism dissolved like a tablet of Alka-Seltzer in your own sweat.

And yet the first explorers were of all things optimists. They told tall tales of hidden riches in this rugged hostile island. The reality was that the island lacked mineral wealth. It lacked the active volcanoes of nearby Java and Sumatra to enrich the soil. Even the trade and monsoon winds never penetrated far inland. Perhaps Borneo's greatest virtue was that it suffered only an average of four earthquakes a year, compared with 55 in Java.

"You get the feeling that nature has put Borneo in a pigeon-hole," said the Welshman. "Some day it'll be dusted down and made to support the big population it deserves."

We were going to a festival known as the Bathing of the Gusi. It took place in a longhouse, supported on stilts, with goats tethered beneath. We climbed the wooden steps into a four-foot wide passage extending down the center of the longhouse for about a hundred feet. A platform ran down one side of the passage, and on the other were family rooms from which cooking smoke rose lazily to the latticed roof.

The *Gusi* were earthern jars of immense value — so valuable that no single family could afford to possess one. The jars were set down one side of the passage, and opposite them squatted young men and women. Each man rested his hands in those of the woman next door, and each man held an egg.

There was nothing that I could see to account for the great

value of the jars apart from the fact that they were the only physical remains of certain human beings. Or so it was believed. The *Gusi* were dead ancestors expatiating their sins and their broken pledges in the form of lifeless jars. They had been handed down through the generations, acquiring a romantic sanctity. The *Gusi* were tended by priestesses, all without exception old but amiable hags.

The festival, lit by resin torches, lasted for several hours to the tireless accompaniment of beating gongs and dancing feet. Only the men with eggs in their hands squatted in silence.

Some of the really big Dyak longhouses boasted of wonderfully elastic "dancing floors" made of wooden strips cunningly curved and interwoven. After a skinful of rice wine the visitor was likely to give the floor undue credit for fluidity. If, having bounced through a night of drinking and dancing, his head seemed to have parted from its moorings, this was not altogether unlikely. Most of Borneo's indigenous tribes had been headhunters at some time. During the Japanese war they were encouraged to revive the practice. Fresh skulls were added to the smoke-blackened relics hanging under the longhouse eaves. A wartime Japanese director of education, Colonel Isao Kidato, still hangs in one such place — or at least his head does, complete with steel-rimmed spectacles.

The more enemy heads a longhouse displayed, in the old days, the more virile the tribe's menfolk were thought to be. From time to time, when a truce was called, feuding tribes would exchange heads in order to facilitate burial rites. It was quite improper to lay away a headless corpse.

There was a striking similarity between the local tribal customs and those I had once found in the jungles along the Burmese border with China. Life was communal, although individual property was recognized. Men did the hunting;

women tended the gardens and performed the household duties and much of the remaining drudgery. The most valuable items of furniture, apart from hunting equipment and bamboo tubes for drawing water, were heavy bronze gongs and large earthenware pots containing rice alcohol and pickled vegetables. There were more magicians than priests; and spirits controlled the elements instead of a single god. This similarity was not surprising because many of Borneo's indigenous people were thought, in fact, to have come from that part of the world. It was not until much later that the Malays came drifting to the island from Sumatra and Java. Later they spread to the Malay peninsula, and the race became adulterated with Indian and Mongolian blood. The common bonds that link the Malay peoples of Southeast Asia today are the Malay language, which has a kinship with local dialects, and the Muslim religion.

I was pondering this background when a cable arrived in Jesselton from my editors agreeing that I should pursue contact with the Indonesian rebels. It had occurred to me that perhaps the upheaval taking place in Indonesia ought to be seen in the light of earlier Islamic influence, for nine out of ten inhabitants of the republic were Muslims. The decay of western imperialism, the withdrawal of the Europeans, might mean the revival of a powerful Malaysian community.

But too many other influences were at work, I thought, as the plane to Singapore began to climb slowly over the flanks of Mount Kinabulu, at 13,455 feet the highest peak between the Himalayas and New Guinea. The mountain dominated the worshipful tribes living in its shadow and its name was Chinese. Perhaps the British knew what they were doing in restricting migration to these territories. Perhaps, after all, the exodus of white colonialists would only reveal an underlying tangle of disruptive native elements and pressure from new centers of power.

I checked the map. Jesselton was only 600 miles from Manila, where the Philippines government eyed Borneo with an avarice backed by pseudo-legal claims. The capital was 1200 miles from Red China, whose population was bursting to find new pastures. It was 1000 miles from Singapore and the Malayan Federation whose leaders were talking of incorporating these territories within a Malaysian commonwealth; and 1500 miles from Port Darwin, where the Australians were uneasily aware of how the winds of change were blowing, and had no intention of standing idly by.

And to the south, the islands of Indonesia arched in a long, forbidding Islamic crescent.

3

Doctor Sumitro

I CHECKED INTO the Cockpit Hotel in Singapore, where Mister Willi had promised I would receive instructions on how to contact Doctor Sumitro. The room clerk said, "Welcome back," and gave me a letter. It was from my wife. The weather in Hong Kong was getting hot again. The house was springing leaks in the roof. One of our Siamese cats had been killed by a car, and one of the dogs had gone off with a village chow. The children were learning to play cricket from Billy Tingle. I made a mental note to write a piece someday about Billy Tingle's athletic club for Hong Kong's children, and about the proprietor himself, a tiny bouncy man who had been teaching future British taipans how to box since as far back as anyone could remember. I stuffed the letter in a pocket, resolutely stifling a desire to take the next plane home, and followed the barefoot Malay bellboy to my room. My route passed through the bar, once employed by the Japanese as a torture chamber for the British upper classes. The bar was now patronized by a devoted group of correspondents, and I paused to catch up on gossip and quaff a lubricating beer.

By the time I had negotiated this hazard, a middle-aged Dutchman was waiting outside my room. He gravely introduced himself, speaking through a smoldering pipe, handed me a large envelope, and with a fleeting smile withdrew.

Inside the envelope was a booklet labeled THE VOICE OF NEW INDONESIA *printed and published in the Revolutionary Area,* containing military sketch maps and battle reports printed professionally on rice paper. An accompanying note invited me to a suburban address that evening.

I sat for a while, wondering what I was getting into and hoping I could justify all this time and expense. My room was a small air-conditioned cell, depressing at the best of times. I began to worry about my eldest son, Andrew. He was eight years old and inclined to overestimate his prowess as a swimmer. The smaller children followed his example. Had I impressed him sufficiently with the dangers of swimming too far beyond his depth? I snatched up a piece of paper and wrote him a dire warning about sharks and undertows; then a letter to my wife explaining why I still could not predict my date of return. Then, suddenly exasperated with the circumstances that had brought me here, I decided to walk down to the cable office.

Singapore was just as explosive an experience as always. All the senses were battered: by the glare of the sun, by the humid smack of the heat, by the too-vivid vegetation and by the wails and squeaks of the shopkeepers' radios tuned to Malay and Chinese music; by the echoes of frantic political argument in the headlines of newspapers, and by the rich mixture of tropical harbor smells. There are few places in Asia where humanity seems to be in such a continuous state of violent eruption.

Down on Raffles Quay you could see the freighters lining up, bow to stern, waiting to rifle or replenish the free port. For Singapore is nothing more than a huge department store. Beyond the ships were the low purple shapes of Indonesia's nearest islets. There was the usual cosmopolitan parade through the downtown streets. Elderly Chinese in long robes and mandarin slippers tottered along the sidewalks, oblivious of the youngsters in western garb, their hair slicked down or cut in the latest Hollywood style. Malay taxi drivers in khaki shirts, oval black hats jammed on their curly heads, swooped through the streams of little English cars and wobbling bicycles. Young Chinese matrons, in tight sheath dresses slashed to the thigh, chattered at the counters of the big emporiums. In Indian bookshops crammed with titles on every conceivable subject, students peered into volumes they could not afford to buy or searched for pirated Formosan editions of the latest best sellers. Outside the big banks stood the customary Sikh guards.

The reason for Singapore's soaring buildings, its diversity of population and ideas, was of course the fact that for 140 years it was a commercial crossroads. It attracted traders from all over the world. Behind them came the professionals. For a long time, Singapore's chief minister was an Armenian Jewish lawyer. One of its best known women doctors, a noted novelist, was partly Belgian and partly Chinese. A leading rubber merchant was an Australian who, in his sixties, worked behind Japanese lines to recruit head-hunting Dyaks for slaughterous wartime expeditions.

The native Malays, more easygoing than the purposeful invaders, had long ago retreated upcountry to farm or work the big Malayan rubber plantations and tin mines. Out of Singapore's total population in 1958 of some 1,500,000, at least 80 per cent were Chinese. Every seven minutes around the clock, a new baby was born. Nine times out of ten, it was Chinese. This was the huge, inescapable fact that underlay all political discussion. Singapore was heading toward independence, but was this going to mean Chinese domination? The new state, which was to become a reality on June 1, 1959, was destined for a socialist government. Yet it had no industries to nationalize. Its existence depended upon free trade, unless it could federate with inde-

pendent Malaya. But in Malaya there was an understandable reluctance to absorb so many Chinese, whose numbers would tip
the racial balance in their own favor.

In the uneasy political atmosphere then prevailing, nobody in
authority looked with favor upon the handful of Indonesian rebel
agents who had established themselves in Singapore. The city
could not afford to annoy its big Muslim neighbor to the south.

This was why Doctor Sumitro employed cloak-and-dagger
methods, although I soon found that he had a natural taste for
intrigue. His chosen rendezvous was a modern bungalow en-
closed in high walls. The Dutchman was at the door, still puffing
his pipe, while his wife trimmed the rangoon creepers entwining
the trellis-work around the patio.

"Major Willi Pantouw sent us word when to expect you," he
said. It was the first time I had heard Mister Willi given a military rank.

The Dutchman took me inside. Rubbing the pipestem against
his nose, he said: "I apologize for the mess. The need to disguise
our activities creates a certain —" he coughed as his wife joined
us — "a certain absence of our customary tidiness."

I made a mental inventory of the room: hi-fi equipment
scattered about the spotless floor, a tape-recording console, Siamese silk drapes, a red-lacquered Korean chest converted into a
liquor cabinet, and modern Swedish furniture. The underground
looked pretty cosy.

He switched on the big ceiling fan which at once blew a pile
of papers from the rosewood coffee-table. A barefoot Malay
girl scuttled across the stone floor to scoop them up. She backed
into the kitchen, clutching the papers to half-exposed breasts; and
then twisted to smile up at someone, baring teeth stained red
from chewing betel nuts. A man in the clothes of a Chinese
coolie brushed gently past her.

The stranger advanced into the pool of light from an over-head lamp. He wore a tattered gray singlet, black cotton pants and open Madrasi sandals. He was thin, with deep shadows under the collarbones. He had a long Javanese face, narrow and sensi-tive, with a quick smile.

"Good evening." His English had a faint Dutch inflection. He moved softly to the center of the room and hitching his trouser legs until they were above his bony knees, he squatted coolie-fashion on the floor, his narrow buttocks resting on his heels. "My name is Doctor Sumitro."

I sat up. This was the legendary Sumitro Djojohadikusomo, financial adviser and representative abroad of the revolutionary government of Indonesia (PRRI). He had been three times a cabinet minister in President Sukarno's government; was once personal assistant to Asia's foremost socialist, Sutan Sjahrir; had been Sukarno's first envoy in Washington; and was a veteran of the Dutch Resistance in Nazi Europe. I drew a deep breath.

"First you must hear this report on the conference of War Administrators in Djakarta, which ended yesterday." He placed a flat package, wrapped in a Japanese *furoshiki* cloth square, on the floor. From it he extracted what looked like photostats. "As you know, Indonesia is officially in a state of war and siege. The republic is divided into war administrations. Here is a full verbatim report of the five-day conference. Present were Gen-eral Nasution—" He tilted the glossy prints and continued reading.

"Microfilm blowups," whispered the Dutchman proudly. "The negatives arrived by today's Garuda flight from Djakarta. Our agents are excessively zealous."

"Should I be hearing all this?" I asked incredulously.

"Why not?" Doctor Sumitro peered up at me. "We have to convince you that we are not playing games. Our espionage is excellent. Also I wish you to understand the risks involved in going to Celebes."

"Celebes? I've no intention of going to Celebes," I said wildly.

Doctor Sumitro sighed. "If you are a good newspaperman, you will want to go and see for yourself. After what I have to tell you."

A group of patriotic Indonesians, said Doctor Sumitro, had tried to set up self-governing areas in the Outer Islands. In February, 1958, they proclaimed the PRRI revolutionary government, having been assured of support from the United States Central Intelligence Agency. Their president, Sjafruddin Prawiranegara, was the former director of the national bank, who fiercely opposed President Sukarno's fiscal policies.

A promise of United States recognition for the rebel government had not yet materialized. Probably it was the invention of an overexcited CIA agent, said Sumitro. His actual words were, "Some CIA men exceed their authority. They get too excited. They believe anyone who says President Sukarno is a communist; and then they make wild promises."

Anyway, the fact was that Sumitro had to find money to buy arms. He especially wanted Hexogen (known in North America as RDX) for mixing with TNT into a rubber compound base. He had the TNT, and the compound was fabricated by his men in the captured rubber estates.

"But what for?" I asked.

"Plastic bombs. We prefer plastic for jungle warfare. It's more stable. You can cut it in strips and move it around easily. Besides," he added mildly, "it sticks to almost any surface.

"We may have to adopt a scorched-earth policy, you see. Destruction of mines, rubber estates, oil installations. *Particularly* oil installations. We don't want to threaten the oil companies but they must be made to see we are determined to succeed. We need more money from Caltex, Shell-Indonesia and Stanvac. Otherwise we may have to blow up their investments."

There was a steady flow of western oilmen in and out of Indonesia at this period. No wonder they looked harassed. They had to pacify President Sukarno, who was always threatening to nationalize them, as well as buy off rebel guerrillas who wanted to blow them up.

"The oil companies may think they can reject us," Doctor Sumitro was saying, "because Sukarno says his troops will smother the revolt. Washington may cut off our military aid."

"You mean the Americans are helping you try to overthrow the established Indonesian government?"

"Not officially," said Doctor Sumitro. "But even the British in Singapore and Malaya are letting us ship our wounded into their army hospitals."

"What are you doing for money now?"

"That's where you come in," said the Dutchman. "As a journalist, you can visit the rebel areas and write about the continuing fight. President Sukarno hopes to strangle us, by persuading the West we're no longer worth supporting. You will see how far from true this is, in the Permesta.

"Also," he added, refilling his pipe and glancing sharply up at me, "you will see we are ready to do business in rubber, spices, gold . . . and copra."

Copra! Suddenly I understood the origin of the stale, sweet smell that haunted Sandakan. It was copra, the dry coconut kernel from which oil is extracted. Indonesia was a major supplier of copra, for which the world's demand was increasing not only because it was an essential ingredient of soap and margarine but also as the result of vastly expanded chemical industries.

"These commodities are helping finance our rebellion," Doctor Sumitro was saying. "They are smuggled out of Permesta into British Borneo."

The name Permesta now rang a bell too. It was a movement launched by Colonel Venje Sumual, the young rebel commander of north Celebes, who felt that the central government in Java was milking the Outer Islands to fatten the Javanese and none else.

The picture was beginning to clear. Not altogether though. I still had a vivid memory of Mister Willi briefing the mysterious Chinese in the warehouse of birds' nests. There was the incident of my searched baggage in the Chinese hotel. Could copra fully account for Sandakan's unnatural air of well-being? I thought not.

I asked Sumitro if all this smuggling of raw materials from the rebel areas would not create just those bad economic conditions that he wanted to end. The Indonesian Army chief of staff, General Nasution, had once said that if the smuggling could be stopped there would be a resultant saving equal to the annual cost of Indonesia's armed forces.

The rebel economist rejected this idea. "Let me give you an example — the island of Sumatra, where the rebel government is now hiding. Sumatra has only 12 million inhabitants, out of 90 million Indonesians. Its oil is worth 108 million dollars yearly and that yields 72 per cent of Indonesian foreign exchange. Yet President Sukarno is going to force the western oil companies out of business. Those that remain will only survive because of our protection. A majority of oil resources will be soon under President Sukarno's exclusive control and he is already arranging for Sino-Soviet technicians to help operate the installations. The money from that oil will be used to pay for communist arms — jet bombers, warships, submarines and so on, which Sukarno is now buying. So where is the benefit to my people?"

He began to pace the room. "What are these communist arms for? To drive the Dutch out of west New Guinea. It is the last Dutch foothold in Asia, and this campaign diverts public attention from the economic chaos at home. The Indonesian communist party, the PKI, fattens on the economic confusion. Ten years ago they tried to seize power. They failed miserably. Now they control more than half of the local provincial assemblies. About one quarter of the army's officer corps and senior officers in the navy and air force sympathize with PKI aims. I know. I see the reports every day. I have my own spies in the PKI."

"But — you're a socialist?" I asked.

He nodded, hesitating slightly. "Yes. I have to be careful who I say that to. Americans think a socialist is a communist. And we badly need American help."

"Don't you think western help for your revolution only pushes President Sukarno closer to the Russians? Particularly," I added, glancing at the Dutchman, "when the Dutch still get mixed up in it."

"My friend here fought with me in the anti-Nazi underground. We are old comrades. He is socialist, like me. And Indonesian by choice."

"Do you think you've got into the habit of conspiracy?"

Several young Indonesians had been filtering into the room. They sat crosslegged on the floor, their smooth expressionless faces belying alert eyes. Now one jumped up. "What are you saying? Doctor Sumitro is scholar. He is, even now, still Dean of Faculty at Djakarta University."

"It is so." Sumitro frowned. "But you are right, I am plotting all the time since school. Talking. It is a drug. I am famous among students for it. For arguing through the long nights.

"It is Arthur Koestler, isn't it, who says, 'There is an intellectual caution that in political and social crises leads the academic mind to suicide.' Too many intellectuals in Djakarta are thinking and talking about revolutionary action. They are brilliantly analytic. At critical moments, however, they find equally brilliant reasons for doing nothing."

He shivered. "It gets light outside. And I talk too much, as usual." He withdrew to a bedroom. A servant brought durians, a fruit whose odor has been unfavorably compared to squashed peaches in urine, although the flavor has won many addicts.

When Doctor Sumitro returned, he wore a crisp white shirt tucked into khaki shorts. His feet were still thrust into sandals, the slender toes protruding like long fingers ridged with coarse black hair.

Outside the sky was bright with a new day. "You will go, then, to Celebes?"

I was drunk with fatigue, and mentally a million miles from the workaday world. I was steeped in Doctor Sumitro's dreams and could only say, "If there really is a story, yes."

He nodded briskly. "We will contact you at the right time. I have good men in navy intelligence who will keep me informed on the blockade patrols." He tucked a few papers under his shirt, at the back. "Even the Nazis never searched us there. Not on ordinary street checks."

He crossed the neat suburban garden and wheeled an old bicycle from the potting shed. It was that hour when the early dew turns to vapor and the sudden weight of oppressive heat squeezes every last drop of sweat from your pores. Across his back and under his armpits the dark patches were forming. The professional rebel flung a leg over his bicycle and wobbled down the garden path and into North Canal Road, where he was quickly lost in the morning stream of clerks pedaling four and five abreast to Raffles Place. Outlawed again, Doctor Sumitro was effacing himself with habitual skill.

4

A Tax on Dutch Bottoms

THE LAST PERSON I expected or wanted to see in the Cockpit Hotel, crawling as it was with busybodies, was Jana. I stared, dumfounded, but she gave no answering signal of recognition. Far from being the prim rebel who led me through the Sandakan's caves, she now wore a tight batik skirt with hand-blocked Balinese patterns in blues and browns, and a low-cut peasant's blouse. Her long glossy black hair had been plaited into a single rope which fell across one bare honey-skinned shoulder. She sat on a stool at the bar, legs crossed, one foot dangling a loose sandal. Behind her stood the bearded portly figure of Alex Josey in his customary bottle-green bush shirt. She had a fierce almost hawk-like expression as she talked intently to another of the British correspondents, John Ridley.

She glanced up, eyes blank, as John gave me a cheery wave. "We're just going to lunch, dear boy. Join us?"

I refused politely. Jana said, "Won't you introduce us, John?" and smiled at me vaguely.

Later she telephoned my room. Could we meet at Prabowa & Company, a shipping agent on Prince Street? I went there and found her alone in an inner office.

"You darn near froze me with that icy look," I said. "Why — ?"

"I am flying to Djakarta in the morning."

"Djakarta! Whose side are you on?"

She smiled. "Indonesia's." There was a gipsy gleam in her eye as she added, "I apologize for being rude. It was not good for us to be seen here as friends. You will come and see me in Djakarta?"

She wrote an address on the pad in front of her.

I said I had no plans for visiting Djakarta.

"Then you have not been to the cable office yet."

"Meaning what?"

"Meaning that they have a cable there suggesting you go. It is something to do with expelling the Dutch."

I made a mental note to inquire about telegrams getting into the hands of unauthorized people and said, "I may not be able to get a visa."

She wrote another name on the pad. "See this man in the Indonesian embassy. He will arrange it. He is a friend of the rebels."

"Is it safe for you to go back?"

"I have excellent connections," she said.

Later I asked John about Jana. "She's frightfully well placed," he said, pinching his nose. "On intimate terms, you might say, with Sukarno."

A cable arrived, as Jana predicted. It was from the Canadian Broadcasting Corporation, suggesting a visit to the Indonesian capital. A more immediate crisis had arisen than the rebellion. It had been simmering ever since the attempt of November 30, 1957, to assassinate Sukarno. On that day a draft United Nations resolution called for renewed negotiations between the Netherlands and Indonesia on the subject of west New Guinea. The resolution was Indonesian-inspired and it failed to get a sufficient majority in the General Assembly. The issue was highly emotional. Sukarno, already enraged by the attempt to kill him, took vengeance against the Dutch families who still remained in Indonesia. He quoted Disraeli: "Colonies do not cease to be colonies because they are independent." Quite so, said Sukarno. So long as Dutchmen kept their financial interests in the new republic, they would continue to hold Indonesia in economic slavery. The quotation had come from one of Sukarno's lesser-known sources of English-language speeches, an exiled Englishman handy with a well-turned and appropriate phrase from the classics.

The idea of taking over Dutch properties, however, came from the extremists surrounding Sukarno and eager to lead him into a Marxist bog. The disappointment over west New Guinea was a convenient goad. Sukarno insisted that the Dutch military bases in west New Guinea were a threat to his authority. He accused the Dutch of reluctance to leave Indonesia alone. They would, he said, always try to promote disunity among the islands. He associated them with rebels who were forever fomenting his internal troubles.

His ghost-writer might have dragged in George Canning, the anti-colonial British foreign secretary of the 1800's, who once wrote in cipher to his ambassador in The Hague:

> In matters of commerce the fault of the Dutch
> Is offering too little and asking too much.

For which sin Canning suggested taxing Dutch bottoms (that is, of course, the bottoms of Dutch freighters) an extra levy.

Sukarno prescribed far sterner measures. In his view, the particular fault of the Dutch had been their haggling over the fate of west New Guinea. It had been a dependency, nearly four hundred years ago, of the Sultan of Tidore, with whom the Dutch had signed a treaty of "union and everlasting alliance" in order to prevent British and Spanish penetration of the territory. The

Hague did not establish direct administrative control over New Guinea until 1900; in 1949 the Dutch agreed that the sovereignty of all former territories of the Netherlands East Indies should be transferred to the Indonesians — without exception. In the final days of negotiation, however, the Dutch suddenly insisted that west New Guinea should be maintained as a Dutch dependency. The question of its political status would be determined through negotiation within the next year.

But discussions led nowhere. In 1956, the Indonesians unilaterally abrogated the earlier agreements, abandoned the Dutch-Indonesian Union and repudiated all debts to Holland. Later, President Sukarno's government committed itself to "action which would startle the world" if the latest appeal for United Nations action were to fail, as now it had.

The first blow fell on December 2, 1957, when the central government withdrew permission from the Dutch KLM airline to operate from the capital of Djakarta. A 24-hour strike was ordered among all workers in Dutch enterprises. This was followed by the physical seizure, by the trade unions, of the offices of all major Dutch enterprises and the premises of many smaller Dutch-owned businesses and plantations in Java. The cabinet legalized the seizure of this property and then appealed to the unions to cease their high-handed actions — an appeal which was partly ignored, apparently with tacit cabinet consent.

In the Outer Islands, local military commanders forestalled similar seizures and placed all Dutch-owned property under army protection. It looked as if the growing breach between local army commanders and Djakarta must develop into a major civil war. The Indonesian economy was seriously damaged. There was a run on the banks. Unemployment rose sharply with the dislocation of trade and business. The seizure of the Dutch KPM shipping company, which dominated inter-island traffic, meant that communication between the islands was almost at a standstill (half the KPM ships had fled to foreign ports and the rest were immobilized). Half of the country's exports could not be moved except through smugglers. Java, and other islands that depended upon food imports, began to feel the pinch.

President Sukarno declared that the people must make sacrifices to win the struggle with the Dutch for west New Guinea. A large number of influential Indonesians were appalled by what was happening. They accused the central government of letting irresponsible groups indulge in melodramatic actions that would hurt Indonesia more than the Dutch. The governor of the Bank of Indonesia, Sjafruddin Prawiranegara, decided he must resign and join the rebels. In his view, the value of the assets seized from the Dutch — about $1.6 billion — could not compensate for the loss of Dutch skills.

The most dramatic aspects of the crisis, from a western viewpoint, were the plight of the remaining 60,000 Dutch and Eurasians, among whom about 12,000 were being forced to leave Indonesia immediately; and the role being played by a resurgent Indonesian communist party, the PKI, which was enveloping the trade unions and which also had other ways of making its influence felt. The Australian foreign minister, Richard Casey, found considerable support for his widely publicized view that Indonesia was "going communist."

In a crisis of this kind, there was little time for the press and radio to analyze matters. President Sukarno was depicted as a pawn in communist hands. The rebels, whose existence was becoming known, began to assume the role of an anticommunist movement. An oversimplified story of conflict between reds and whites went into general circulation.

The difficulties confronting President Sukarno as the result of outside interference were typified in the case of an Irish-Canadian convert to the Islamic faith, Tyrconnel Fay, who was busily spreading anti-Sukarno propaganda in Singapore. He represented the Darul Islam, one of the dissident movements which had recruited ex-guerrilla fighters who preferred pillage to demobilization. They sought the transformation of Indonesia into an orthodox theocratic Realm of Islam. The main support came from west Java, where Moslem religious leaders exercised strong influence in the villages, although the movement also had armed Moslem adherents in the other islands as far away as Borneo and Celebes. One of the Indonesian Army intelligence reports, photocopied by the rebels and shown to me by Doctor Sumitro, identified the Darul Islam as "the biggest threat to security in the Republic." There were "armed D.I. bands" in east Sumatra and Borneo, "a serious situation" in west and central Java, where 1100 people were made homeless by the destruction of one village alone, and fighting in south Celebes, where the D.I. insurgents had tried to force villagers to join the movement by destroying their homes.

Tyrconnel Fay saw all this as a glorious crusade against communism. He told me that he fought the communist terrorists in Malaya as a British paratrooper, at which time he had been converted to the Islamic faith. I asked if he thought the Darul Islam guerrillas were not helping to create the very chaos in which communism prospered. "In the jungle we shoot first and ask questions later," he said, sipping his ginger ale. "The place is full of communists. It's better to be wrong twice than let even one of the bloody bastards get away."

I found myself beginning to sympathize with President Sukarno. An interview with a Dutch refugee next day convinced me that if I had to be involved once again with these stormy islands, I had better take another look at the other side's case. The refugee was one of several thousand provided with temporary accommodation by the British in Singapore. My heart sank when I saw them. It was such a familiar spectacle. I had to do a television interview and we set up the sound cameras between tin-roofed army huts. The women and children were making the best of the primitive conditions they had to contend with; and some talked tearfully of the homes and, in some cases, the husbands they had left behind. The men were bitter. But they were less resentful of the Indonesian government's actions than they were angry with The Hague for having failed to understand Indonesian feelings.

Finally a middle-aged Dutchman stepped in front of the cameras. He looked defiantly at his attentive companions. "I have no hatred for Indonesia," he said, speaking slowly and deliberately. "I have lived and worked there all my life. We, the Dutch, have tried everything to bring about the collapse of President Sukarno's government. We did nothing to help the new republic. We learned nothing from our past mistakes. We did nothing to adjust to the changing world around us. Now a few of us have got to suffer. I have lost everything. I do not know how I shall ever begin again, because Holland is like another foreign land to me. I would gladly go back to work for Indonesians but I cannot blame them for not wanting me."

The men around him nodded. His wife, with two blond infants tugging at her skirts, pulled him away. "It is not good to be saying such things," she said. "Come."

5

The Cautious Intellectual

IT WAS TIME TO LEAVE Singapore. I arrived late at the airport
and passengers were already boarding the morning flight to
Djakarta. A grinning Malay customs official took one sympathetic glance at my untidy suitcase, crammed with the debris
of three weeks' note taking, and waved me through. The
Chinese passport clerk examined my passport with its freshly
stamped visa from Jana's friend in the Indonesian embassy. He
seemed surprised that I had one. Roving newsmen were not
popular in Djakarta just then.

A Dutchman walked beside me to the plane. We caught
sight of a blond head in the pilot's cabin. "See," said the Dutchman. "They pretend they fly their own airliners. But they
cannot do without us. They hide the Dutch fliers behind cur-
tains and only let us see the Indonesian stewards."

The remark typified an attitude among many Dutch businessmen. They ignored their own responsibility for failing to prepare a colony for independence. They were unconsciously
patronizing, and unable to believe in their own unpopularity.
There was a Dutch phrasebook circulating at the time, full of
harsh imperatives, reflecting this unconscious arrogance. It was
not an exclusive Dutch trait. You found it wherever a foreign
community wielded too much economic power. The rulers were
corrupted by their own strength; by the small daily testimonials

to their own superiority; in the cringing of servants dependent
for their very livelihood on the whims of the white memsahibs.
In such an artificial relationship between the "natives" and the
colonialists, artificial judgments were inevitable.

As we flew the 600 miles south, I wondered if anyone would
ever put the problems into proper perspective. The Dutch were
a dramatic illustration of it. They were hard-working, conscien-
tious and kind. In their own overcrowded flatlands they had
long ago learned to respect the individual whatever his station in
life. They made excellent emigrants to North America. They
were reliable and brave comrades in war. They undoubtedly
believed that enlightenment and protection followed them to the
savage tropical islands they colonized. But like many of us, they
could not believe in any other form of civilization than their
own, and since their motive for coming to the Indies was chiefly
a commercial one, they had little patience with people whose
values might be different.

There were armed sentries and nests of antiaircraft guns
dotted around Kemajoran Airport when we landed. The air
was hot and sticky in the crowded waiting rooms. My Dutch
friend was swallowed up by a knot of uniformed Indonesian
security guards. He was returning on business and had resigned
himself to a complete and humiliating examination by customs
officials. There were large numbers of troops wearing guns and
an unmistakable air of hostility. I braced myself for the inevitable
delays and irritations, knowing that this was the other side of the
coin. It was all very well to see where the Dutch had gone
wrong, at an elevation of 20,000 feet. It was much easier to share
their frustration when you came down to ground level.

I was resignedly laying out my camera gear for inspection
when I was thumped on the back. "So — you are back?" It
was an officer of the airport security guard, a man I had always

known as Captain Flick. He shouted something in Indonesian to the customs men. "It's all right," he said, turning back to me. "Everything is passed."

I managed to look grateful without suggesting, by too extravagant a display of relief, that I had anything to hide. One excellent reason for the careful customs examination at Djakarta is the black market in Indonesian rupiahs. The currency had been progressively devalued to a pegged official rate of something like 30 to the American dollar. But the same dollar in Singapore or Hong Kong would buy 200 rupiahs. For anyone willing to take the risk, it was possible to live extremely well for three dollars a day on black rupiahs.

Captain Flick said, "You're not smuggling rupiahs, I hope?"

"Good heavens, no!"

"Nor American dollars?"

I shook my head.

"Then come and have some coffee. They'll send your bags out later."

I stopped dead in my tracks. "Later?"

He flashed me his most disarming smile, a row of gleaming white teeth set in a narrow face of light mahogany. "Yes, yes, old friend. Do not be alarmed. It will save us all much inconvenience if you will come and have some coffee and talk to me."

I glanced back at my suitcase and typewriter, already vanishing into one of the small back rooms. An efficient young man was opening the back of the Rolleiflex. Another was unscrewing the lenses from my 16-mm Bolex Paillard. "Oh, very well," I said, marveling at Captain Flick's tact and hoping nobody in the small back room could read my shorthand. At least it was painless this way, and you kept your dignity.

After two cups of coffee with Captain Flick, I was completely at home again. It was, in some ways, a pleasant sensation to sink back into the familiar routine of an Indonesian conversation: the infinite courtesies, the swift allusion to some sensitive subject, the little things left unsaid as you sat opposite each other with frank and open smiles concealing a feverish conjecture. You weaved a tortuous path through these conversations, relying upon a kind of mental radar. I had expected Captain Flick to make some polite noises while his men conducted their search of my baggage, but it became apparent that he wished to warn me of a deepening hostility between the authorities and the western press. Some correspondents had foolishly allowed themselves to be impressed by the claims made by a few isolated groups of dissident army colonels. Of course, the rebels were of no importance. They would be eliminated, destroyed . . . although one must understand that in some cases their motives were patriotic.

I gathered that Captain Flick did not want me to antagonize his government. I also understood that he was wondering if the rebels really had much of a chance. Since I did not know, I could not tell him. My reticence was naturally interpreted as being in itself significant. We parted in another flurry of good will. I knew, by the same combination of telepathy and half-sentences, that I would be seeing more of Captain Flick.

At the Capitol I found an old friend from Ottawa, Jim Wilde, who was then with Associated Press. We sat in the restaurant overlooking one of Djakarta's many canals, while Jim recounted the dim outlook for newsmen. "If you rewrite the government handouts, you're okay," he said, staring morosely downstream at a group of young women knee-deep in the muddy canal water. They had untied their sarongs and were bathing with graceful but discreet gestures that afford brief glimpses of naked brown bodies. An elderly washerwoman was beating the laundry against a stone with slow, rhythmic movements. Several men beneath us had stripped and were washing their glistening torsoes without embarrassment. All these figures were held in the soft radiance of the stormy evening, slender bodies twisting and curving above the sluggish brown waters.

"If you get out of line," said Jim, "these people can find a million ways to make your life miserable. And the more they mess you about, the angrier you get. It's a vicious circle." He brushed away the circle of flies balancing on the rim of his glass. They were replaced by more flies, fresh from the canal, where an old man crouched a few yards upstream, defecating with ritual dignity.

I went to see Sutan Sjahrir, one of the best loved of Asia's socialists and a former leader of the underground resistance against the Japanese. He was a small, quiet man and expected any day to be arrested. Much later he was, for being a close friend of Doctor Sumitro, the rebel economist. "There's a breakdown in administration," said Sjahrir. "And it's not a bit of use our continuing to blame the Dutch. Before the war, there were 40,000 civil servants. Now there are more than a million. They get in each other's way and slow everything down. But, in effect, they're on the president's payroll. You would call his policy one of 'jobs-for-the-boys.' So long as the president plays this game, the communists will prosper. They've been very clever, pretending to be patriots, flattering Sukarno and making him feel he can't do without them."

Sjahrir sat in a suburban bungalow, surrounded by books and interrupted from time to time by visitors. He was a short, rather thick-set man of middle years who seemed to command the devotion of a large number of young intellectuals. "You see," he said, "we have to work out our own salvation. I mean, we cannot rely on the West. The Americans are becoming prisoners of an ideology nearly as narrow as that of the communists. They equate capitalism with freedom. Communism is an evil, in their minds, almost as absolute as murder."

He stood up. "Let us walk. This is the only way I can escape

my friends." He led the way out, and we began strolling along
the banks of yet another canal. "If only the West would open
its mind. You all seem to think that if a nation undertakes to
nationalize its industries, it is already on the way to communism
and perdition. You won't believe that in Asia it may seem desirable and practical to nationalize. So you back the worst of the
reactionary elements, instead of understanding that our economy
has to be developed quickly through intelligent planning. The
reactionaries are out of touch with the people, and the people
finally turn in despair to the communists. It is a self-defeating
policy."

We walked along in silence for a few moments. "Of course
communist techniques are dangerous and difficult to fight. But
why help the Russians? Communism can only succeed in very
limited conditions unless the Russians have military control.
These conditions are poverty, backwardness, feudalism and oppression. And in Asia, they include — above all else — anticolonialism."

He paused to light a cigarette, cupping it inside his hand,
watching the match curl and the flame die. "Until colonialism
is buried and forgotten, the West will always be at a disadvantage
in countries like Indonesia. The dangerous temptation is for the
West to intervene in every little country that flirts with Marxist
ideas. This only confirms communist propaganda that the West
imposes, under United States leadership, a new and disguised
form of imperialism."

"But supposing the communist party here is clever enough to
build up its strength within the existing system, and forces President Sukarno to follow communist policies in order to maintain
his own position?"

Sjahrir nodded thoughtfully. "Well, the local comrades have
promised us: Not communism today, nor tomorrow, but perhaps

in fifty years." He shrugged. "It is a risk you must take. First win our confidence. Make the newly independent nations like Indonesia truly believe you will respect their independence. Leave them alone and they will see, in time, the much greater faults and more selfish ambitions of the Soviet Union."

"Supposing it is too late by then," I persisted. "You said yourself that if the communist bloc gets a stranglehold on the economy here, it will be hard to escape."

"Too late to escape?" He was heading back home now, a small man in a short-sleeved white shirt, taking the air beside the quiet canal waters. "I cannot believe it will ever come to that. They would arrest me before that happened."

He was arrested in January, 1962.

Sjahrir, like other Asian socialists, was the target of communist intrigue. His subsequent arrest placed an effective gag upon his influential voice. "This country is in the slogan stage," he had once said. "There is no planning, no systematic approach to our problems. The present regime lives by exploiting nationalist feelings and contents itself with haphazard measures."

He never could bring himself to openly support the rebels, believing they were doomed to become pawns of the West and therefore bound to be suspect in the eyes of ordinary Indonesians. At the time he left a deep impression on me. Looking back now, I ask myself if Sjahrir's fate is not typical of the fate of all reasonable and just men when confronted with the iron discipline of their enemies. It was not merely that his intellectual caution led him to political suicide. His philosophy, so appealing to the sophisticated western mind, had no force against the crude rock of communist ideology. It was like hammering a nail with candy floss.

6

Purple People-Eater

I HAD TO WAIT two weeks in Indonesia before calling on Jana. She began almost at once to tell me a story then current in Djakarta. Scientists testing the sewage-filled canal waters, she said, could find no germs. "The germs had eaten each other up," said Jana. She laughed. "Anyway that is how my people choose to interpret the story. Evil germs cancel each other out. The same in politics. It is quite safe to have communists advising President Sukarno because the evil will destroy itself."

We sat in a small Dutch-style house belonging to Jana's "Uncle Arnold." This could mean that he was her cousin thrice removed or merely somebody for whom she held a deep affection. Indonesians promote their closest friends into the upper ranks of family relationships. It is a charming gesture that carries with it the practical advantages of mutual help. In a land that suffers from an unreliable administration and an erratic application of the law, the healthiest citizens are those with the widest variety of aunts and uncles. Jana's collection was one of the best and unquestionably spread an umbrella of protective influence over her dubious activities.

She was stretched out on Uncle Arnold's settee, notebook in hand. On shelves and side-tables around her squatted little wooden Chinese gods, grinning and pouting. There were other bits of chinoiserie: sandalwood fans, ancient bronze utensils and a shocking-pink thermos flask from Shanghai in which Uncle Arnold kept his tea.

I said, "How do you keep a balance between Doctor Sumitro and Uncle Arnold?"

"I just told you." She recrossed her legs, smoothing her sarong. "We mix up good and evil, and it comes out good."

"And yet you go on taking risks for Sumitro and the revolution?"

She smiled. "The rebels are good customers for copra. And my family owns a considerable interest in copra. Anyway, Uncle Arnold is a very amateur communist. He went to China and thought he saw how the communists did things there and came back to do the same here. He thinks communism means giving everything away. He would give the coat off his back to a poor man. Sometimes that is exactly what he does do."

"What about this business you make in copra?"

She waved the notebook at me. "I will tell you, perhaps, some day. Now, tell me who else you have seen of importance. I will arrange for you to meet the others."

I ticked off a list of cabinet ministers and politicians. It was not a bad list, considering how little time I had to arrange the interviews.

"What about President Sukarno? Do you want me to help you see him?"

"Is he another one of your uncles?"

"Not exactly," said Jana.

There was a noise at the door and a young man, grinning sheepishly, walked through the room.

"That means Uncle Arnold's coming home," said Jana. "I'd better go."

"Well, look," I said, rising. "I didn't expect you to help me see people on the government side. I mean, you can't be *persona grata* with *both* camps."

"You don't understand Indonesians." She walked to the door as Uncle Arnold, a small wrinkled man with an intent look, burst in. There was a swift exchange of greetings and Uncle Arnold shambled off again in the direction taken by the graceful young man.

"He's very happy," said Jana, watching the departing figure with affectionate interest. "He says he is really in love this time."

It was twenty minutes before Uncle Arnold returned to the living room. "I told Jana it would be very nice to speak to you," he said. "You do understand this is confidential? I am still in the diplomatic service. Please come here as often as you wish but do not mention my name to anyone."

He had a cheerful gnome's face, like a wrinkled walnut. I was at a complete loss to understand his evident fondness for Jana. I had to assume that he knew nothing of her job as a rebel courier.

He unscrewed the thermos flask. "I am not a communist," he said, splashing tea into my empty glass. "In spite of what Jana might tell you."

I blinked. "I am," he went on, "a Trotskyite. This is why I wish to tell you that my countrymen are no longer caring what the West thinks about Indonesia. My people think that Russia and China are their true friends, because it is the Russians and Chinese who have supported our claims for west New Guinea. I want you to see some friends of mine who come from west New Guinea. But first, tell me what is your impression of Djakarta?"

I said it was a tiring city. I probably added that it was an ugly city, suffering from administrative constipation and hardening of the traffic arteries; a frustrating experience for the foreigner, lost in the labyrinthian departments of government. You seemed forever to be chasing permits down long hot corridors, or scuttling from one bureau to another across downtown streets choked with oxcarts, Russian jeeps and honking little European cars. Through it all, the bureaucrats moved with slow grace and tranquil smiles, closing their desks with arbitrary speed when you hove into sight, urging you gently in pursuit of the unfilled form that had just been forwarded to another department across town, and leading you courteously along an endless paper chase.

"If you were in less of a hurry," said Uncle Arnold, "you would seem less like a Dutchman and so have fewer problems."

I said something about lacking time. Uncle Arnold sipped his tea. "Dear boy," he said, picking up a copy of the *New York Times* and putting it down again. "It is because you white people are in such a hurry that you create resistance. It is like riding a *betjak*. The faster you pedal, the more resistance you create."

He sent me to his New Guinea friends in another part of town, and his words came back as the *betjak* boy strained away in the front seat of the tricycle rickshaw. The boy had stretched elastic bands across the front wheel and these thrummed gently in the wind created by our slow progress through streets fragrant with frangipani. These deep vibrations underscored the shrill scissor-grinding call of the cicadas, producing a melancholic two-tone melody. We creaked past hawkers lighting their charcoal braziers for the cooking of *saté* — spiced bits of meat grilled on bamboo skewers. Moving sinuously along the roadside were the graceful forms of young Indonesian girls "walking-walking," which is to say that they were out admiring an enormous moon inflating itself behind the distant volcanic peaks. Later they would gossip beside the *saté* stalls, twisting white buds of frangipani into their glossy black tresses.

These people had been easy prey for Europeans who came

to build fortunes from nutmeg, pepper and cloves. There was little Dutch response to the ancient cultures. All that the Indonesians seemed to have taught them were phrases like "It's as costly as pepper!" coined by an Amsterdam merchant impressed only by the rarity and risk attaching to his spices. The islanders for their part learned that sewage is for foreigners, and canals the proper place for natives to defecate and wash.

Uncle Arnold had said, "The West forgets how the Dutch clung on, formenting rebellions, trying to establish separate states in the Outer Islands. Why do these so-called statesmen in Britain and Australia say Java is going communist? Perhaps because it is the most heavily populated island and the center of administration? Why do they think it is better if Indonesia breaks up into 'manageable units'? Perhaps because the Dutch would get back, hah! The Dutch treated us like children for three centuries. We are not children now. We know who is behind Mr. Richard Casey, the foreign minister of Australia. It is the Dutch. Making him say the republic will turn communist, that only the rebels prevent it."

I had been somewhat dazzled by this outburst. In his patriotic frenzies, Uncle Arnold was like all Indonesians. This probably explains why, during the years of postwar revolution, there were few pitched battles between rebels and government troops. The rival commanders were likely to fall into a discussion of the nation's future instead. There was a make-believe quality to the revolutionary plottings, as witness "Auntie Emiria" Sounassa, to whom Uncle Arnold had now sent me.

She was the sultana of a Papuan community in Dutch New Guinea, but now lived under house arrest in Djakarta. Not being sure about relationships in a country where everyone called President Sukarno "Bung" (or Brother) Karno, I could not guess Auntie Emiria's true position with regard to Uncle Arnold.

Certainly she bore no resemblance, being an enormous old lady with a grin like a split lemon. She was imprisoned in a ramshackle wooden house and spent the daylight hours in a losing battle with jungle growths that marched across her untidy garden and thrust white spiky fingers through the wooden slats of her doorstep. At night she painted, wildly and excitingly, huge canvases of blazing colors and lovely geometric forms.

Guards posted around the house winked as I negotiated their barricades, and let me pass. Auntie Emiria hauled me into a bedroom riotous with spilled paintpots and flaming canvases. Wiping her hands down the front of a plum-colored smock, she sagged onto a four-poster bed with an alarming creek.

"Can you help me escape?" she hissed. (She is now back on good terms with President Sukarno, who knows of her previous restlessness and has characteristically forgiven her.)

In some fright, I hissed back, "Where to?"

"Major Pantouw."

I searched my mind. "Good heavens. Not Mister Willi in Sandakan?"

She nodded with such energy that the bed twanged and groaned like an untuned harp. Instantly a tiny man in a gold-embroidered skullcap entered and studied me with the unwavering and disconcerting stare of a child. "He's the rajah," she said, waving a plump hand at him. "I'm primitive but he's even more primitive."

She winked with grotesque coquetry. "He is only my paper husband. We do not sleep together. Among my people, the ruler is the woman. In the old days, we killed the male issue until a female came along to inherit the throne. We were," she added, "cannibals."

"But you cannot live in Sandakan," I said, eager to move the conversation on.

"No. From there I can get to Dutch New Guinea and be with my people again."

"Under the Dutch?"

"No." She scowled at my stupidity. "We wish for a United Nations trusteeship. I am in touch with my people by courier."

She dug into the bedclothes and produced a few enamel buttons on which her likeness appeared in silhouette.

"This is proof they are loyal to me. They risk much to show their love. They want me back. *They do not want Indonesian rule.*" She spat out the last words.

I explained, feeling a little foolish, that a foreign correspondent might have certain difficulties in smuggling a Papuan monarch out of Indonesia. She was quite crestfallen for a moment. Then a slim young girl entered, smiling shyly, and removed one of Aunt Emiria's several small dogs. The older woman beckoned the child back and touching her fondly on the head said, "She is my adopted daughter. Someone left her as a baby on my doorstep. She is my princess."

I taped much of our conversation, aware all the time of being observed by the many guards hovering in and around the house. They wore no uniform but carried in their jacket lapels the small badges of a workers' union. Their automatic weapons were piled near the front door. Once in a while Auntie Emiria would raise a finger to her lips and nod in their direction, but they interfered very little and when she decided to bring out some of her paintings for me to photograph alongside her strange little family, a couple of the guards helped to carry the huge canvases.

Auntie Emiria at this time enjoyed a certain amount of freedom because her enemies of the PKI were not yet strong enough to hurt her. Nor was it in their interest to interrupt the flow of information from west New Guinea. She was popular with

President Sukarno, who owned a number of her paintings, and her husband in his innocent way had been placed on the National Council as the representative of west New Guinea so as to lend an appearance of authenticity to Indonesian claims to that territory.

She and the sultan invited me to visit their "niece" next door. We toddled through the adjoining gardens and on entering a much larger and better appointed house Auntie Emiria became a jollier and noisier companion. There was a record-player which she insisted on turning on, and soon I found myself whirled through the living room in the old lady's arms. Later, exhausted, she crooned some Papuan songs into my tape recorder while stretched out in a large wicker armchair.

Suddenly she stopped and then exploded with laughter. "You have heard the song called 'The Purple People-eater'?" she demanded.

I said I had. She smoothed her plump hands over her purple smock and patted her stomach. "That is me. I come from a cannibal family. I am a purple people-eater."

The sultan, a silent onlooker, twitched his little head to one side as she translated for him. From the blank look on his face I gathered that the joke fell flat. There were others in the room however, including the Americanized niece, and they shook their heads in mock despair at Auntie's outrageous suggestion.

We had a spiced lunch, this huge boisterous queen and her wizened little sultan, the orphaned princess and the niece and several nephews and although we were not always communicating with each other — for one thing there was a kind of palm toddy going the rounds — we all seemed to find each other uproariously funny. From time to time a thin-faced guard would peer at us through an open window and once, soon after the sultan retired clutching his embroidered "crown," there was a loud crash from the outhouse followed by the shrill and not altogether unhappy squeal of a kitchen maid.

Auntie Emiria was taken with the idea of her primitive origins. On hearing the noises from the outhouse she leaned heavily against me and announced, "I'm primitive but —" pointing a finger at the kitchen — "he's even more primitive." She thought about this a little more, recovering her equilibrium while I edged nervously in the direction of the palm toddy. "But I am a queen," she said with fresh dignity. "Come. I will show you."

Four or five of us trailed back to her own house. The sultan was no longer with us. Auntie charged heavily into her bedroom and from under the swaybacked bed she pulled a large parchment scroll. This she unrolled, displaying an intricate family tree denoting her royal ancestry embellished with small maps. It was a painstaking piece of work and as she spread it out on the rumpled bed, we grouped ourselves around it in respectful silence. Auntie anchored the scroll with a couple of brass knobs and proceeded to trace her lineage. Unpracticed as I was in these matters, I could only express a proper degree of awe at what seemed an irrefutable — or at least highly impressive — document.

Auntie now became very sober. "If I escape," she said, "perhaps the Dutch would try to use me. These rebels — are they playing a Dutch game? I went to school in Holland, did you know? I have seen how the Dutch do not give up without a struggle." She shook her head in sad perplexity. I was enormously sorry for her; not so much because she was old and ought to be living life in her own boisterous way; but because she felt herself to be inadequately qualified to examine her situation. She knew that she was being used, and that wherever she went, and whatever she might do or say, there would be powerful forces always eager to make her a puppet. But what aroused my pity was her conviction that she was not clever enough to cope. Such a wise and humorous old lady deserved to know that even the most ingenious young gladiator would have found difficulty getting out of the trap she was in. But she blamed her plight on her own stupidity. That much the Dutch had taught her — a sense of her own inferiority.

She brightened up later. "When you see Major Pantouw again, tell him my bank in Switzerland has not received any payments lately for the copra. Ask him if he has bought a new mistress or have all his ships been sunk?"

Seeing my surprise, she added, "I was once known as a copra queen too." She unrolled another map to pinpoint her plantations of coconuts in the area of Celebes. In selling copra to finance the revolution, the rebels were depleting her estates.

"I am not really angry," she said as we parted. "In Indonesia we are all brothers and sisters in trouble."

And aunts and uncles, I added mentally.

7

The Dancing God

"O RICKSHAW BOYS — my brothers — we were born in the flames of revolution. We have bathed in fire for many years. We must fight together to drive the Dutch from New Guinea —"

A great roar went up from the crowd. "*Merdeka! Merdeka!* Freedom! Freedom!"

President Sukarno lifted his swagger stick for silence. A black cloud darkened the sky. "O my sisters, ye women who fight for our beloved country. There are spies, imperialist agents among us! Face your country's danger."

Again the pause. Again the shouts rolling in stupefying waves over the lawns and flowerbeds around the white palace.

"When I die —" A shudder passed over the upturned faces as if the approaching storm had riffled a field of golden rice. "When I die, do not write in flaming letters on my tomb: 'Here lies His Excellency Doctor Engineer Sukarno, first President of the Republic of Indonesia.' Just write: 'Here lies Bung [Brother] Karno, Tongue of the Indonesian People.' "

The voice of nationalism paused. The storm clouds parted. Sukarno, in his favorite dove-gray uniform garnished with gold, was bathed for a moment in the bright tropical sunshine. Around me, the crowd sucked in its breath.

"*Bismillah* — Godspeed!" The little president raised his pock-marked face to the morning sky. "*Merdeka!*"

He sat down again in a gilt chair on the palace steps, nodding agreeably as thousands of throats took up the chant.

I turned to Jana and Uncle Arnold. "Let's go."

Jana, the patriotic rebel, gave me an angry look. "Don't be a fool." She stood on tiptoe to see over the heads in front. There was an unmistakable look of rapture on her face. Uncle Arnold, the amateur communist, said: "He is a great man." He had to speak in a shrill voice to be heard. In front of us, tiny soldiers in white U.S.-style army helmets shifted uneasily, their automatics pointing into the heaving mass of humanity.

"It wouldn't be hard to throw a grenade from here," I said. Jana turned on me, furious. "Well, it wouldn't," I persisted. Uncle Arnold looked away, disowning me, pretending not to have heard. Jana, her long black hair uncombed, her dark eyes blazing, said, "Do you want to be torn apart?"

Sukarno was gathering up his entourage with quick little gestures. His attendants fell obediently in line as he rose and led the way indoors: generals, ministers, young men in crisp uniforms and pretty girls swaying gently as they moved across the palace steps. The crowd began breaking up. I lost my paradoxical companions and let the cheerful, chattering citizens of Djakarta carry me along into the street outside.

Merdeka. Freedom. The word buzzed and hummed like a magic incantation, a golden note flashing through the low murmur of many voices: softly muttered by an Arab sailor from one of the *prahus* in the central canal; sung with a Welsh lilt by a fat Bombay merchant too struck by the music of *merdeka* to understand what it was doing already to his legitimate business; shouted by a bunch of little girls hopping between the puddles and sheltering their sleek black heads with huge banana leaves against the big raindrops suddenly splashing down. *Merdeka*, the new ju-ju to replace the gods toppled by war and the idols crumbling under the impact of white technology.

The white man had not yet found a cheaper and better umbrella than the banana leaf, I reflected, dodging under the spreading arms of a banyan. The storm had broken with routine
violence, suddenly, predictably, sweeping down the damp slopes
of the volcanic hills and pattering across the city with a purifying
roar. The girls under their banana leaves danced through the
red mud. Beside me a young Javanese woman absent-mindedly
lifted her hair and tied it above her head with a strip of toweling,
her breasts tip-tilted against her thin tight blouse of yellow
cotton, the nipples hard and dark under the wet fabric. There
was a subtle aroma of jasmine released by the casual movement of
arms.

"Let us remember, Sisters and Brothers, that for the sake of
all . . . we Asians and Africans must be united." It was strange
how Sukarno's compelling voice lingered in your ears; a voice
to which you could put the other eager appealing faces from
Egypt or Algiers, from Cuba or the Congo. Black, brown and
yellow faces. They spoke in different tongues the same message.
Not feed my people. The people would go hungry if need be.
Not shorten my people's working week. The people would
work twice as hard to pursue a dream. Not fill the empty bellies,
nor take the burdens from bent backs, nor teach my people.
Just let my people free.

Well here they were. Free. They jostled each other under the
banyan, crouching between its bent arthritic fingers rooted in the
earth. Free, but still crying for freedom.

An elderly Dutchman shuffled out of the rain, his battered
planter's hat dripping, his bared legs caked in the red mud.
He had powerful shoulders and the back of his thick red neck
was a network of wrinkles. He must be a rubber planter, I
thought, from one of the families who put two or three generations into this fertile soil. He smiled and nodded at the men
and touched the wet brim of his hat as he squeezed between the

chattering laughing women. "They used to say you only had to fill an Asian's belly to make him feel good," he said, glancing sideways at me with red-rimmed eyes sunk in a wrinkled brown face. "What a mistake. What a mistake. We could have given them ideas. We could, you know. They were hungry for ideas. They eat Marx. They eat Mao Tse-tung. They can live off Sukarno forever."

He lit the dottle of tobacco in his pipe with large mottled hands, tamping the glowing bowl with a stubby broken-nailed finger. "We had already started. Before the Japs. I had a school on the plantations. My own school. I treated my workers' children as if they were my own. You know? We were very happy, my wife and I. And then there came the shit-disturbers."

I gave him a startled look. A couple of eavesdropping youths grinned.

"I was a language officer with the British when they came here," he said. "And that is what we called Sukarno and his lot. The shit-disturbers. Creators of discontent. Making promises. Filling the workers' heads with dreams of glory. And now my workers have the plantations and Sukarno has the country and nobody has very much to eat except Sukarno's words."

"And you?"

He shrugged. "I have nothing left," he said, not asking for my pity but just stating the fact. "Oh, some worthless rupiahs of course. My pockets are full of rupiahs. They will not buy me even a little shop in Rotterdam in which to sell tobacco." He peered up at the sky with forget-me-not blue eyes, blinking the fatigue-reddened lids. "The rain has stopped," he said and moved off, lifting his hat to the jasmine-scented woman, nodding at the attentive youths, his pipe smoking and bubbling between his clenched teeth.

A squad of armed motorcycle cops thundered out of Merdeka

Palace and down the rain-washed street. My companions under the banyan tree began to disperse. I saw Jana and Uncle Arnold appear from the shelter of the palace walls and joined them.

Jana had twisted her hair up, revealing features that were more finely etched than first appeared. She had high cheekbones and a stubborn profile, but her narrow nose and round figure were not oriental. Her skin glowed in the clarity of light that follows a Djakarta storm. Dressed in western clothes, she would be difficult to identify with any particular race or clime. I remembered how enraptured she seemed when President Sukarno was speaking. Was it a chameleon's talent she had for blending with the political landscape? Or something more dangerous, like divided loyalty?

"What did you think of the president's speech?"

She tossed her head. "It was not improved by your remarks. Do you know how dangerous it is to have a crowd turn against you after the president has won them over?" She paused. "Besides, I have been arranging for him to see you."

I glanced warily at Uncle Arnold. I supposed anything was possible in this make-believe country. Even a lady revolutionary with friendly contacts in the palace.

He read my glance as one of inquiry. "You foreigners cannot understand," he said gently, "that in Indonesia we have much easier access to our leaders. Jana is one of many people who may call on the president and speak with him if they wish. It is one of the secrets of his popularity."

It was not an aspect of President Sukarno that foreigners were likely to discover for themselves. He had an unhappy talent for traveling abroad in royal state. At the United Nations, he had once tried to take a procession of nine army officers with him to the rostrum of the General Assembly. The number was whittled to five, then to three, and finally to one. The one man

was Lieutenant Colonel Mohamed Sabur, who stood slightly behind Sukarno while he made his speech. As he finished each page,
Sukarno handed the sheet back to the colonel, who put it away
in a satchel. Asked about this procedure later, Sukarno explained
that it was his custom to have an aide hand him each sheet, while
another aide took away the pages when he finished them. The
other seven aides were standing by, in case of need. "What sort
of need?" the president was asked. He smiled blandly. "Oh,
this and that."

From the time he took power, Sukarno had been building up
a personal army of bureaucrats who did "this and that" for him.
Their duties ranged from the investigation of geisha houses prior
to one of Sukarno's frequent sojourns in Tokyo to the summon-
ing of his personal "spiritual teacher." The teacher was a seer
who advised the president on the eve of any important decision.

To most Indonesians, there was nothing odd in having a
president who believed in soothsayers. Sukarno, who was convinced that destiny and Allah chose him for his present role,
shared the common conviction that supernatural powers did
exist and could be profitably employed. The fact that Sukarno
had escaped from would-be assassins on five occasions between
the end of 1957 and the summer of 1962 was widely regarded as
proof of his special immunity.

This supernatural agent acting on behalf of goblins and
ghosts is called a *bomoh*. Indonesians appeal to him when orthodox means have failed to cure the sick, or in order to rid the
home of mysterious noises or to save a crop. Their lives are so
plagued by evil spirits that a *bomoh* is accepted in the community
as if he were a doctor or a priest. The *bomoh* himself is emi-
nently respectable. No gaudy rags, no charlatan tricks. He
knows, just as surely as a surgeon exploring the internal organs,
what is likely to be wrong and how to cure it. Perhaps a polter-

geist is smashing the pots in a village *kampong?* Possibly an enemy has mobilized the powers of darkness to destroy a farmer's health? A good *bomoh* has an answer for everything; and every sensible citizen, no matter how exalted his rank, will know of a good *bomoh*.

It seemed as if President Sukarno provided a symbolic link between the world of the *bomoh* and the world of Marx. He consulted his seers, like anyone else. He observed the Islamic laws. He took a vigorous interest in attractive women, as any virile Indonesian male should. He could quote fluently from the Koran, tell an anecdote from Hindu mythology and delve into Buddhist philosophy to make an effective point. He stood before the adoring masses like a many-armed Siva, his golden throat pouring forth a reassuring flood of familiar analogies as he pointed the way to a political utopia.

The peasants prayed:

> *The dancing foot, the sound of tinkling bell,*
> *The songs that are sung*
> *And the varying steps.*
> *The form assumed by our dancing god,*
> *We find these things within ourselves*
> *And so our follies fall away.*

Sukarno had the gift of assuming a form readily understood by any of the crowds he played upon. He voiced their fears. He proved that their inadequacies were the fault of the white colonialists. He restored their pride by heaping indignities upon their former masters. He salved their wounds with promises of better times. Like the tribal witch-doctor, the temple god, the *bomoh* and Hitler, he resolved their fears and dissolved their guilt and gave substance to their dreams. And for a while, hearing him, their burdens fell away.

Was Sukarno, at bottom, a communist? Most Indonesian intellectuals would have laughed at such a question. They found it funny to watch the earnest witch hunt conducted by western observers in Asia. What *is* a communist? they asked. Their dancing god was only himself, embodying Marxist ideas perhaps, but also rising from the ashes of outmoded beliefs; a being supreme, dominating the narrow doctrinal groups around him.

The men who led the communist PKI had very different ideas. Sukarno knew this. He knew his armed forces had, to some extent, a counterbalancing effect. He gambled on his own skill at fascinating the masses. If he should lose the magic of his tongue, he would dance in vain between the power-hungry groups assembled in Djakarta; the colonels from other islands where Java's rule was resented; the right-wing fanatics; and the left-wing players of political chess, aware that if they hoped to inherit the nation whole, they must keep this man who single-handedly united it.

This national hero had a background not untypical of Afro-Asian leaders. He was born in eastern Java in 1901 and went to Holland as a young engineer. He became the leader of a new nationalist movement, the Partai Nasional Indonesia, which fought single-mindedly for social justice and total independence. In 1929 Sukarno was arrested with other PNI executives and sentenced by the Dutch to three years in jail. He was freed at the end of 1931, when he resumed his activities with another nationalist movement, Partinda. The Dutch arrested him again and imprisoned him on the island of Flores.

Sukarno was accused of collaborating with the enemy after the Japanese released him in 1942, when they invaded the islands. Later they used his popularity to further their own ambitions. Sukarno made speeches that the Japanese hoped would win them widespread sympathy and support. His friends said that the speeches were two parts Indonesian nationalism to one part Japanese propaganda; and that he used this opportunity to continue his fight for independence. His enemies said that Sukarno was egotistical enough to believe that the Japanese really meant to make him a national hero and leader, and that he was quite prepared to play ball.

The best tribute I know to Sukarno's patriotism came from the Indonesian socialist leader Sutan Sjahrir. He told me: "The president's role during the Japanese occupation was a difficult one. He realized very quickly that the Japanese were fascists of the worst kind. He decided we had to use every cunning means to defeat them. We agreed that I should organize an underground resistance movement while he pretended to work with the Japanese." Sjahrir told me this at a time when he was being bitterly critical of the president's administration, and when his close friend Doctor Sumitro was in open rebellion against the president. He had no reason to praise the man, other than his own intellectual honesty.

The Japanese picked Sukarno as the leader of several pseudo-nationalist organizations. They made him a partner with Dr. Hatta, another nationalist; and the two became known as "the Mother and the Father of the nation."

Like many Indonesians, Sukarno had no first name, although he was often incorrectly called "Ahmad." His father was a light-skinned Javanese; his mother had the rounded beauty of the Balinese. He had the large, brilliant eyes, flat nose and sensual thick-lipped mouth of Bali, and the quick wits of Java. The mixture was not likely to have much immediate appeal outside of Asia. "A slippery fellah," was the verdict of an English diplomat. "Pinning him down is like trying to catch a piece of soap in the bath," said an American aid expert. "Just when you think you've got him, he's gone."

Sukarno's job of fostering pro-Japanese feeling included recruiting a militia to defend the country against Allied invasion.
The military formation, Peta, later became the Indonesian Republic's army.

The Japanese, despite what Sukarno later claimed were his
true designs, kept nationalist feelings under control. In other
parts of Southeast Asia, they had established "independent local
regimes." But it was only in August, 1945, between their first
offer of surrender and their final capitulation a week later, that
the Japanese gave approval to an independent Indonesian state.
When the Dutch lieutenant governor general arrived in October
in the company of British Commonwealth troops, he found the
whole machinery of government and the economy in the hands
of Sukarno, who had proclaimed the republic with himself as
president.

He remained an idol of the masses for thirty years or more.
Yet he had no perceptible talent for running affairs. Whatever
industrial and technical progress there had been since the so-
called Revolution of 1945–1949 was largely a result of western
aid which found itself in competition with the Soviet bloc. Sukarno's contribution to economic progress did not lie in his administrative abilities. It was in his skill at playing off one foreign
power against another. Having fostered the impression during
the Japanese occupation that Sukarno was for sale, Sukarno
could intimate to each side of the cold war his continuing availa-
bility. Neither of the power blocs dared risk calling his bluff,
and the foreign aid continued to pour in.

"He's like a highly successful tart," said a visiting Tokyo
editor. "Each lover is made to feel superior to the last one."

The blackmailing aspects of this technique are familiar enough
these days. There was some excuse for them, perhaps, in the
postcolonial period, when the West was eager to make up for

past mistakes. Later, however, even the Russians must have been concerned with the corrupting effects of foreign loans and charity. They saw Sukarno enlarging his bureaucracies at an alarming rate, strangling initiative and encouraging among his people an attitude of "why-worry-when-the-stupid-foreigners-are-always-eager-to-pull-us-out-of-the-mess." The Russians saw this, Nikita Khrushchev alluded to it during visits to Indonesia, but neither they nor ourselves could afford to be first to quit the merry-go-round. Meanwhile Sukarno waxed poetic when he described Indonesia's growing influence in the Afro-Asian world, pointing the way for all underdeveloped countries.

I watched him one evening near Bandung, in central Java. Thousands were gathered between the thatched huts and in the *kampong* square. "Silence," said the trim well-tailored figure in the brimless cap and dark glasses. He spoke softly but around him the voices fell silent in a widening circle, as if silence was a bomb exploding noiselessly, swallowing sound.

Then, his own voice rising to a strident pitch, he launched into an impassioned speech. The phrases were standard. The ideas had changed very little. The crowd quivered with almost the same responses. Sukarno touched them on all the sensitive areas. The wickedness of the Dutch colonists. The great prospects for Indonesian socialism. The need to liberate west New Guinea. And when he had gone, the excitement lingered in the villages like the warm afterglow of sexual passion. Indeed, it was an Indonesian intellectual, an aging professor, who said to me, "He makes love to us. But even the best of lovers begins to pall if he has nothing else besides his manhood."

Sukarno's concern to keep his manhood had created a number of legends. He was allowed four wives under Muslim law but he had divorced two, he had separated from a third and was keeping a fourth. His aides went to some lengths to make it known that his journeys abroad involved a great deal of nocturnal activity. The stories circulating among his critics were not printable. Those invented by his admirers paid tribute to his physical prowess, as if the peasants unconsciously understood the intimate nature of their relationship with him. When Sukarno reached the climax of a speech, the shrieks of the women and the deep murmurs of the men were like a mass orgasm. "Le Grand Seducteur" was the name given to him by a Paris magazine and characteristically he took it as a compliment.

Seduced or raped, the villagers were gripped in the man's passionate oratorical embrace. The younger intellectuals, however, had begun to agree with their elders that Sukarno was a national debit, grinding out slogans to camouflage his failure to establish either economic or political stability. The mutterings of discontent had started to spread again.

To some extent, attacks on Sukarno could be deflected by the familiar technique of labeling critics "unpatriotic." The president long ago identified himself with a campaign to wipe out the scars of inferiority, insisting on a celebration to mark every "Indonesian achievement," from matchsticks to culture. He became the impresario of all the arts. Ambassadors were put through back-straining, knee-buckling hours of Indonesian dancing.

"Sukarno *was* culture. If you were not in favor of Sukarno, you were against culture and against Indonesia," editorialized the *Indonesia Raya*, foremost in its exposures of corruption until the editor, Mochtar Lubis, was arrested on charges of treason.

Both the Russians and the Chinese recognized how susceptible Sukarno was to flattery, how eager were his people to be told that they were admired and loved. The president made his first tour of the communist bloc in 1956 and came back convinced that the leaders in Moscow and Peking regarded him as a brilliant revolutionary, a political genius, and the man to bring Africa and Asia out of the wilderness. They had offered him support in any military campaigns against either the dissident factions at home or the Dutch in west New Guinea, and unlimited arms. But most important of all, Russia and China provided Sukarno with the prestige he required to tell the West to pay strict attention to what he had to say. Covered in flattering unction, he left the communist bloc with a deep impression of the wisdom and perception of its people. After all, they liked him.

His views on government underwent a sharp revision. He could now see a great deal of merit in the communist system, although he was careful to avoid expressing unadulterated admiration. His new theories might be summed up as follows:

1. Priority should be given to securing freedom from want (to which the communist world gave maximum attention) in preference to freedom of expression (which was more highly valued in the West).

2. The people must be "organized, guided and taught from above" because this kind of leadership had accomplished much better results in the Soviet Union.

3. "The system of Opposition, aimed solely at the defeat of the government of the day" should be abolished and replaced with an advisory council in which members competed to bring forth fresh and constructive ideas to solve national problems.

4. There should be a dissolution of political parties, after which Indonesians would decide if they wanted a single party system or a limited number of "rational parties." *

Sukarno made his plans clear early in 1957, when he called for the appointment of an all-party cabinet, including the communists, who could not be ignored because they had commanded six million votes in the last election. He proposed to establish a

* These were points made in later speeches.

non-elected National Advisory Council, headed by himself and representing all sections of the community. This council would give solicited and unsolicited advice to the cabinet.

The constitutional setting, prior to Sukarno's introduction of "guided democracy," was this:

The president, who was also head of the state and commander in chief, and the vice-president ("assisting in the president's exercise of duties") were elected by the Chamber of Representatives, this being a fusion of members from the former upper and lower federal houses and of consultative and legislative organs of the Jogjakarta republic. The chamber could be dissolved for new elections by the president within 30 days.

The constitution of August, 1950, was explicitly termed "provisional." It contemplated the election of a Constituent Assembly with one representative for every 150,000 resident citizens, in conjunction with a new "properly elected" quadrennial Chamber of Representatives, each representing 300,000 citizens.

The president could nominate one or more cabinet "formateurs." In accordance with their recommendations, the president would approve a prime minister and cabinet. The government could promulgate emergency decrees which would have to be confirmed by the Chamber in its next session.

The preamble to the provisional constitution enunciated the five principles (Pantja Sila): belief in God; nationalism; internationalism (apparently the promotion of good international relations); representative government; and social justice (which Sukarno said was missing in the purely "political democracies" of the West).

Sukarno dissolved parliament on March 5, 1960, and assumed vast executive powers. He explained, blandly enough, that the parliament elected in 1955 had failed to live up to "the hope for mutual understanding and co-operation between it and the government." He formed a new parliament a few days later. It consisted of 261 members appointed by Sukarno and supposedly representing all parties, plus labor, the armed forces and other sections of the community.

The similarity between this extraordinary piece of political architecture and the communist Chinese "people's assembly" was not lost on some Indonesians. The president requested that the new Parliament should employ the traditional Indonesian method of mutual consultation "in order to arrive at unanimous decisions" — in other words, to give a stamp of authority to Sukarno's own dictates. Later that year, he announced the formation of a Provisional People's Consultative Congress. Again, the model was China. The congress would meet every five years to determine basic national policies. A Preparatory National Front Central Board was sworn in by the president in September, 1960. Its job was to marshal all forces in the country in support of government policies. At the same time, Sukarno announced the dissolution of his most outspoken critics, the Masjumi and PSI (socialist party of Indonesia) on the grounds that these parties opposed his objectives. The Masjumi was regarded as the second largest party in the country. The PSI had attracted a small but devoted following among intellectual circles.

It may seem somewhat academic, in the circumstances, to examine the political scene prior to Sukarno's assumption of dictatorial powers. Sukarno delegated many of his executive powers to the army, however, and a glance at the four main parties and the lesser ones with which they were associated is worthwhile. They are useful guides to the army's own political divisions.

The complexity of these parties, their numbers and variety, also contain a lesson. At the time of the 1955 general election, there were 169 parties and individual factions. In the delirium of independence anyone who could spout slogans and invent theories of government was likely to win an audience and might, with luck, become a politician. All over the world, new states were suffering from this excessive appreciation of political freedom. Indonesia was merely a more spectacular specimen. Sukarno took advantage of this political carnival, drawing on earlier Dutch experience to make the best of squabbles which prevented an organized resistance to his moves.

Sukarno's party, the PNI, had a socialist, chauvinist wing which was opposed by a more moderate faction. It moved steadily toward the left, cooperating more and more with the communists.

The socialist party (PSI) lost one of its leaders, Amir Sjarifuddin, to the communists in 1948. The other was, of course, Sutan Sjahrir.

The Muslim groups were divided among four parties, of which the largest was the Masjumi. This was composed of prewar political, social and cultural Muslim organizations, and its predominant sympathies became increasingly pro-socialist. Two of its members were prime ministers at different times; a third was governor of the Bank of Indonesia. All three fled to Sumatra in 1957 to join the rebels. There were two Christian parties.

The Indonesian communist party (PKI) joined the Communist International in 1921, and was an offspring of a group founded by the Dutch Social Democrats. It sponsored the first "nationalist uprising" in 1926, which collapsed from lack of support. The communist leader Tan Malaka, who later died in mysterious circumstances, started a separatist movement, and the PKI was not heard from again until November, 1945, when an irregular "Red Army" was formed. It tried at regular intervals to form "Popular Front" coalitions until a former leader, Muso, came back from the Soviet Union after 23 years' residence and called for a national revolt against Sukarno's government. That was in 1948, and although the revolt was crushed and the PKI badly discredited, the party survived. It is now thought to have the largest support of any party in Java and it works closely with the biggest Indonesian trade union federation, SOBSI, which is affiliated to the communist World Federation of Trade Unions, ruling workers on plantations and in shipping industries, railroads and oilfields.

"I am a leftist, not a communist," Sukarno continued to claim. After so many years surrounded by sycophants, the possibility of domination by communist flatterers did not impress him as a serious possibility. Embarked upon the dangerous experiment of uniting all factions behind a national front, Sukarno knew what had happened in similar situations elsewhere in Asia; in China, for instance, or in Communist North Vietnam or Laos. The example of Ho Chi Minh, the Vietnamese figurehead propped into position by Chinese communists, was not lost on Sukarno. The Chinese had been unusually frank in explaining how the technique worked. "Uncle" Ho was a national hero, he had led a popular revolt against the French, he was fascinated with Marxist ideas, and it was natural that he should accept Chinese aid until it swallowed him. The president of Indonesia remained convinced, however, that he could venture into the communist quagmire and not fall in.

Red China began offering Sukarno military and financial aid after the Indonesian campaign against the remaining Dutch exiles hit its stride. Peking's agent was the man who jostled his way to Sukarno's elbow, a stubby and humorless strategist named Dipa Nusantara Aidit. Aidit helped to plan Sukarno's assumption of enormous executive powers. He recommended the dissolution of the Boy Scout movement ("There is something wrong with it," Sukarno explained. "If it was any good, there would be 23 million Boy Scouts instead of only half a million. I therefore declare the formation of the Vanguard Association — with myself as chief").

Aidit became the political *bomoh* that Sukarno must always consult. He was secretary general of the Indonesian communist party, whose support had become essential to Sukarno's survival.

8

The Vanishing *Bomoh*

AIDIT WAS an elusive man. I tried to catch him before breakfast at Party headquarters on the outskirts of Djakarta. The red banners were limp above the squat concrete building. The dawn rains had swept through this part of town, bringing no breath of cooling wind. Puddles gleamed in the driveway and the white walls were steaming gently in the heat.

Young men with red badges in their lapels glanced up uneasily as I entered. A girl received my request to see Mr. Aidit with a discouraging frown. The atmosphere was familiar. The shabby converted house flaunting its communist identity with crimson banners, the watchful air inside as if the inmates waited with one ear cocked to catch the sounding of the last trump. All over Asia there were similar buildings filled with anxious bespectacled poets waiting, mostly in vain, to give their lives to the cause. You could not laugh at their deadly serious faces because there was never anything amusing in the spectacle of young and intelligent people driven to desperate measures. Nor could you dismiss them. Not after seeing their coreligionists march in silent discipline to take over the temples of Peking, or the palaces of Hanoi, or methodically scraping up the mess of a Malayan ambuscade.

They always looked the same. Drawn faces, martyred eyes. You surprised them in their barren offices and they were leaning on their silent typewriters, reading. Sometimes their lips

moved as they tried to translate. Sometimes they copied unfamiliar letters into notebooks. Always they looked like dili-
gent students, unnaturally quiet even in the absence of a teacher.

Taking them by surprise this way, you were rebuffed. No,
the comrade qualified to answer your question was not in. No,
it was not known when he would be back. No, do not wait.
But there were other times when the tight suspicious faces fell
back and someone with greater authority was suddenly plying
you with cigarettes and the stiff scented magazines printed in
Moscow or Peking.

I had come to see Aidit but the secretary general was away.
A lean Sumatran comrade interrupted my ceremonious rejection. He wore authority like the collar of purgatory and once
again, as had happened before at other times and in other places,
the earnest apprentices drew back. Advancing into the middle of
the room, the older man said, "Would you please come inside."

He had an aquiline nose and sharp but not unfriendly eyes.
He had a girl secretary whose hair was cut severely short, but
she too had a friendly smile now and brought us tea in thick
mugs. Why, I wondered, do Asian communists always drink
tea?

The conversation could have been packed into a brief sentence.
Courtesy demanded that we spin it out. I knew that only Aidit
could answer my questions, but I was anxious not to humble my
host by an abrupt departure. At the same time, I knew that he
knew how well I understood the situation. So that my lingering
there in his cluttered dusty office was proof of my delicacy, a
small token of good will, devoid of any doctrinal significance
but simply the recognition of a more ancient code. We parted
amiably, the ritual ended. And as a seeming afterthought he
took my name and the number of my room at the Hotel
Transaera.

I bounced back to the hotel in an elderly bug-shaped taxi. The level-crossing gates were down. The traffic continued to pour into the blocked street like broken toys shoved into an old sock. Behind us, tin-roofed trucks and pony carts and trishaws and Russian jeeps and battered Cadillacs were piling up in a noisy logjam. Horns sounded on the narrow canal bridge. I paid the driver and got out. It was going to be a long wait and I was hungry.

Breakfast at the Transaera was a Dutch concoction of cheese and jam and chocolate flakes, with an irresistible but bowel-jolting glass of mango juice. I peered at *The Times of Indonesia*, fascinated by a verbatim report on the front page of my private interview the previous day with the foreign minister. The papers filled their columns with curious items snatched indiscriminately from the agency teleprinters, but this one must have come from the minister's own office. There was also a tantalizing dispatch from Prague, where an old woman aged 123 had learned, it was said, to lay bricks. A cow named Nusi was having a statue named after her in Budapest. All over the world, I assured myself, truth continued to outdraw fiction. And such was the force of this revelation that I could watch with comparative calm the sudden and inexplicable entry through the hotel lobby of Jana.

She said: "I tried to phone."

I folded the paper. "They never really mastered the theories of Mr. Bell here," I replied in my best well-Sherlock-what's-new style.

Jana smiled, crouching into a chair. "I am taking the plane to Palembang. At noon."

"That's in Sumatra, isn't it?"

"Yes." She stroked the black rope of her hair.

"What for? I mean, why go to Palembang?"

Jana pouted and twisted in the chair, her green eyes alert and roving. "The revolutionary government is moving into the hills. They're under military pressure. I have to see Sjafruddin [the rebel president]. Doctor Sumitro is in Washington asking for more help."

"What happened?"

She tapped a Javanese cigarette out of a shoddy paper packet and I noticed how brutally she had cut her long curved nails. "General Nasution caught us by surprise. He landed amphibious troops and a parachute unit on the west coast. Our brave soldiers were not prepared, it seems." She spoke with soft sarcasm, tossing her head back angrily. "Our commanders talk a great deal but they do not really expect to fight. They hope always for easy solutions. President Sukarno was going to capitulate just as soon as they declared their revolutionary government — or so they thought."

I said there was nothing in the newspapers about this obviously large-scale military operation. "At least," I added, "nothing directly. Now I think of it — yes — there's a report here that flights to Sumatra have been suspended. You can't go."

Jana smiled. "My connections here have arranged for me to go on a military flight."

"But how will you get to wherever the rebels are?"

"I'll take a bus from Palembang. There's a bus to Bukittingi and I should find Sjafruddin somewhere around there."

So Jana went off to the wars, aboard an aircraft in the service of what I presumed were her enemies, and by bus. I suspected that a personal reason for her journey was the presence in Sumatra of Colonel Zulkifli Lubis, a tough and clever army officer who had established the Indonesian army intelligence service. Some time ago, Lubis had broken with President Sukarno and after threatening to assassinate him, threw in his lot with the rebels. Lubis, one of Jana's more intimate "uncles," felt that Sukarno was getting dangerously involved with the communists.

Jana had left me some addresses and an invitation to attend a ceremony at the presidential palace. "You will have an opportunity to talk privately with him," she had said. "And don't forget to go — it would be discourteous to break the arrangement." These were odd words, coming from a courier for the president's sworn foemen.

Shortly before noon a young man appeared from Party headquarters. I was sitting in the tiny patch of garden outside my hotel room, trying to type under an old-fashioned fan. It was too hot inside the room, and too dark and dismal, quite apart from the fact that I had to share it with a total stranger who was lying on his narrow cot there now, snoring gently, one leg slung over the narrow hard bolster known as a Dutch housewife. My visitor accepted a glass of mango juice while I unfolded the message he brought. It was unsigned and said merely that Comrade Aidit would be addressing a meeting in a certain *kampong* that evening if I wished to go.

I walked back through the hotel garden between the creaking palms into the lobby. A couple of Indonesian Army captains watched. They sat with their automatics in their laps, their hairy forearms bared, trim in their pressed khakis. I had forgotten that the hotel was under military requisition. They listened as I asked the hotel clerk to hire me a car and then one of the officers walked away. Abruptly excusing himself, the clerk followed.

When he returned, it was to apologize. Finding a car would require a little time. There would be the necessity to telephone. And if I was going out of Djakarta, permits might be needed. I recognized the opening moves of a delaying action and agreed with the clerk that this would be a good time to take lunch.

When I got back to the room, two hours later, the stranger in the next bed was leaving. He shot me an angry glance and disappeared at the head of his baggage boys. I was puzzled by his sudden and unexplained departure. The answer turned up in the form of Mr. Kan.

"Excuse, please." He waddled in, a fat little ageless Chinese, and began directing traffic. "Over there, *boy*. No, put the big suitcase *here*." The porters streamed through the room, wheeling and backing under his orders.

"I am Five-Stroke Kan," he said finally, extending a fleshy hand. "Shipping agent from Singapore. Sorry to disturb you. I am called Five-Stroke because I belong to the millions of Chinese called Wong. However, I do not write my name with three strokes, as is usual, but with *five* strokes — like this." He drew a Chinese ideograph on the palm of his hand. "Care for a drink?" He pulled a whiskey flask from his briefcase.

"Well, thanks all the same." I hesitated. "But I'm waiting for a car. Perhaps not. But thanks."

"It may take another hour," said Mr. Kan. "Hired cars in Djakarta are never reliable. Come. Just a small peg."

Now I could hardly refuse. How did Five-Stroke Kan know the car was hired? It seemed rather obvious that the hotel's military masters had seen me fraternizing with the comrades and having chucked out my unknown roommate, had planted this voluble Chinese gentleman upon me. If my guess was correct, the army must be watching Comrade Aidit and the Party pretty closely.

We had almost emptied Five-Stroke's flask when he excused himself and rolled away down the garden, his fat dimpled legs wobbling beneath faded blue shorts, his enormous shoulders straining the seams of his flap-tailed shirt. There were no telephones in the rooms and I supposed he had gone to use the manager's. I had told him all he wanted to know, without being too obvious. Doubtless the car would show up.

It arrived soon after Five-Stroke's departure, driven by a Muslim in tattered clothes who introduced himself as Ahmed. Our objective was the cluster of villages where Comrade Aidit had called his meeting. They lay some distance along the road to

Bandung, on the other side of the mountains. The road was potholed but Ahmed had a heavy foot. Once clear of Djakarta's suburbs he trod on the accelerator. I was glad when we tangled with the weaving tail of a crawling military convoy, effectively cheating Ahmed of his ambition to race a ten-year-old Dodge as if it were a jet-propelled tank. After his reluctant application of brake, he was good enough to smile apologetically at me as he reached down to fit his feet back into their torn boots.

Now that I had time to look around, it felt good to be free of the city, away from bumbling bureaucrats and tight faces, shuttered shops and swirling traffic. Here the young rice gleamed in brilliant green crescents on the terraced hillsides, sometimes blotted out by a sudden plunge into the chilling gloom of a deserted rubber plantation. In the distance a volcano puffed a tired little gray cloud from its jagged crater.

The convoy slowed untidily to a stop. Up ahead, an army checkpoint plugged the road. "Bandits," said Ahmed. "They are checking for bandits."

Battered buses cluttered the roadside, their rooftops creaking under the weight of bags and baskets. The drivers squatted comfortably like crows along the edge of a ditch and their passengers spread around them in colorful pools of resigned humanity. At the head of the line, seated at a table in the road, a young officer stamped travel permits with that familiar and universal air of a petty functionary endowed with the power to complicate the lives of the humble citizenry. He sat very erect, waving this passenger through with a sharp flourish of his pen, sending that one back with a look both stern and magisterial.

"What kind of bandits, Ahmed?"

"The Darul Islam, sir. Very bad fellows. They have been killing one of my friends, sir. His head. Cutting it off and giving it to his wife. Not good to be doing such things, sir. They are saying bad words about him. That he was a communist and then tearing out his eyes." Ahmed let in the clutch and we shot forward past the waiting line of traffic.

We stopped with a jerk beside the duty officer. Ahmed leaned out of his window, his brimless black hat jammed so tight it almost covered his eyes. He spoke rapidly, gesticulating. The officer got up and walked slowly to the car. He wore an American-style paratroop uniform with a pistol at his belt that protruded below his groin. He growled at Ahmed, who pulled in his head. The officer ducked, removing his sunglasses to get a good look at the interior. Ahmed said something that made the officer straighten up, salute, and wave us on.

"Golly. How'd you do that?"

Ahmed spat through the open window. "I said you were going to the president's week-end palace."

I did not believe him. But whatever imaginative lie he had told, we were through. There were few reports of banditry at this time, and the roadblocks seemed to be more of a formality. Perhaps they were a precaution against attacks on Sukarno's country palace at Bogor. It was a white regency mansion built by Raffles, where deer grazed under the banyans and Ionic columns twinkled like icing sugar in the sun. I thought about Tyrconnel Fay, tirelessly telling heroic tales of the Darul Islam, whose troops were said to be hiding up in these hills.

"You're a Muslim. Why do you call them bandits?" I asked Ahmed.

"They are trying to rule our lives, sir. They are very strict. If a woman walks in the village at night, or dresses like a white woman, she is stoned. Anyone they are not liking, sir, is a communist."

It was here that local Islamic leaders had proclaimed their own theocratic state in the chaotic days before the final Dutch withdrawal. The thugs and remnants of the wartime militia invaded the movement later, using it to justify what might be otherwise regarded as pure villainy.

We reached the village by late afternoon. Red flags fluttered from the attap rooftops. There was a whitewashed mosque and two rows of open-fronted shops with their Chinese owners sitting inside on wooden stools like little mandarins. A layer of woodsmoke hung over the thatched houses. The air was fresh after the mosquito-ridden swamps of Djakarta.

We left the car and walked over the rutted road to a single-story building in the middle of the *kampong*. Ahmed walked with the insolence of the townsman, enjoying his role of guide. He found me the *penghulu*, the village headman, who nodded gravely when I explained that I had come to see the meeting and Aidit.

It was an attractive village, prosperous, filled with the cheerful noises of evening. Most of the villagers, said the headman, were smallholders. They grew sweet potatoes, maize, soya beans and cassava enough to satisfy their own needs. The rice was grown communally. Once, the people had worked in larger numbers on the nearby Dutch estates. Now many of these estates were lying neglected, their owners gone. The headman gave a regretful sigh. "The Dutch were kind masters."

Ahmed stirred his foot, the oversize unlaced shoe scraping on the cobbles. "That is so," he muttered, and suddenly I knew he was not being polite but really did miss his former overlords. It had been easy to hate them once. Now that they had gone, however, who was there to give advice, fix the machinery and protect the rubber trees from disease and neglect?

We sat in a Chinese teashop, watching the children herd the gleaming black water-buffalo out of the village pond. There was a distant rumble like thunder and Ahmed said, "They are shelling the Darul Islam. Up there in the hills." Then, anxious to reassure me, he added, "It is mostly exercising, sir."

"What about the rebels? Are they up here too?"

"Rebels, sir?" Ahmed's face turned blank.

"The rebel colonels. The revolutionary army of President Sjafruddin."

Ahmed bent over his glass of tea, shaking his head slightly. "No, sir." He took a sip and then faced me with eyes too direct and honest. "No, sir, I am knowing nothing about such people, sir."

The communist meeting was a disappointment. Aidit failed to show up. The audience was meager and consisted mostly of young people. A Party official from Djakarta said he was sorry about Comrade Aidit. It was hardly worth our staying, in his opinion. In fact he rather thought he would return home before the meeting got underway. Perhaps we could give him a ride?

This approach in other circumstances would have made me more determined to stay. But it was already late enough. There were military patrols out on the road and I was not at all sure that we were wise to go plunging around the countryside late at night. Martial law was in force and my presence among these timid-looking comrades had undoubtedly put a crimp in their plans. All in all, there were any number of face-saving reasons for returning to Djakarta. But the fact was that I had no wish to expose myself needlessly to danger. Aidit, for his own inscrutable reasons, had not arrived and it was time to cut bait.

During the drive back our extra passenger glared unhappily out of a side window and seemed to enjoy smothering my feeble attempts at conversation. He was unwilling to speculate about Aidit's absence from the meeting and spoke in predigested phrases. "Comrade Aidit has said we cannot achieve communism in Indonesia in less than forty or fifty years," he said, using the treadworn phrase intended to reassure prospective victims. I had no means to match his half of the Party's instant dialogue and Ahmed was no help.

Once he showed interest. "You were in China? Ah. I too was there. We must all learn from China, how to unite and struggle." I forbore to mention that after some time in Red China, I was appalled by the sophisticated technique by which Mao "collaborated" with those he was about to devour.

We dropped our cheerless companion at the former Dutch KPM shipping lines office. Unexpectedly he asked me inside.

The building had been occupied by trade unionists. There were army cots in the cavernous marble hall, borrowed or stolen by the self-styled "activists." The men stood in small groups, talking softly, barely discernible in the flickering yellow light from paraffin lamps.

"At night," said my communist companion with ill-concealed pride, "this becomes a people's university." I suddenly realized that the whispering groups were, in fact, classes. The students were union members who ran the KPM office management by day, and who now lived and slept on the premises too.

We climbed the great curving sweep of the imposing staircase and paused beneath a statue depicting the Netherlands as a bountiful mother embracing native children who symbolized her colonies. "Not a very good mother," said my companion, shrugging. "She even wanted us to pay the cost of our war of liberation."

He took me into the office formerly occupied by the KPM president. A stocky figure sat at the big desk, working by several hissing storm lanterns.

"Comrade Kussain," said my new friend.

He introduced me, speaking rapidly in his own tongue.

Kussain was far from friendly. "I understand you are curious about the takeover," he said. He walked round to the other side of the desk, perching above where I sat. He nodded to a young man lounging near the huge old mantelpiece. The youngster took an automatic rifle by the muzzle and slouched away, letting the butt bump along the parquet floor. I hoped the safety catch was on.

"You Americans think we cannot run the ships," said Kussain, glaring down at me and pulling on a cigarette in short, rapid puffs.

I explained that although I was not an American, I felt sure that Americans did not doubt Indonesian ability to run anything.

He sniffed. "This will be like Suez. The western imperialists said the Egyptians could not keep the canal open. But they did."

He slapped the desk with the flat of his hand. "Why do you Americans want to know so badly if we are communists? If we are, we are not afraid to say so. What is communism? It is to work for the people, yes?"

He harangued me for some time then, in the familiar stilted phrases.

I left the building a bit shaken. Kussain and his armed workers had taken over with nobody's authority but their own. If the PKI had never put an overt communist into the cabinet since 1948, they still wielded their own kind of influence. They expanded their "front" groups, tightened control of the labor movement and lulled Indonesian fears of their ultimate goals and orientation. The measure of their power was this well-organized seizure of the republic's major shipping line.

It was to be a long time before I met Aidit and then the only impression he left was that of a small dedicated fanatic whose power resided in less obvious talents than that of mesmerizing the crowds. He was the puppet-master, content to manipulate Sukarno. He was a graduate of that much older school of mummery in China where more cunning and ancient devices are employed to keep the audiences spellbound.

Aidit's self-effacing task was to ensure that a popular national hero like Sukarno should remain unalarmingly "neutral" while increasingly dependent upon communist good will. To the simple-minded western taxpayer, the fact that Sukarno himself remained a self-avowed neutral made him eligible for aid. The fact that he would be forced to consult Aidit to retain his popularity was much too complicated an idea to alienate western friends of Indonesia. Furthermore, the vast Indonesian territories could be utilized to sustain "national liberation armies" operating in adjacent countries without those armies — despite their communist direction — appearing to be supplied or trained by Peking. The value of this device, it will be seen later, was that it prevented the effective mobilization of western military forces to suppress uprisings disguised as patriotic movements.

A casual visitor to Indonesia was unlikely to sense this hidden communist power. Few foreigners had the means or opportunity to explore the countryside in such an intimate way as to discover the real extent of Aidit's influence. Those foreigners who had settled into village life — and there were quite a number until the mid-1950's, including my own friends — were ruthlessly squeezed out. A retired Indian Army surgeon, a gentle soul and well known to me, was forced out of Bali for the reason that he exercised a distracting influence by his services to the community.

The strength of the communist PKI lay in these rural communities. By 1957 it was on the way to becoming the biggest political party in Java. In general elections that year, Java produced 89 per cent of 6.2 million PKI votes. This astonishing improvement in Party fortunes, less than ten years after the abortive coup that discredited communist leaders and broke their treasury, was Aidit's work.

Dipa Nusantara Aidit was born in Sumatra in 1923, two years
before Moscow attacked the Indonesian communist movement for
its lack of flexibility. Thirty years later, he won his fight within
the PKI for the adoption of flexible tactics. He insisted that
communism be made understandable in existing Indonesian conditions, and he defined the PKI's primary task: "To draw the
peasants who comprise 80 per cent of the population into the
united front."

There was a great similarity between Aidit's grasp of Indonesian realities and the earlier experience of Mao Tse-tung in
China. This was no coincidence. Aidit studied Chinese methods
in Mao's territory and returned to Indonesia after the Chinese
communist regime was firmly established. He spent a significant
period with Ho Chi Minh in the communist Vietminh regions
of Indochina. From these men he learned lessons which were
reflected in later Party directives.

Aidit had always been careful, however, to create an impression of independence from either Red China or Russia. For
one thing, a general hostility had developed among Indonesians
against Chinese residing in the republic, and it would not be wise
for the PKI to become identified with the Chinese motherland.
For another, the PKI's bitterest enemies among the socialists had
done much to popularize the idea that Indonesian communists
were loyal to foreign powers whose imperialist design masqueraded as an international ideology.

Aidit represented a second generation of Indonesian communists, who emphasized their nationalist spirit. When he returned from Peking in 1950, he became the guiding force of the
PKI's Agitprop and by 1953 he had redirected the Party into
a new phase of National Front policy. A year later, after a bitter
factional struggle, he won control as the PKI's secretary general.

His fight within the Party paralleled that of Mao Tse-tung's in China. Both men defeated the original leaders, who tried to make the communist movement exclusively the organ of an industrial proletariat and the peasantry, with complete disregard for local conditions. The industrial proletariat was as yet insignificant and the peasants were too bound by tradition to respond to a doctrinal appeal.

Aidit was a skillful organizer and mobilized mass support for popular national issues with great agility. President Sukarno would be scarcely finished launching a campaign for volunteers to invade west New Guinea than Aidit's organizers and Agitprop would rally the peasants. He was content at this stage of the game to increase President Sukarno's dependence upon the PKI and to advance behind that demagogue's mask. But he was obliged to share Sukarno's power with his enemy, the army chief of staff, General Haris Nasution.

The general had, at this time, crushed a plot to seize the Anglo-Dutch Oil Company in Djakarta. Workers had been directed to take over the oil installations by SOBSI, the trade union federation, and later evidence made clear Aidit's complicity. The seizure should have followed the same pattern as (and it should have coincided with) the occupation of the Dutch KPM shipping line.

General Nasution evicted communist-led workers from the big Dutch estates they had occupied by force, and in other ways he had proved to be a thorn in Aidit's flesh. During the initial negotiations for Soviet arms, he concluded a contract with the United States for light weapons without consulting the president, forestalling at least that Soviet-bloc sale.

But the general remained something of an enigma. He had banned, for example, political organs of extremist views on both left and right; and he had placed Chinese Nationalist schools under close government supervision.

He led an army which performed a distinctive role in national affairs. It looked upon itself as the guardian of the revolutionary spirit and the protector of national unity. Its leaders interfered in politics and threatened to disrupt the administration. In turn they suffered interference from the politicians, with reactions that were sometimes violent.

Nasution was a man impossible to ignore.

9

Compulsive Partners

MR. FIVE-STROKE KAN was bouncing happily around the shower when I woke up next morning. He had found the secret of coaxing lukewarm water from the cold tap. I congratulated him. "Come," he cried, "I will exhibit for you my method."

So I kicked aside my Dutch housewife, the bolster whose main function in the tropics is to soak up the night's perspiration, and stumbled through the mosquito net to witness Five-Stroke's technique. It consisted of giving the cold-water pipe a couple of lusty kicks with his bare foot. Unfortunately in his enthusiasm he struck the hot pipe. There was an ominous gurgle and water engulfed him in a scalding cascade. The Chinese shipping agent streaked out of the bathroom with a towel clutched to his plump behind.

"Well," I said, "that's one way of waking up. You know, that hot tap has never worked the whole time I've been here."

"For me," said Five-Stroke, sitting gingerly on the edge of his cot, "things always work at the wrong time. It is an irritation, a disability such as having a wooden leg or being afflicted with an interfering mother-in-law." He became philosophical with pain. "Is it not strange that medical science recognizes our physical disabilities but fails to consider that a man may be pursued all his life by an intangible and hostile fate?"

I said that he appeared to have survived quite comfortably.

"You may believe so." He gave his bald pate a worried rub. "However, it is my conviction that many endeavors in which I engage turn out differently than expected."

There were a number of Chinese like Five-Stroke in Djakarta. They transacted business for the government, for the rebel agents, for corrupt officials and occasionally for correspondents trying to reach the rebel areas from the capital. I was to meet Five-Stroke again, in other circumstances, when his purpose in visiting Djakarta became clearer. He was in fact the owner of several small ships in Singapore, profitably carrying cargoes from the more remote parts of Indonesia to foreign ports without the central government's knowledge. The Indonesian Navy at this time was intercepting perhaps one ship in twenty, but the authorities were beginning to tighten their controls. One result was that Five-Stroke's business interests in Djakarta were placed under constraints that foreshadowed a more vigorous attack on all those Overseas Chinese who were actually resident in the archipelago.

Five-Stroke could see trouble ahead. He had misguidedly adopted the role of a devout anticommunist. This was not going to help him at all in the future, but at this stage he felt he was betting on the right side.

It is hard to convey the atmosphere of chaos that prevailed in Five-Stroke's strange world, where thousands of dollars of illicit business might be done on a man's word alone. The Chinese in particular wanted nothing on paper. To them it appeared impossible to judge where a man's loyalties might lie, and foolish to talk frankly to a stranger who might report your conversation to the local military commander in order to win approval. For instance, Ruslan Abdulgani, the man who had done most to gild Sukarno's image in the West, was foreign minister when the army arrested him on the eve of his departure to attend the conference of Suez Canal users in London. A Chinese black market-eer had denounced him. He was released after the intervention of higher authority. A commission of inquiry in April, 1957, cleared Mr. Abdulgani of charges of corruption. He was convicted, however, of "unintentionally taking abroad bank notes and valuable papers without the approval of the foreign exchange department." Later he was appointed by President Sukarno to the position of chairman of the National Council, which made him the most powerful figure in the republic next to General Nasution. From this dizzy height, Abdulgani was able to drop bolts of fire on his Chinese accuser, whose sufferings after this unexpected turn of the wheel can be easily imagined.

Major General Haris Nasution was not as resilient nor quite so adaptable as Abdulgani, who told me one day in his grandiose office that Indonesia's guided democracy was not like Red China's system of government because the Chinese were all under the communist party's thumb, whereas here the leadership was in the hands of Bung Karno, whose wisdom could be relied upon. One of the declared aims of the Indonesian rebellion was to have General Nasution forcibly retired. Yet there had been a time when the general himself surrounded President Sukarno with tanks and demanded his resignation. In any other country but Indonesia, this would be a mystifying state of affairs. Here it was par for the course.

All this made western support for the rebels very risky. It was impossible to guess which group was likely to switch sides next.

I wanted to see General Nasution and then get away. My chief purpose had been to assess the effects of President Sukarno's seizure of Dutch businesses. But this was tied up with the rebellion, with a new economic crisis, and with the need to stir up nationalist fervor again over west New Guinea. To disentangle all this confusion would take far longer than I could spare; and compressed into a news dispatch to be read ten thousand miles away, it would be meaningless. The conspiratorial atmosphere of Djakarta, in the damp heat of the coastal plains, depressed my spirits. I longed to return to a situation more tangible than this foggy melodrama filled with ambivalent personalities. The rebels, it seemed to me then, could hardly fail to provide a tonic.

There was a screen of bright young army officers around Nasution, and picking my way through them was almost as instructive as talking with the general. They were bitter in their denunciation of the rebellion.

"It is led by British and American spies," said one.

"How do you know?"

He shrugged. "British bases in Malaya and Borneo refuse to interfere with rebel activities there. And our own agents have recorded conversations between rebel leaders and men of Central Intelligence."

Another said: "It is always hard to prove that a man is spying for a foreign power. However, here is a list of Americans recently in contact with rebel headquarters, and here are details of the sums of money and arms which they have promised." Among the names was that of a retired United States Army general.

It was not easy to check on the veracity of these statements. But later I discussed with Paul Hurmuses, then of *Time* magazine, a military report on his own visits to rebel areas. He agreed that the report was surprisingly accurate and ventured his own opinion that Nasution had sown the rebel ranks liberally with agents and informers of his own.

Other news of the rebellion kept trickling through, distorted by censorship and often delayed by weeks. Fourteen Indonesian diplomats had deserted their foreign posts to side with the rebels. The ambassador in Rome had taken $500,000 in government funds and was shopping for a warship "to give the revolution."

Rebel funds were rolling in from mysterious foreign sources, which also provided arms and ammunition. Doctor Sumitro had issued a widely publicized appeal to noncombatant sympathizers to remain in their places unless they could abscond with money or equipment to supplement rebel resources.

General Nasution's men were holding, for later public exhibition, captured rebel weapons bearing United States markings. These weapons, they said, had come chiefly by air.

The general took a dim view of what he clearly regarded as a poorly disguised attempt to bolster the rebels. He did not, at this time, blame official American policy, but his senior officers had been empowered to discuss more fully the charge of intervention by the Central Intelligence Agency. The United States embassy in Djakarta had denied all knowledge of, or responsibility for, secret service operations in Indonesia. These denials were received with cynicism. What about Western Enterprises Inc. on Formosa? asked the army men. What about the so-called naval purchasing agency on Formosa? Weren't these dummy organizations which had for many years disguised United States espionage against mainland China?

I went to see General Nasution in his suburban villa, riding there by bicycle-rickshaw. I parked, and ambled onto the front verandah. Sentries pottered into the front yard and gave me a casual inspection.

Nasution, informally dressed in khaki open-necked shirt and drill trousers, was not eager to talk for publication. I think he had been warned of Sukarno's resentment at the favorable publicity given him by the western press. *Time* had delivered something close to the kiss of death by proclaiming Nasution a staunch anticommunist. The general put me straight on this at once. "The West," he said, "must stop branding as communist every action taken by an uncommitted Asian country. We do not want to be involved in any East-West conflicts. The Dutch, for instance, still interfere in our internal affairs."

This oblique reference to the rebellion was not pursued. He preferred to play down its importance. The group of dissident army colonels, he said, had nominal control over part of central Sumatra — about 250 miles by 350 miles in area — centered on Bukittinggi. "But," he added with a bleak smile, "they will not resist my troops." He made the revolutionaries seem dreary and unimportant. When he waved a stubby hand, dismissing them, you could almost believe that the gesture had dissolved their ranks.

Was Nasution dreaming of a military coup of his own? I found it hard to believe that this handsome, alert young army chief did not nurse a secret ambition to lead an army junta. He had promulgated a number of decrees over his own signature. One of his targets had been the press, which he forbade to "indulge in destructive and provocative news reporting."

His sensitivity to the printed word was, I reflected, reassuring. Only the professional scribbler knows how little of what he writes ever sinks in. The potential despot is revealed by the extraordinary importance he attaches to what the press thinks.

The general denied any dictatorial ambitions of his own. The army, he said, should be the protector of the state. So long as he lived, no religious or military or political force would take command. "The army was born in revolutionary upheaval and it has a right to make its voice heard — but not to engage in politics."

His position was clearly a delicate one. He was deeply religious, being a Muslim from Sumatra, and he was still reputed to be (despite his expedient disclaimers) critical of communism. "I am," he said, "neither anticommunist nor anti-West but pro-Indonesia."

He had been maneuvered into a political cul-de-sac. His army might have played a still more important political role by keeping its independence. If, for example, the rebellion achieved its purpose of dislocating communications and dividing the republic, the results might be so chaotic that only the communists could benefit. Then, too, many of the rebels were old friends and comrades of Nasution, and while he sympathized with their wish to wipe out corruption and achieve a more equitable distribution of government benefits, he had a bitter conviction that the Dutch would never stop trying to break up the nation.

Before he could deal directly with communists in his own army — 25 per cent of the Javanese army officers were regarded as communist sympathizers — he had to secure law and order, introduce sound administrations and put a stop to widespread corruption. But this he refused to do on terms dictated by rebels financed from abroad.

Eighteen years younger than Sukarno, the general was well advised to keep in the background, nursing his strength. Any bid for power that he might make, now, could not seriously challenge the popularity of his supreme commander.

It suited Sukarno this way. It suited the communist PKI. Time, the compromise of principles and the galling necessity to swallow pride for the sake of ambition, all these must erode Nasution's firmness of purpose. The communists meanwhile gave him the toys he wanted; the sophisticated weapons that the West for various reasons refused. And from time to time they assured the general that Muslims had full freedom of religion in a communist state.

Nasution was a Batak, a tribe in north Sumatra who fifty years

ago filed their teeth and ate human flesh. Dutch missionaries
were a notoriously frequent delicacy. The Bataks were regarded
with amused contempt by other Indonesian communities, mostly
because of an alleged thickness in their cannonball skulls. It was
a psychological handicap to be a Muslim Batak but at least it
made the young general more than usually aware of the futility
and self-destructive nature of intolerance. He was, he said,
trying to break down racial and religious prejudices within the
armed forces, in the belief that this would provide the basis for
unity later. It was these variations of race and creed, of course,
that obstructed the spread of communist ideas.

As Nasution took me back to the front yard his guards sprang
alert, gun butts scraping, boots clicking. There were two Soviet-
model jeeps in the driveway. Out of the martial glitter emerged
the waiting bicycle-rickshaw boy. He wore the cocky look of
a city sparrow and grinned hugely as we wobbled away from all
that spit and polish, swaying on the broken springs of our awkward conveyance.

There was no easy way to label Nasution. He was a super-
patriot but was he clever enough to escape a web of communist
intrigue? During the so-called Indonesian Revolution of 1945–
1949 he commanded guerrilla forces against the Dutch, and later
he took charge of the Siliwangi Division, which crushed the west
Java communist uprising of 1948. He had acted against Aidit and
the communists when they stepped out of line in too public a
manner. But he had also placed Indonesia under a state of war
and siege while he tackled the rebels.

He had something in common with the military chieftains of
other Islamic states, and also with army leaders of similarly
underdeveloped countries. Like General B. M. Kaul of India,
he was impressed with the role an army could play in stabilizing
affairs; and he saw no essential difference between the methods

used in Red China and those employed, say, by Field Marshal Ayub Khan in Pakistan.

In this treacherous area of political speculation, General Nasution was attracted to theories that have always tempted military commanders, whatever the label: communist or fascist. General Ne Win in Burma had used much the same measures to purge his country of corruption and indolence, as had Nasser in Egypt and Mao Tse-tung in China. The essential view was that a multipurpose militia could be employed, when not fighting, to mend the economy and streamline the administration.

The history of the Indonesian Army was not unlike that of other Afro-Asian states. First there were soldiers recruited by the colonial power; then a sprinkling of officers trained in conventional western methods at some imperial war college. In the case of Indonesia, the army's most rapid expansion followed the creation of self-defense forces by Japanese invaders, with officers who (like Nasution) had first studied at the Dutch-run academy in Bandung. It was now in the process of shaking off western military traditions which did not meet Asian needs, having already dealt with a great many nonprofessional problems of civic administration. For example, when the Indonesian Army became fully responsible for security after the reluctant Dutch withdrawal of 1949, the new republic had barely enough trained civil servants to run a medium-size city. (In the last year before the war, there were only 157 Indonesian students in Dutch colleges and universities, which gives you a measure of Dutch efforts made in this direction.)

The army found itself increasingly responsible for maintaining Indonesian unity. If local army commanders did not help the administration in their areas, if they did not provide vehicles to move supplies and people, if they did not put their communications equipment at the service of regional civic offices, the republic was liable to break up into self-governing units.

Nasution, then a colonel, was satisfied that Dutch forces (with or without The Hague's consent) were trying to achieve this dissolution. In 1952 he supported the minister of defense, the Sultan of Jogjakarta (and a cousin of Doctor Sumitro), who wanted the Indonesian Army streamlined into a disciplined, non-political force of 100,000 men. This would mean getting rid of another 100,000 ex-guerrillas, of whom far too many owed allegiance to local warlords. Among them were trained communist agents who were in those days as eager as the Dutch to see the republic fall apart.

Nasution was one of 17 high-ranking officers who called upon President Sukarno to resign when the sultan's proposals were dismissed. The sultan, said Sukarno, wanted to "destroy the Army's revolutionary zeal." The communist PKI carried the anti-Army motion of censure, with President Sukarno's support. It was the one moment in Nasution's career when he openly challenged the president's leadership.

Sukarno averted disaster with characteristic skill on that famous day of October 16, 1952, when Nasution's troops occupied Djakarta. Their tanks and armored cars surrounded the palace. A riotous mob stood in the palace yard shouting for Sukarno's resignation. But as the president began to speak, the shouting died. He talked of the long fight for liberty. What was the purpose of a sacrificial struggle if, at the end, the people must submit to the dictates of military commanders? He had no anger in his heart at the actions of these misled miscreants. Let them come and speak with him, and cast out the fear that etched men's actions into curious patterns.

"Sisters and Brothers," Sukarno cried, "we live in a world of fear. Fear of the future, fear of the thermonuclear bombs . . . and fear of ideologies. Fear drives men to act foolishly, thoughtlessly, dangerously. I beg of you, do not let fear guide your actions this day. Do not destroy what has been so dearly won."

The mob melted away. The old magic had worked again. "Destroy me," the president had told them, "and you destroy the republic — for we are indivisible."

One of the 17 officers with Nasution on that day was Colonel Kawilarang, who was to become commander of the rebel armies in Sumatra and Celebes. But whereas Kawilarang refused to be hypnotized, Nasution saw a prospect of gaining his own ends through this spellbinding president who groped so obviously for some new technique of government.

Although Nasution was obliged to resign and remained in limbo until the "Officers' Strike" of 1955, he began to voice expedient agreement with the president's view that Indonesia needed disciplined government. The welfare of the state should not be at the mercy of squabbling political factions, they both insisted. They nevertheless professed a deep dislike of dictatorial rule.

President Sukarno had a soaring imagination and could easily persuade the masses that totalitarianism was in fact popular democracy. He reinstated Nasution as army chief of staff to put an iron fist inside the velvet glove.

For Nasution, it became a pact with the devil. If he broke away from President Sukarno, the resultant upheaval might destroy the republic, which was barely holding together anyway. Even if the country did not fly to pieces, to be pounced upon by others, Nasution's departure would make room for communist-trained officers, whose numbers and influence were growing as the result of closer liaison with the Soviet bloc. Air force recruits were being sent to communist flying schools via Burma and China. Some pilots were being trained by communist flying instructors in Egypt. Soviet technicians and advisers were beginning to trickle into Indonesian bases.

The longer he stayed in partnership with President Sukarno,

however, the harder it must have been for Nasution to swallow some of the leader's policies. As a Batak from Sumatra, he was not insensitive to the rising clamor from the Outer Islands to end "Javanese colonialism." There was growing resentment of Java's domination of the national economy, and political writers recalled that before the Dutch came, there had been nothing but wars between the islands.

10

Captain Flick Thinks Twice

JANA HAD KEPT her promise to get my invitation to the presidential palace. Her departure from the scene, however, left me at the mercy of Djakarta's vagaries. I was listening again to President Sukarno. But the circumstances had changed.

"East Wind," he shouted, "means the wind of freedom and justice. The East Wind today is breezing over the West."

He was paraphrasing Mao Tse-tung and the meaning of the parable was clear to the drenched crowd gathered at Kemajoran Airport. Heads turned in our direction as the people cheered. My companion was Marvin Farkus, a New York cameraman who had joined me on a last-minute television assignment. We were under a leisurely form of military detention, a white minority of two.

What had happened was not unusual. Western newsmen in Djakarta faced the hazard every day. Farkus and I were luckier than most. As the briefest of visitors, we could hop on the next plane. Our unimportant story merely illustrates the bigger difficulties under which the semi-permanent correspondents worked.

We had planned to go to the presidential palace on Jana's wangled invitation, where Sukarno would be the center of a brief ceremony before his own departure to Japan. There would be an opportunity to get answers to a list of questions from the president.

An enormous crowd had gathered outside the palace. Ahmed, who was still driving me around, tried in vain to get through. Police barriers were going up in streets approaching the palace and we were stopped finally by an army major. There was a long argument and then Farkus unwittingly put his foot in it. He said, turning to me with an amiable grin: "We should never have stopped to feed those bloody monkeys."

Farkus was talking about the time we had wasted feeding bananas to a brace of monkeys outside the Transaera. It had delayed us ten minutes, long enough for the crowds to thicken disastrously. But the major, to everyone's astonishment and dismay, whirled on Farkus. "Bloody monkeys, is it?" He poked his automatic through the window. "Bloody monkeys, you call us. I will show you what is bloody monkeys."

He had the door open and Farkus by the arm before Ahmed, babbling wildly, sprang to his side. There was a long exchange between the two Indonesians while Farkus was dragged out in a series of agonizing yanks. "Come!" the major would yelp, giving another heave on the arm, while Ahmed gesticulated and bawled his explanation in the major's ear. The major would pause, consider the plea, reject it, and give another tug on Farkus. It was some time before he reluctantly let go.

Even after accepting Ahmed's version of what had been said, he made Farkus apologize. "For something I didn't say?" cried Farkus, not unreasonably. "But why?"

"Because," said the major, "you are an American."

We were too late now for the palace ceremony and decided to race straight out to the airport. The major, hearing our change of plans, said he would like a lift to the airport barracks. And so Farkus, the outraged American unjustly blamed for something he had never said, made room in the back of the car for his Asian accuser.

One of those sudden Djakarta cloudbursts had flooded the

airport. We dropped the major and drove to the passenger lounge. A platform had been placed on the tarmac for Sukarno to make yet another speech before boarding his aircraft. Farkus decided to put one microphone from his sound camera on the platform and to film Sukarno there.

It began to rain again, steadily. We hauled the equipment from the trunk of the car and wrapped it in borrowed plastic raincoats. A friendly security guard found us two oiled-paper umbrellas. A couple of porters offered to help. They hoisted the equipment on their heads and jogged ahead, dodging the puddles with storklike jerks of their bared legs, which stuck out from the corners of their capes. Soon we had an impressive safari assembled. One by one, we hopped and skipped across the puddled tarmac and erected our little jungle of tripods and sound batteries and cameras and mikes. The paper umbrellas were lashed above the cameras. The plastic raincoats were tied around the microphones. We were all soaked from rain and perspiration.

An officer of the security guard had watched from the shelter of the restaurant. Taking his time, he let us shake the water from our hair before delivering the ultimatum. "Dismantle your equipment or you will be arrested."

Useless to argue. Futile to display airport permits, cable cards, Blue Cross certificates. The art of survival in modern Asia is knowing when to give up.

Back we crept, hopping the smaller puddles, raising our trouser legs to wade through the bigger ones, flinching under the downpour, wondering if it wouldn't be easier to strip to the buff. Down came the little trees of lenses and reels, the trailing vines of cable, the small blossoming plugs and leads. And down, too, came the rain.

When we got back to the restaurant the officer had gone.

Farkus, with all the guts of Brooklyn, said, "Let's go back and put it up again."

A kind of insanity now gripped us and infected the porters. Out across the tarmac we streamed. Up went the cameras. Once again the green umbrellas sprouted. Farkus was gambling, of course, on Sukarno's cavalcade of cars arriving and causing so much confusion that we'd be forgotten.

We were unlucky.

Tapping his short malacca stick against his leg, one hand on his revolver butt, the officer was back in the restaurant and Sukarno was still — for all we could tell — a million miles away.

Meekly we accepted the inevitable reprimand, the order to pull it all down again. Halfway through these damp and doleful proceedings, a thought struck me. I trudged back to the security officer and fished from a wet pocket my crumpled invitation to the palace. Was this not proof of the validity of our efforts to film the president?

He faltered. If, perhaps, I could produce some further evidence . . .

It took ten minutes to find Captain Flick. I could only hope that he felt as amiably disposed toward me as on the day of my arrival. He sat in the small police office and listened to my request for help. Then he nodded. "Give me your airport pass," he said. "I will endorse it." He selected one of a dozen rubber stamps and pounded the pass. "There." He scribbled his initials. "This should take care of things."

It did. Without bothering to read Captain Flick's endorsement, I ran back to Farkus and told him to reassemble his equipment. Already we could hear the distant thunder of army motorcycles escorting the president. Sukarno arrived as we put the microphone for the third time on the platform.

It was at this point that a dozen young army men, guns cocked, surrounded us. Triumphantly I waved the pass with Captain Flick's signature. The officer with the malacca cane examined it. "Aha!" He waved the pass under my nose. "We are right, you see." He turned and issued fresh orders. This time it was his soldiers who dismantled our gear. I retrieved the pass. Stamped across it in smudged purple ink, as I should have known had I looked earlier, were the words PHOTOGRAPHY STRICTLY PRO-HIBITED.

Later, after Sukarno had gone and our cameras had been im-pounded, I thanked Captain Flick rather elaborately for his help. "Oh yes," he said with deceptive mildness. "I believe I used the wrong stamp." He paused. "By the way . . . the major that your cameraman called a bloody monkey this morning is my commanding officer."

It was too late now to kill the slander. The story would be circulating already about the American who insulted a senior officer and how the insult was avenged.

Such stories are quickly coined, especially against American correspondents who are valued by their colleagues in countries like Indonesia where the domestic press is severely restricted. The foreign press then becomes the outlet for protests and criti-cism, and efforts are made to curb its activities. In a state border-ing upon totalitarian rule, nobody near the center of power wishes to be disturbed by the probings of a foreign newspaper.

In Indonesia in recent years the *New York Times* has been the only western newspaper willing to maintain a staff corre-spondent in Djakarta. It is an astonishing fact that millions of dollars are spent annually to spread western propaganda and to shore up the economies of tottering Asian allies, while very few news organizations are willing to spend the modest sum required to keep one good reporter in these vital regions. The argument seems to be that nothing tangible is obtained from these expenditures. A correspondent closes no money-making deals, influences no trade negotiations — in short, is a dead loss in the accountancy department.

You can hardly blame the communists for taking advantage of this pocketbook mentality and putting pressure on the few newspapermen in the area. It is no coincidence that in "neutral" Asian countries, needless difficulties and frustrations are thrown in the way of correspondents in the hope of eventually forcing them out.

The incident at the airport had an unexpected sequel. Captain Flick came to see me two days later, to apologize. He had heard Ahmed's version of our argument with the major. He now believed we had not intended to insult his colleague.

I bought him a beer. Quite soon, he steered the conversation around to the rebels. "Many of my soldiers are listening to the communists," he said. "They are saying the rebellion is a foreign conspiracy to keep the imperialists in control of the Indonesian economy."

The rebels had laid such emphasis on the crusade against communism, hoping thereby to win western sympathy, that the communists had smartly reversed the effects of this propaganda. It proved, they said, that the rebels were mere pawns in the cold war and on the side of the imperialist-capitalist camp against the people.

Captain Flick said he was a good Muslim. He was disturbed by the number of communists among his comrades. He had noticed, when examining my passport, that I had been several times inside Red China. Was it very bad there? I told him, as fairly as I could, that the good and the bad were mixed. He seemed relieved that I did not lecture him upon the evils of communism. "You see," he said, "we are simple people in Indonesia but we are also not fools. We know there are many men in the West who frighten us and tell us communism is wicked in order for them to keep control of us."

It was difficult, said Captain Flick, to tell the true from the false. "I am not ashamed to say we are like children. That is why we are listening to Bung Karno and trusting him."

He asked me to share a meal at his home. I gladly accepted. Indonesians were often shy about inviting westerners until the initial barriers were overcome. They felt, quite understandably, that the difference in living standards created a gulf. It was a feeling common throughout the poorer countries; an inhibition that often prevented the English in the postwar years of austerity from extending hospitality to visiting Americans, not from unfriendliness but from a simple despair at being unable to cope with more pampered tastes.

It must have been a bit infuriating to hear so many westerners complain that they were excluded from local society ("I invite these people to party after party and they never ask us back"). The accusation had been made in my presence in so many Afro-Asian capitals that I sometimes forgot how sincerely it was meant to support some fantastic generalization about local traits ("Of course you can see they really don't like us, my dear." Or "Take all, give nothing, that's their national motto." Or "They're just too lazy to plan — can't think ahead, y'know. Let the women do all the work.").

I found it hard to believe that by some odd coincidence the Somalis should have the same unsociable and miserly habits as (say) the Burmese or the Trincomalese. As I knew from bitter experience, when you're hard up you hesitate to impose your own austerities on others.

The complaints, and the general conclusions to which they led, were usually voiced by small diplomats with large entertainment allowances.

Captain Flick was a good host, as Indonesians always are. He lived in a two-room hut, hardly big enough to accommodate a family of four although his wife seemed to manage it. I wondered how it would be to leave this austere home each day and spend the next ten hours on customs duty at an international airport. For Captain Flick's chief concern was to prevent the smuggling of currency and taxable luxury items. One could better understand how, after a sleepless hot tropical night with perhaps a baby crying and the mosquitoes swarming, Captain Flick might betray a little impatience with a well-heeled and evasive passenger. And, unfortunately, the western visitor was more likely to fall into that category than a Russian technician.

We decided to shoot a brief television story in Captain Flick's home. Setting up the equipment one morning, Farkus was trying to keep the usual crowd of spectators at bay when a ragged figure said to me in English: "They are saying here you are from Canada? Is this true?" I said it was, and the man shook my hand fervently. "I spent two years studying on a Colombo Plan scholarship with your National Film Board," he said.

He must have seen the disbelief in my eyes. He stepped back, suddenly aware of his broken shoes and patched clothes. "I'm sorry," he mumbled. "You are busy. It was good to see a Canadian again —"

I grabbed his arm. "Of course. When were you there?"

His story was not unusual. Expensive technical training, another statistic for the West to boast about, and no follow-up. He was in worse plight than being merely unemployed. He was unemployable. His qualifications were too good for the work available, and he was afraid to take humbler employment because this might thrust him back among unskilled laborers. For North Americans this is hard to understand. But once a man in Asia has made the incredible leap into literacy and perhaps a skilled trade, he dare not work with his bare hands again. He feels, unlike ourselves, the suffocating danger of being sucked back among the faceless millions.

This chance acquaintance, with his useless knowledge of film-making techniques, was skirting the fringes of communism. I could well understand why. But he was also intensely patriotic and he was deeply suspicious of Aidit's loyalties. He got his hands on a series of articles written by the PKI secretary general and left these for me with Captain Flick.

The articles had been written by Comrade Aidit for future publication as the basis of a new Indonesian communist manifesto. They were set up in galley proofs. Later they appeared in the official communist newspaper *Harian Rakjat* as the outline of a new Party program. Their indigestible prose revealed a great deal. The PKI, like other Asian communist movements, recruited frustrated young intellectuals who needed a cause to serve. It was not made easy to join the PKI. There was a period of probation and once accepted, the novitiate was prepared in the communist catechisms as if his life were dedicated to the church.

Aidit's plan covered all the causes of discontent among intellectuals, and I have dealt more fully with it in Chapter 23. It is enough here to say that it masqueraded as a genuinely nationalist movement with sickening chauvinism, supported President Sukarno while warning against the cult of personality, and sought to put General Nasution firmly in his place.

Aidit demanded "mutually helpful relations between the diumvirate of the Army and the people, and between officers and their subordinates, maintaining the right to vote and other democratic soldiers' rights; removing from the Army all traitors, corruptors and others wishing to destroy parliamentary democracy [sic] and to establish a military dictatorship or junta."

This was a clear statement of communist intent not to permit

General Nasution's climb to military power. It disturbed officers like Captain Flick, loyal to their chief, worried about the struggle going on within the armed forces between the two major factions.

Another kind of struggle was going on in Captain Flick's mind, a typical inner conflict. Should he join the rebels or could he fight the dangers of extremism more effectively from within the central government army?

The answer for many such men was No. They felt that open rebellion was tantamount to treacherously assisting the old colonialist powers. Their distrust of the Dutch was profound.

"In historical perspective we learn to be a little more sorry for both parties than they knew how to be for each other," Sir Herbert Butterfield once remarked. It is possible to feel such compassion for the Dutch and Indonesians, whose enmity could only benefit a third party plotting to undermine the independence of both. There were many Dutch at home who had long ago recognized the changes wrought by World War II, and who wished to move forward with a free Indonesia into an era of constructive and cooperative endeavor. Even the returning Dutch governor general, Dr. Hubertus J. Van Mook, after a tour of Java, had reported "I have talked with many people I knew in former years . . . I asked 'What is for you the essential thing that has happened?' I received the same answer . . . 'It is the feeling of human dignity.' "

Van Mook was unable to convince thousands of Dutch colonialists that changes had taken place while they were interned in Japanese prison camps. That was the tragedy. By the time the Netherlands Foreign Minister Joseph Luns could tell the United Nations, as he did in 1961, that "The Netherlands wishes irrevocably to terminate its history as a colonial power," it was too late.

Too late, for example, to guarantee that the peasants could

keep their feelings of human dignity. There had been no interval between the abrupt interruption of old-fashioned colonial rule and the forced withdrawal of the Dutch, no time to prepare the Indonesians. They were unprotected from the effects of maladministration. Their lives were disordered. They were prey to all the fears mischievously created by the PKI's efficient propaganda apparatus, and somewhat more exposed now than before to the crudest exploitation.

It was dawn on the plains of Jogjakarta when I drove through the villages of Java for what seemed to be the last time. The smoking volcano of Merapi threw its shadow across the sculptured fields of rice. The teak forests were threaded with mist. An old peasant jogged toward us, a wide palm hat tied under his chin, sheaves of rice dangling at either end of the pole slung across his thin shoulders. Ahmed slowed down to avoid dusting his countryman. The old peasant trotted past, the pole bouncing, the sheaves of rice shivering and shining like gold.

His dignity was ageless. It had little to do with recent political upheavals. It might have been diminished, even, by the recent years of civil war and banditry. Plans had been shelved to develop the rich virgin lands. The population explosion had made it necessary to import thousands of tons of rice from Burma and Siam. With one million new Indonesians every year, Java now contained 1246 people per square mile compared with only 86 in neighboring Sumatra.

To adjust the balance, Sukarno proposed to organize a mass migration of villagers from Java to its underpopulated neighbor. Even the Dutch had never considered such a draconian measure. Indonesian communists wanted to go still further. They suggested "adjusting" the density of population by a long-term program of forced migrations, in which millions of "worker volunteers" would be transferred to new development areas on a scale similar to China's ruthless movements of population.

By a familiar paradox the dignity of the peasant was exposed to greater perils *because* the Dutch had gone.

General Nasution had acquired a reputation for ambiguity. One of his lieutenants, flying with me from Djakarta, observed that it was difficult to divine the general's mind. "We have to translate him to the troops," he said ruefully. "He tends to talk above their heads nowadays."

There was a mystical quality about the general, and some said that he had allowed his devotion to the Islamic faith to get a bit out of hand. Often he interrupted staff meetings at the hour of prayer, withdrawing to a private room.

On his return from one of these abrupt departures, a staff officer is reported to have asked: "Well, did you see him?"

"Who?" asked General Nasution.

"God of course. Who else would you be talking to?"

Whoever it was that Nasution consulted, the advice augured nothing good for the rebels. British military observers in Singapore, when I got there, believed that the general was mobilizing all the support and forces he required to deal a decisive blow against the rebels.

How had a situation developed where this basically generous-hearted man was forced to destroy some of his old friends?

They had formed regional councils after losing patience with Sukarno's unfulfilled promises to decentralize the government. Some of them had a vested interest in decentralization. It meant a loosening of Java's control, already so inefficient that many local army commanders were running their own small kingdoms, which were financed out of the sale of their local resources.

The first striking evidence of a movement to break off relations between the islands of Sumatra and Java was given at a secret meeting of three dissident colonels, whose motives seemed the least selfish. This took place on September 8 and 9, 1956, following the significant journey made by Sukarno to communist capitals, from which he returned with the proposal for virtually one-party government. The colonels signed what became known as the Palembang Charter, calling for a ban on communism, the decentralization of government, and the ejection from the armed forces of General Nasution and communist sympathizers. News of this gesture soon reached London and Washington, and it was swiftly followed by the arrival of couriers seeking western aid. They brought fresh reports of a fermenting discontent which had some active and solid ingredients. There was opposition to an administrative system which ignored ethnic and cultural ties, and which strengthened Java's domination of the other islands through the selection of civil servants and the allocation of money for developing resources.

In vain the central government argued that most of the initial developments should take place in Java, the center of the new republic. To the islanders of Sumatra the important fact was that although they contributed the major part of Indonesia's income from abroad, they got only 12 per cent back. In Kalimantan (Borneo) the percentage was rather less; and in Celebes, less still.

These grievances were aired locally by army district commanders, who were natives of the territories they commanded. The deputy army chief of staff, Colonel Zulkifli Lubis, had attempted his coup against the capital. Now Colonel Ahmed Hussein, the local military commander in central Sumatra, announced that his own organization of ex-servicemen, the Banteng Council, would assume control of provincial affairs. He was joined by the commander of the First Military District in Sumatra, Colonel Maludin Simbolon. The two men proclaimed their loyalty to the president but prohibited all financial remittances to Java, where they said the money was being wasted by a corrupt and muddled bureaucracy.

The cabinet replaced Colonel Simbolon by his chief of staff, Colonel Djaman Gintings, who kept some support among Javanese plantation workers around Medan in north Sumatra, although the Banteng Council had the more popular following. It recruited another government emissary, Colonel Jambek (who, like Lubis, was a deputy army chief of staff) and then arrested a number of alleged communists.

The Provincial Security Co-ordinating Board of South Sumatra Province (which by itself was earning 40 per cent of Indonesia's foreign exchange) declared its financial autonomy. Money withheld from Java would be used "for financing reconstruction projects." A revolutionary council, Garuda, demanded that all officers in south Sumatra should be Sumatrans and invited Colonel Barlian, the commander of the Second Military District, to take over administrative power. At the other end of the archipelago, Colonel Ventje Sumual, commander of the Seventh Military District (East Indonesia) proclaimed a temporary military government.

The Permesta Charter of Universal Struggle was signed by 51 local leaders demanding full autonomy for all four eastern provinces, including west New Guinea, and a reduction in the central government's demands on local income and produce. A province of North Celebes was proclaimed by the local authorities, and Colonel Sumual transferred his rebel headquarters there from Makasar in the south of the island.

The cabinet took strong measures in Java, where separatist feelings were stirred by the defection of Colonel Lubis. But it moved cautiously. It made financial concessions to the two Sumatran provinces and tried to settle other differences by discussion. Special "committees of reconciliation," however, had to admit failure.

President Sukarno's "concept" that the people must be led and guided from above helped to harden opposition. He appointed a "cabinet of experts" which included three members generally acknowledged to be communist sympathizers, one of whom held a new and peculiar portfolio: minister for mobilization of the people's energy. The president, calling for a mental revolution among Indonesians, launched a New Life Movement. He established a national Planning Council, which drew its sixty members from many walks of life and which had the task of executing a grand plan in accordance with "messages of guidance" received from Sukarno.

President Sukarno thought a bloody clash with the rebels could be avoided right up until two of his former cabinet ministers and other "intellectual leaders" joined forces with the rebel commanders and proclaimed the revolutionary government in February, 1958. There followed a heated discussion between the president and his army chief of staff. A detailed report was later smuggled to the rebels by a senior member on General Nasution's staff. It showed President Sukarno still unwilling to take military action against his own countrymen. "Why should we go before the world as a nation divided against itself?" the president is quoted as saying. "Our enemies will seize upon any evidence of civil war and accomplish what we have all been trying to avoid — the division of the republic."

The general stubbornly submitted evidence that the leaders of the revolutionary government would not fight. If the republic was to endure, he must develop strong security forces. What better way than to exercise them in action against a weak and irresolute enemy?

President Sukarno still did not like the idea of bloodshed.

The people had suffered enough at the hands of the colonialists. It should be possible to negotiate a settlement.

The general this time refused to yield. He had a final conclusive point to make. The revolutionary government had been persuaded by its western friends to rush into a premature proclamation of its aims. He submitted further evidence that the United States Central Intelligence Agency and other foreign agencies were supporting the rebels with arms and money. If the rebels survived long enough, there was a danger that they would win more open recognition. They could be defeated at this stage. Later, they might win enough popular support among the peasantry and establish strong enough bases in Sumatra and Celebes to resist attack. The result would be a stalemate and eventually the loss of these rich and strategically essential islands. This argument was the clincher.

II

Musjawarah

GOVERNMENT AIR ATTACKS against rebel territories began on February 21, 1958, and General Nasution's troops began to establish themselves on islands off the Siak estuary on March 7, followed a few days later by full-scale operations on the mainland of Sumatra. Paratroops seized the oil region of Pakanbaru and a few weeks later more Javanese troops made a seaborne landing in west Sumatra and captured Padang. The fall of the rebel capital at Bukittinggi was announced on May 4, and the revolutionary government withdrew into the hills.

At the other end of the archipelago, the rebels had obtained light bombers and fighters and were using these against shipping and other targets in the region of Borneo, Celebes and the Moluccas. How the aircraft were being fueled and armed remained a mystery. The central government in Java accused the United States and the Nationalist Chinese in Formosa of providing weapons, and it was hard to believe a rebel claim that the bombing attacks were sustained solely from airfields within the Indonesian Republic.

The rebels provided a reason, or at least an excuse, for President Sukarno's government to buy arms from communist countries. Added incentive came from the Soviet and communist Chinese governments. Both issued statements blaming the civil war on United States intervention. By the end of April, the first military aircraft from the Soviet bloc were arriving in Djakarta.

It was painfully apparent that the rebels had neither the means nor the determination to resist General Nasution's forces. Furthermore, the rebellion was having the opposite effect on domestic affairs to what was wanted by the revolutionary government and its foreign backers. There was a greater assertion of central authority. The trend away from the party system and orthodox parliamentary democracy now became irresistible. General Nasution was making decisive use of his powers under the state of emergency, which was now further extended. General elections were postponed indefinitely.

The United States Secretary of State of the time, Mr. John Foster Dulles, announced on May 20 that his country having once suffered civil war too, believed the Indonesian situation "should be dealt with as an Indonesian matter by the Indonesians without intrusion from without." In the months that followed, the United States issued licenses for the supply of police equipment and undertook to sell military equipment for internal security and self-defense. The Indonesian foreign minister, Dr. Subandrio, said these events possibly marked "the start of a new understanding between both countries."

During this period I was elsewhere, traveling in parts of Southeast Asia where Chinese business communities had started to express alarm at the anti-Chinese feeling developing in Indonesia. Sukarno's government was not so forgiving toward the Formosa-based supporters of the rebellion as it had been with Washington. Its anger rebounded upon Chinese within the republic. All the Nationalist Chinese press in Indonesia was banned. Fifty-two Nationalist organizations in Djakarta were suppressed after the minister of justice claimed he could prove the strong links between the rebellion and the Nationalist Chinese. It looked as if the unhappy Chinese had been left high and dry;

and indeed this was made apparent by Doctor Sumitro, who contacted me about the proposed visit to the revolutionary areas. Washington, he said, had withdrawn all assistance for the rebels. I asked if he meant "official Washington." He replied that he meant those influential Americans who in the past had been able to dispatch funds and arms to the rebels.

The rebels had opened "business" offices in Hong Kong to cover their operations in that area. Late that spring, when I was home there, Jana turned up. She had seen the rebel retreat in central Sumatra and she was cynical about the fighting spirit of the guerrillas.

"This is the real test, now," she told Glenys and myself one evening. "Everything has been running against us. We have few foreign friends left. The Nationalist Chinese want to be paid in cash for every weapon delivered. But on the other hand, the Indonesian Army is not more than half effective. Its strength on paper only is 200,000 — *nothing!* Most of these forces are loyal to their regional commanders. If we hold out, Djakarta can be brought to heel."

This extraordinary woman left me bewildered. When Sukarno's fortunes were low, and I had made that undiplomatic remark about bowling a bomb at the president, Jana had sprung to his defense. Now she talked enthusiastically about bringing about his downfall once again.

"Is this characteristic of Indonesians?" I asked her.

"What?"

"Well, this habit of passionately arguing one side of the case today and just as passionately arguing another side tomorrow."

Jana frowned. "But I have always been arguing the rebel case."

"Hmm. In Djakarta I thought you showed quite a loyalty to Sukarno."

She tossed her head. "Sukarno *the man?* Yes. Not his government or his politics."

"You put up strenuous objections to my joking remark about assassination."

"Did I?" She turned her hand over and examined her clipped fingernails. "That is quite natural, no? I do not believe in *killing* another Indonesian. Do not forget that we are accustomed to settling our differences by means of discussion."

My wife's eyebrows flew up. "Discussion? I thought you were all out there shooting each other."

"In a way, yes," said Jana. "However, it is our tradition to try and settle matters by peaceful discussion. *Musjawarah* is the word. It means talking, listening, arguing, negotiating, compromising — but not, unless absolutely necessary, resorting to violence."

Musjawarah, it seemed to me, explained a lot of things about the rebellion, Sukarno and Indonesian "guided democracy."

While Jana stayed in Hong Kong she talked a good deal about her own people. "I often believe myself to be two persons," she said one day in a flash of self-revelation. "Part of me is very wild." We nodded in silent assent.

She turned up one day with a remarkable painting. It was an underwater scene and conveyed with an exciting fidelity the physical sensations of swimming down through a tropical sea. Jana had painted it, giving the sea that peculiar translucence you find in shallow depths.

"The water's a bit like a strong gin and lime, isn't it?" said Jana. "In a very clear glass, that is."

There was a large oyster on the seabed, several anemones of brilliant hue, and a cuttlefish oozing across one corner of the canvas. "You must have done a lot of skin-diving to paint this," said Glenys.

"I used to dive for pearls," said Jana. "As a child we lived in and beside the sea. I can paint any number of pictures like that, just from memory."

Another day she brooded about the effectiveness of plastic explosives, having forgotten for the moment her faith in *musja-warah*. She had purchased a consignment from her Formosa sources. While she was arranging for its shipment to a sabotage training center in Sumatra, she brought us a sample. It was light brown in color, like putty, with a slight marzipan smell.

"See, it's wonderful because you can carry it around in your pocket and it won't go off," she said. "You can fit it to any target. Stick it to a truck, for instance, or mold it round a tree." We gave her a wide berth until she explained it needed a small tube-shaped detonator to set it off, together with a short gunpowder fuse.

She was trying to arrange a meeting in western Europe between Doctor Sumitro and two leaders of the Darul Islam, which would result in a new Federal Republic of Indonesia. The rebels needed any allies they could find, but the idea of a partnership with the atavistic Islamic State seemed a thoroughly bad one. The religious fanatics had antagonized Indonesian Christians and were repugnant to the socialists who had rallied to the rebel cause. All the same, an agreement was finally arrived at between Doctor Sumitro and the Darul Islam's Prince Mohammed Daud Bereuh and Colonel Abdul Kahar Muzakkar to jointly attempt the overthrow of President Sukarno. If anything, this misalliance hurt the rebel cause, although it added considerably to its paper strength in south Celebes and in Achin.

The Achinese occupied the northern tip of Sumatra. They had fought holy wars against the Dutch throughout the last century and their present leader, Prince Daud, claimed he had 85,000 trained and armed men. The figure turned out to be a gross exaggeration, but it was generally agreed that the Darul Islam in Achin could never be overpowered by force of arms.

The seat of the rebellion was farther south, in central Sumatra, only a short sea trip across the Strait of Malacca from Malaya. Jana had been gone from Hong Kong for some time when a message came to the house, delivered in the usual dramatic style by a strange voice on the telephone. Doctor Sumitro hoped I could come to Singapore "to make a journey."

There were a number of correspondents waiting in Singapore for passage to rebel territory. Some had made the trip and returned with disillusioning stories of disorganization and muddle. The biggest hazard, they said, was the bus service in Sumatra. You could board a bus to a rebel area and wind up among central government troops.

In the end I traveled comfortably in a freighter to Palembang, a seaport in southeast Sumatra. The Indonesian Air Force, for some mysterious reason, was running the town but this did not appear to interfere with its role as a thriving outlet for rebel smugglers. The rebels bought rubber and copra in the interior and delivered it to Chinese merchants in Palembang for gold and United States travelers' checks, and with these proceeds they were able to purchase military supplies, medicine and food.

Despite its untidy appearance and seedy reputation, Palembang had a considerable history. It was for many centuries the capital of a maritime empire controlling the two channels through which ships had to pass between China and India, and its Muslim rulers held commercial sway over the islands of Java and beyond. Sir Stamford Raffles, during his brief period in Sumatra, had seen the port's great possibilities and encouraged the sultan to resist Dutch rule. Years later this provided the Dutch with one more reason for suspecting British motives after World War II in seeking a settlement between the Netherlands and the Indonesian Republic.

There was a lot of talk in the town of secession from the republic, and of some form of association with the Federation of Malaya across the strait. This was natural enough. The town was populated mostly by Malays, and like so many coastal areas of Sumatra it had strong links with Malaya and Singapore.

My problems now began of distinguishing between prorebel and pro-Sukarno officials. The first day was spent looking for the former and avoiding the latter. The town straddled both banks of the Musi River, which was deep enough, even at this point 50 miles inland, to take ocean steamers. I wandered down shabby streets and across greasy canals, searching for addresses scribbled on the backs of airline tickets and old envelopes. Most of the addresses were those of Chinese shipping agents whose warehouses were either filled with raw materials from the rebel areas or with imported goods destined, I suppose, for the guerrillas of the interior.

It all seemed rather casual and off-hand. There were numbers of young army officers clanking around with weapons dangling from their belts and fancy canes twirling. I came to the rash conclusion that these were the pro-Sukarno boys. The prorebels generally wore beards and blue jeans, made vigorous little speeches about the uncrushability of their forces, and looked like beatniks.

My search led finally to a courteous old Chinese gentleman sitting on a high stool in the front of a medicine shop. It was crammed from floor to ceiling along three walls with wooden drawers labeled with the names of herbs and other natural cures. There were glass display cases with revolting shriveled black objects laid out tidily on sheets of white paper: tiger bones, the shavings from deer antlers, bears' paws and little packets covered in Chinese ideographs. On shelves near the street were huge glass jars to catch the eyes of passersby, crammed with the curled bodies of civet cats and salamanders pickled in alcohol. My eye fell upon an old friend: a box of Dr. Yapp's Masculine Pills for Lasting Strength and Happiness.

12

A Mass Beheading

"I SHOULD THINK," said the Chinese medicine man, "that it would be better to take Cheng Fu's bus to Djambi."

"Bus?"

He nodded, fingering a silky thin beard with twiglike fingers. "At Djambi you may speak to my friend" — here he gave me an address — "who will direct you to another bus."

I sat on the adjoining stool, rather heavily. "That'll take *days*."

He nodded, either from fatigue or in resignation. I suspected the latter. Doubtless he was constantly challenged upon his choice of route by travelers to the revolution. "Three days," he said, "to Bukittinggi."

"Which has been captured," I said quickly.

He laid both hands gently in his lap and remained quite still, an old man with a black mandarin hat and a traditional Chinese gown of dark blue, a button nose and wise wrinkled eyes and lips that hinted at an unexpected lasciviousness. I had a feeling that if pushed, he would topple over and splinter on the earthen floor of his strange dark shop with its dead relics and the musty odors of the tomb.

"At Djambi they will tell you where to go," he said after an agonizing silence.

Seeing little prospect of learning more, I thanked him and checked myself from walking backwards out of his imperious presence. It was raining hard outside and I was soaked by the time I rediscovered my Chinese hotel for the night. It was near the town's largest mosque and there was a pleasant murmuration of prayers from inside, a soothing sound that spread like balm over an otherwise dismal evening. The hotel was built on four sides of a courtyard and my room was on the far side, across a sea of mud. The room was a concrete cell with a tiny barred window set in the thick walls near the ceiling. A big overhead fan creaked and whistled as I turned on the switch. I fiddled with the loose knurled knob which in theory controlled the fan's speed. The knob spluttered and threw out blue sparks while I tried to accelerate the whirling blades. Finally it stuck at *avancer* (it was, it seemed, a French fan) and I had to go to bed under a miniature hurricane.

The cot was hard and narrow. The mosquito netting breathed a familiar tropical odor of human sweat and rotting linen. A naked electric light bulb shone dully near my head, the fan casting weird black shadows above it. I lay for a long time studying the fan. Should I turn it off and suffer? Or leave it on and feel compelled to watch for the moment when it must surely fly loose from its slender moorings and descend in a slaughterous arc into my belly? Would torque cause it to perform a circular flight, like a boomerang, possibly swooping low enough to decapitate me before soaring back to the cracked ceiling? I began to devise a murder mystery . . . and hastily groped for the light switch.

I had a restless night. The Chinese tend to wake up at midnight to hammer on sheets of tin or roll garbage cans down the hotel steps, singing out to each other in harsh accents. Or that is how it sounds. Now and again female whispers came from the courtyard and a door slammed. Once or twice, it seemed to me, objects bumped against the fan. I tossed and turned. The room was hot and stuffy and the sweat trickled between my shoulder blades.

It was scarcely light when I woke up and threshed through

the mosquito net, rubbing myself dry with the corner of a crumpled sheet. The stone floor was warm — and sticky. Before I was fully on my feet, they skidded away from under me. One hand fell on a warm, wet furry substance and I leaped across the room, sliding on fresh patches of unmentionable stickinesses.

The floor was strewn with beheaded bats. They had flown through the small barred window and then collided with the fan. Why they should have done this, and how they accomplished it despite their built-in radar, remains an abiding mystery. They were big, vampirelike fruit bats whose mass flights were usually made at twilight. The luckless ones, minus heads, were strewn around the room like black echoes of a long nightmare.

I made as decent an exit as I could from the hotel. Breakfast had no appeal and I mooched through the awakening street to find Cheng Fu's bus station. It stood a short distance outside the town. A strange assortment of ancient wooden vehicles squatted in a circle around a small vegetable and meat market. The cobbled lanes between stalls were covered in thick slime. Black clouds of flies hovered above raw lumps of meat. In the middle of all this confusion, a pool of tranquillity in the midst of the noisy shouts of hawkers and the cries of children, a young girl squatted beside the public tap and bathed as if in utmost privacy.

The buses were destined for points all over Sumatra. They were operated by a family of Chinese who were clearly determined to squeeze every last cent out of the fleet. Not one of the buses appeared to be less than fifteen years old. Their bodies were monuments to Chinese ingenuity, patched with flattened gasoline cans, and held together here and there by wooden stakes and rope. Their roofs were burdened with bedrolls, hampers of ducklings and vegetables, battered suitcases and crates of fruit. Seeing one of these charge round a bend in the road was like meeting a circus elephant head on, its square front daubed in brilliant colors and the rooftop cargo leaning dangerously toward the inside curve.

The bus to Djambi was tastefully decorated as a pink Chinese dragon. The driver's cabin was the head, with two carved wooden horns and two bulbous green eyes serving as sidelights on either side of the battered hood. By the time I found the bus, it was already full and overflowing with passengers of all sizes and sexes, including Malay schoolgirls in white blouses and black pinafores. The driver grinned when he saw me and yelled something that sent his passengers into paroxysms of mirth. Dozens of heads were stuck out of windows and I caught the word *Bellanda*, Dutchman. "No," I said to the driver. "Not *Bellanda*. Canada."

"Never mind," he said consolingly.

The presence of a white stranger caused considerable upheaval inside the bus. Large Malayan grandmothers courteously gathered up their children and moved to the rear, baskets were shifted, and a protesting pig ejected into the road. The pig, trussed in a kind of wickerwork, had been *seated* between two slender young men on the front seat. It was now hoisted to the roof of the bus and I was ushered into its vacated place, my entry being illuminated by radiant smiles.

The road to Djambi ran northwest behind the broad coastal swamps, in the shadow of the mountain chain of volcanic peaks known as Bukit Barisan, Parade of the Mountains. It was a rich countryside, with dense rain forests blanketing the damp slopes of the mountains, and with broad expanses of savanna. Once we rumbled to a halt while a green peacock paused in the road, shivering its quills before whirring over the bank into a thicket of bamboo.

One of my seat companions unwrapped a bag of curried eggs and offered me one. We grinned and nodded at each other but it was impossible to talk above the grinding of gears and the rattling motor. Behind us someone played a mouth organ and the schoolgirls sang. Despite the physical discomfort, it was oddly comforting to sit in that bus among these cheerful people and feel a member of the family.

Many of the passengers were university students on an indefinite vacation caused by the rebellion. They were in high spirits at the outset but slowly subsided as the journey wore on. The road was badly broken and much of the time was spent dodging potholes and crawling around swampland. By nightfall I felt like a plug of tobacco, tamped well by the constant jolting, encased in a bowl formed by the hips and shoulders of my seat mates. In front of me beside the bus driver was an open shelf jammed with dusty bric-a-brac — a plastic pink comb, a Japanese mechanical monkey, a thick wad of Chinese-language newspapers. Whenever I nodded off to sleep, an extra jolt of the bus would jerk my head back and I would find myself staring at the same red-hatted monkey whose glass eyes mocked me from the dashboard.

We bounced into Djambi early the next morning. The night had been full of minor mishaps and my back ached with the effort of helping to heave the bus out of ditches and creeks. The brisk morning air helped me to rally briefly, enough to haul my belongings out of the cargo that cascaded from the roof of the bus. It had taken us ten hours to cover some 140 miles.

A coolie stood on the other side of my kit and said, in excellent English, "Carry your bags, sir?"

I waved him impatiently aside. Still he stood there, a scarecrow of a man whose rags mocked my crumpled drip-dry suit. "Are you certain, sir, I cannot be of assistance?"

I was very hot, very hungry and very tired. But I had a fixation about making others carry my few small possessions. "No,"

I said, and bent down to hoist a strap of my rucksack over one shoulder.

"Perhaps, sir, I am taking you to your revolutionary friends?"

I stopped, bent double, and looked at the dirty splayed toes of this persistent creature, the skinny knobby legs and the stained loincloth visible beneath a torn old shirt. My eyes traveled up in slow wonder to the familiar smiling face of Doctor Sumitro.

13

The Shadow Boxers

DOCTOR SUMITRO'S reputation as a chameleon was well known but I could hardly conceal my surprise at this fresh encounter. He had been reported on previous occasions, and by various "authorities," to have shaved his head and donned the ochre robes of a Buddhist monk or grown his hair to his waist to pose as a Hindu holy man. One senior member of the United States Central Intelligence Agency, who has now left that organization, Peter Sichel, insisted that Sumitro had changed his face entirely through plastic surgery. So far as I could see, confronted so unexpectedly by the rebel leader, Sumitro had only combed his hair differently and dressed completely out of character. It transformed his appearance.

This casual adoption of disguise has, of course, a long and honorable tradition in the Far East. Another example that springs to mind is that of Colonel Masanobu Tsuji, a member of the Japanese Diet until recently,* who planned the capture of Singapore and later dodged Allied searchers for many months by posing as an itinerant monk. He once told me that he flung himself so completely into his role that he became in fact a devout Buddhist.

Doctor Sumitro had not risen to these histrionic heights, being content to don the guise of the humblest coolie. He took me to

* He vanished in mysterious circumstances during a visit in 1962 to his old stamping grounds.

a wooden bench under a black tarpaulin where, under a sign that spelled KAFE, we gulped sweet black coffee and tried to forget about the swarming flies.

His instructions on how to find the revolutionary (PRRI) were splendidly vague. ("Take the morning bus to Muaratebo and go to this rest house. . . .") He had just come from the rebel headquarters and was now returning to Singapore. An amphibian plane would pick him up off the Hari River estuary.

The rebels had been chased out of Bukittinggi in ignominious disarray but he remained philosophically calm. They would just have to lick their wounds and ponder the lesson. Already General Nasution's speed and efficiency of action had gained him a third of rebel territory in one bold stroke and the PRRI leaders would have to justify the price of this harsh experience.

I asked Sumitro about the highly publicized capture of United States military equipment by Nasution's forces. They had struck first in the east, his 700 paratroops dropping near the Caltex Oil depot at Pakanbaru, where they seized United States arms abandoned by the fleeing rebels. The weapons and ammunition included light antiaircraft and automatic guns, small arms and mortar bombs. They were all stamped with United States insignia. This discovery seemed to confirm Djakarta's claim that "imperialist" aircraft had been dropping supplies to the rebels, and the captured equipment was later put on public display.

Sumitro said the supplies were dropped by "chartered" aircraft from Civil Air Transport, the Formosa-based airline which had inherited the equipment and personnel of General Claire Lee Chennault's "Flying Tigers." This American will be remembered as the former aeronautical adviser to Chiang Kai-shek who organized a group of freelance pilots to fight for the Chinese Nationalists in World War II, mostly in defense of the Burma Road supply route.

It came as no surprise that Doctor Sumitro finally admitted

that aircraft were being chartered from Formosa. Ever since China had turned communist, CAT operations had been associated with airdrops to Chinese Nationalist guerrillas in Burma, to the French at Dienbienphu in Indochina, and wherever else the satrap armies and saboteurs of Red China might be at work.

Did Doctor Sumitro regard the Chinese Nationalists as desirable allies? He wriggled. They were a source of the modern arms he needed.

Well, I asked, did he feel they were joining his revolution for ideological reasons or to make a fat profit? Doctor Sumitro said, with a sudden flash of anger, that the Nationalists talked valiantly of an anticommunist crusade, but their prices for airdropping arms and other aerial operations over Indonesia came very high.

On the other hand, Soviet Russia had already started delivery to President Sukarno of MIG-17 jet fighters and Ilyushin bombers with Czech instructors. These Russian planes had not been used in the Sumatra operations but they had released older aircraft for operations against the rebels. "We have no air cover of any kind," said Doctor Sumitro. "It has been very demoralizing for our men."

Nasution's airborne invasion was followed, of course, by the landings, already described, of seaborne forces at two points on the coast. They met with no opposition. The rebel army commanders had a difficult time assembling their small and scattered forces, and retreated without a fight. A major handicap was the lack of field radios, whose delivery by air was vainly awaited.

Doctor Sumitro clothed these humiliating defeats in the bold language of a military strategist, and what at first appeared to be the scattering of a disorganized rabble became "defense-in-depth." The rebel commanders had not been *driven* out of towns like Pakanbaru and Bukittinggi. They had "decided upon a form of guerrilla warfare" in which the enemy was to be lured into the towns and then cut off.

There was nothing wrong with this interpretation if the rebels possessed the will to fight. They had the best of all precedents in the example of Mao Tse-tung and the Chinese Red armies. But all reports indicated that Doctor Sumitro was a good deal more persistent and devoted to his cause than were the troops. They talked boldly in terms made familiar by Mao's textbooks on jungle warfare, and meanwhile awaited miracles. They seemed to think Djakarta's use of aircraft unsporting and the spilling of blood not really necessary. The civil war often seemed for them to be an exercise of the imagination with an occasional sharp jab from reality.

Doctor Sumitro was aware of these little rifts within the lute. "We *have* suffered a severe setback," he agreed. "These defeats will weed out the weaklings. We may have to go into hiding for two or three years, and engage in hit-and-run tactics. It will strengthen our revolutionary spirit." He left me in the same abrupt manner as before, a tiny tough man whose resolution and courage were more than some of his followers deserved.

I stayed overnight in Djambi at the house of a Dutch oilman. He was a technician, married to a pretty Sumatran girl, and reluctant to leave. "But our lives are made miserable every day." He bounced a black-haired, almond-eyed daughter on one knee. "The anti-Dutch campaign here has been vicious and the local tax office gives me a rough time." He stroked the child's hair. "I've given the best years of my life to this country. I hate to see what Djakarta is doing to it. They're forcing out the oil companies and they've nobody to put in their place except Russians." He shook his head. "I just don't understand. They seem bent upon ruining the economy simply to spite us."

The bus to Muaratebo left just before noon. It was a sober

vehicle with narrow hard benches and what felt like square wheels. The driver was engaged in an endless dispute with a pair of dignified matrons in the seat behind him so that his hands, being a necessary instrument of discussion, were seldom on the wheel while his eyes were almost never on the road. A warm steamy mist rolled off the forested mountain slopes and at first it cut visibility to a few yards, which really did not seem to matter. It was a relief when we fell into a shallow ditch two hours later. Having anticipated an accident of some kind, I was quite happy with the little one we got.

Before we parted, Doctor Sumitro had suggested that I see the rebel president, Sjafruddin Prawiranegara. My own inclination was to see the rebel army. Sjafruddin and the other revolutionary leaders were gifted talkers but they had failed to demonstrate why the West *should* give them any further support. They did not appear to have the support of the peasantry, and there was no record so far to show that the rebels could and would fight. The casual way in which everyday life continued even on the fringe of rebel territory was proof enough of their incompetence.

Their territory began north of the Tembesi River, but there was little to indicate this. The citizens of Muaratebo had discreetly removed the rebel signs after General Nasution began his military operations, leaving blank spaces on the walls of eating houses and shops. One or two portraits of President Sukarno had been taken out of hiding, and General Nasution's Javanese troops had posted up signs proclaiming the "liberation" of central Sumatra. There was a notable absence of young men. Those not drafted into the rival armies had wisely hidden themselves. I missed the students with their unfailing courtesy and their eager interest in a foreign traveler. They were free from the backward-looking bitterness of their parents, and you did not automatically brace yourself to argue with them about past injustices. It was ironic, and perhaps significant, that instead of rallying to the clean-cut young colonels who had rejected corruption and dishonest government, many of them were rallying instead to the absolutist philosophies of Marx and Aidit.

The dust of the town had been swept away by heavy rains. That evening the skies cleared and the air was cool and filled with distant country sounds; the creaking of wagons, the snorting of water-buffalos submerged in the public ponds, and the faraway tinkling of *gamelan* music like an endless waterfall. There was a sense of peace and well-being, a sweet melancholy in the squeak of bats and the soft brief glow of fireflies among the trees. The tang of woodsmoke and a faint sandalwood perfume hung in the air. An immense comfort might be taken from this slow twilight pace of people following an anciently civilized way of life.

Soul restored, I found the rest house to which Doctor Sumitro had directed me. It was an extraordinary building, two stories high, made of wood and flush with the roadside. There seemed to be no windows. I hammered at a small door, which was opened by a pale young creature with a kind of white sandalwood paste on her face. The effect was gruesome. The woman stared at me uncomprehendingly, long enough for the hot fetid smells to escape from inside. I began to mumble an apology, anxious to leave, when another face appeared over the woman's shoulder.

"Come." The second woman elbowed the younger one aside and grabbed my bag, leaving me little choice. I stepped over a stone in the doorway, into a narrow and dimly lit passage. The second woman, a moon-faced Hakka Chinese, shuffled ahead of me to the foot of a perpendicular ladder. She pointed up it with her chin.

The younger woman, a Malay to judge by her ankle-length sarong, was already scrambling up the wooden rungs. There was an explosion of shouts between the Chinese holding my bag and a man on the floor above. I heard him scuffling near the top of the ladder, and then his face appeared in the hole above. It was almost a bald skull, the eyes showing merely as sockets in the lamplight. He said something in a voice that seemed suddenly very near and intimate, and then withdrew. I heard him a moment later hawking and spitting and felt reassured. The sure sign of a bonafide Chinese hotel is the presence of brass spittoons.

The hotel, such as it was, consisted of tiny stuffy cells with wooden walls that reached only part of the way to a low ceiling. The rooms were all on the first floor, each one secured by a solid door protected by an enormous padlock *on the outside*. I was taken to an end room, presumably the best. It had a small window overlooking the latrines. There was an old Chinese calendar tacked to the wall, an enamel bowl on a broken wooden chair, and a wooden bed covered with a thin pallet. The young woman who had first opened the door fussed about the room, lighting a candle, shoving my bag and typewriter behind the chair, throwing me flirtatious glances and finally withdrawing to the door, where she stood in a gesture of coquetry, winding a jasmine bud into her black shoulder-length hair. I gave her a weak smile and indicated that she had discharged all responsibilities. Indeed, if an entire regiment of General Nasution's troops had arrived at that moment and ordered me out, I would have found it impossible to move, such was the anesthetizing effect of that stuffy room. I made a mild and unsuccessful attempt to open the window, which was securely cemented in its frame, and collapsed on the bed in a lather of perspiration. I woke up hours later with my head ringing, to hear the muffled snorts of my neighbors in adjoining rooms, and the faint but unmistakable scent of jasmine cutting through the thick mixture of earthier smells.

There was a light tap on the door, and it creaked open. A flashlight shone through the darkness. A man's voice called my name and when I answered, the new arrival turned the beam of light on himself, revealing a chubby Sumatran face under a red beret.

"We are to leave at once for Colonel Jambek's headquarters." The hoarse whisper seemed abnormally and unnecessarily emphatic. "There is a jeep outside." I was still fully clothed, and within two or three minutes I joined my visitor in the corridor. With him was the Malay girl. She giggled at my evident surprise and lowered herself down the hotel's unconventional stairs, her pale face shining like a ghostly luminous ectoplasm as she descended slowly and ceremoniously through the floor.

The streets were deep in a silence so profound that the barking exhaust of the jeep made me jump. "What time is it?" I mumbled to the rebel guide, a major. He sat at the wheel, the girl between us, and let in the clutch. "Half-past two," he said as we lurched forward into the moonless night.

We reached the rendezvous shortly before noon the next day, first discarding the jeep at daylight and climbing on foot into the mountains above the Inderagiri River. We were, by my reckoning, on the slopes of Mount Kerintji, one of the chain of volcanic peaks that runs along the western coast and is part of a mountain system beginning in lower Burma and extending by way of the Andaman Islands the full length of the Indonesian archipelago.

Colonel Jambek was the minister of the interior of the revolutionary government, with headquarters in a high valley guarded by troops. As we climbed up from the road I remarked on the absence of Djakarta's military forces and asked the major if there had been much action. "Much fighting," he said. "Much fighting. We were completely victorious." But he offered no details.

The girl tagged along with us, although I had the impression that the major had only picked her up at the hotel the previous night. They left me at the first rebel checkpoint on the village outskirts.

The checkpoint was a peasant's hut. Above the gaping doorway was a shield carved of wood and depicting the Indonesian coat of arms cradled by an eagle with the words PEMERINTAH REVOLUSIONER REPUBLIK INDONESIA. From here I was escorted to a European-style house. The windows were shuttered and after the blinding sunlight and the brilliant colors of the countryside, it was difficult to see inside. I could hear children's voices upstairs and the low murmur of women talking. Someone said, "Welcome," and a neat figure in faded khaki fatigues appeared in the doorway.

It was Colonel Jambek, the former Indonesian military attaché in London. He was a small, powerful man in his late forties, with a disciplined manner and a clipped English accent. He was, in addition to his duties as a cabinet minister in the rebel government, the leader of the Movement Against Communism in Central Sumatra.

Colonel Jambek was more interested in discussing the threat of communist subversion in Indonesia than he was in analyzing the defeats inflicted upon the rebels thus far. "The West must understand," he said, "we are in the forefront of the battle against communism. We need your help."

I suggested that self-proclaimed crusaders against communism were likely to defeat their own purposes unless they had something positive to offer.

"We offer good government, a sound economy, proper respect for regional interests," he said portentously. "We are ruthless in one thing only. The only good communist is a dead communist."

How many communists had he killed? Well, replied Jambek,

British customs checks smuggled copra from Indonesian rebel areas after it is landed at Sandakan.

Twin outboards drive this low-lying and very fast smuggling *kumpit* unloading its contraband under the flag of the British marine police.

Right, above: Skippers of blockade-runners like this one, aboard a Chinese cargo vessel sailing to Celebes, made a month's salary in one trip.

Below: Rebels were supplied in Indonesia by a variety of vessels from Okinawa fishing boats to old tramp steamers.

Air travel in Borneo is informal.

The home of Emiria Sounassa, "Queen" of west New Guinea, on the outskirts of Djakarta. Emiria was under house arrest, but relatively free to
roam around this small estate.

MF 275, the rebel blockade-runner which plied between Celebes and Borneo through seas infested by pirates and the Indonesian Navy's patrols.

Right, above: "Mister Willi," the rebel courier, and author aboard the blockade-runner

Below: MF 275 had a tiny "bridge." Captain Ling is on the right. His navigator with sweat band is a Bugi

A Bugi rebel sailor.

he had killed none so far. But he had locked up a few hundred suspects in a special camp. He thought that the West should help him more in the task of destroying communism. "It is," he said, "your fight as much as ours."

He agreed, however, that weakness and vacillation on the part of some rebel commanders might justify our slackening interest. "Time is frightfully short," he said. "Do you know that here, in Sumatra, the communists have organized the young people in preparation for armed revolution? Let me show you." He produced a file of papers listing secret communist organizations: the Rebellion Front, the Destruction Front, the Moral Breakdown Front. There were names and addresses of citizens said to be connected with these units, and lengthy reports on so-called Secret Directing Cells. The reports were printed on good quality light-weight paper and evidently on foreign presses.

"Here is a report on plans to subvert young people in British Borneo," said Colonel Jambek, fishing out another file. It included a copy of the *Manifesto on Establishment of the Borneo Communist Party*, with instructions on how to infiltrate the schools and clubs of the Overseas Chinese.

This was all very interesting. I had no doubt of its authenticity. But was the PRRI the best way to eliminate the dangers of political extremism? Was it not likely that an unsuccessful armed rebellion would only create the administrative and economic chaos in which communism or any other -ism could thrive?

Colonel Jambek was confident that the rebellion would succeed. "You will see," he said. "We will fight Javanese colonialism everywhere. Attacking from the hills and in all the islands. Attacking and withdrawing. Attack! Withdraw! We will force Sukarno to meet our terms."

He spoke with a kind of defiant boastfulness. I could imagine the splendid effect these fine sentiments and melodramatic poses must have had in Washington. "We must win American support by emphasizing the communist dangers," he said. "We must win popular favor in the Outer Islands by attacking Javanese colonialism. We must attack communism as anti-religious to win Muslims to our side."

Meanwhile, the PRRI cabinet was in hiding and Colonel Jambek's men looked anything but ready to fight.

I went off to look for "President" Sjafruddin, who had quit his office as chief of the national bank with $3,000,000 in state funds to give the rebels. He was at a meeting with Mohammed Natsir, the leader of Indonesia's second largest political party, the Moslem Masjumi. Both men were living in the village and it soon became apparent that whereas Sjafruddin was having private doubts about his desertion from Djakarta, the Masjumi leader was not. But both were depressed. They had misjudged the ability of General Nasution's army to conduct an amphibious campaign. They had overestimated the support that Sumatra's peasants were prepared to give them. They had counted upon distinguished men like the republic's vice president Mohammed Hatta, and the Sultan of Jogjakarta to join them, when in fact these men were not prepared to jeopardize their country's new-won freedom for the sake of a rebellion that required foreign assistance.

The PRRI leader, Sjafruddin, had not expected to become the revolution's chief figure. He had counted upon Hatta to occupy that position, bringing to it all the prestige and influence that Hatta had always commanded despite many years of apparent fence-sitting. On the other hand, there was no question of Sjafruddin's sincerity. "President Sukarno is giving us slogans when the country needs good administration," he said. "We shall be bankrupt within a few more years." He sat in his small bungalow, rubbing his tired eyes with knuckled fists. "We fought for independence all these years. Now it seems we must become pawns of either Russia or of the United States." Later, when poor Sjafruddin abandoned the revolution and (in August, 1961) swore an oath of loyalty to President Sukarno as "the great leader of *the* Revolution," this unhappy man publicly concluded that the PRRI rebellion was not a genuine expression of popular dissatisfaction but merely satisfied an irresponsible and blindly anticommunist group of Americans. This was being hinted by Sjafruddin even during his experimental career as a revolutionary guerrilla. He told me with some bitterness that he and his colleagues had been badly advised to proclaim the PRRI government on the basis of "United States promises."

Natsir, the Masjumi leader, had a different outlook. He was preparing himself, mentally and physically, for a long guerrilla campaign because he believed any form of collaboration between the existing authorities and the Indonesian communist party to be entirely wrong. He was convinced that President Sukarno was becoming the prisoner and the "front-man" for communism and therefore must be opposed. He planned to continue the fight from Celebes, at the other end of the archipelago, if this was necessary.

He had faith in those Americans who, he said, had promised support and recognition for the PRRI government once it secured the two strategic islands of Sumatra and Celebes. "The British," he said, "have turned away from us." I suggested that he might be attaching too much importance to statements made by Americans not qualified to speak for the State Department. He would not have this.

And yet the possibility had been growing in my mind that a great many of these reported contacts with "CIA men" might have been nothing of the sort. What was there to prevent any American citizen passing himself off as an agent in order to secure purchase orders for surplus weapons? Equally, of course, there was nothing to stop the Central Intelligence Agency from disowning its agents if things went wrong. There were many precedents for this sort of thing.

Both the rebel leaders and the Djakarta government had provided some convincing evidence to show that at various times there had been Anglo-American help and advice for the revolutionaries, and this had never been denied. But I was prepared to take the word of one responsible British diplomat, who insisted that no help was being given now. "The difficulty for the Americans," he said, "is to put a stop to aid supplied by all their different agencies. It involves a clear-cut decision to abandon the rebels — and I don't believe this decision can be finally given so long as the rebels maintain their anticommunist line."

There was an air of unreality about this whole revolutionary enterprise. Despite the undeniable existence of rebel troops, whose shadowed faces peered at me from under camouflaged tin hats in every hedgerow, I felt like the cynical spectator of a poorly acted play. Even the battle reports, which seemed so impressive when relayed over the rebel transmitters, evaporated on close examination.

From somewhere the rebel army commanders had obtained information on the techniques of sabotage. "We shall blow up the oilfields," Jambek had said. "We shall destroy the rubber estates. We shall adopt a scorched-earth policy. See. Here are instructions for patriotic acts of sabotage in our harbors."

The directions for destroying cargo were to be issued to dockyard workers: "Mix sand with sugar. Put methyl telluride into rice, causing contamination by smell. Puncture all sacks of rice and cereals. Encourage vermin below decks by ignoring fumigation rules. When handling hides, add salt water to assist bacteriological action. At night, connect ship's firehose to the washdeck line after opening appropriate valves, then lead hose to hold, allowing water to infiltrate."

A great deal of imagination and ingenuity had gone into these instructions. Their great value was the ease with which a worker, without special instruments, could create havoc. Officers and crews of ships were told how to alter the position of magnets under compasses; how to interfere with steering compasses shortly before landfall; how to get rid of the vital Azimuth mirror from the chartroom.

Jambek said: "As you know, the Java government is trying to get the inter-island shipping traffic back into operation and any act of sabotage will have serious results." Later I heard that Djakarta's biggest setback came, however, from the Russians. With many of the Dutch KPM inter-island steamers laid up or gone, the Djakarta government obtained an emergency supply of Soviet vessels. Moscow, heeding the special requirement for shallow-draft ships, sent ice-breakers with steel decks. Under the tropic sun, the decks became unbearably hot and miserable Indonesian crews spent most of their time hanging in the rigging to prevent their bare feet from frying.

I was fascinated by the rebel do-it-yourself sabotage kit. Mechanics working on army vehicles were told, for instance, how to incapacitate trucks and jeeps by putting rice or sago in the radiators, fluff in the gasoline tanks, sharp rocks between twin tires close to the bead; and how to distort the toe-in of tires, loosen bolts on the drag-link of the steering mechanism and cause intermittent short circuits by removing insulation leads.

There was one big flaw. These methods, to be effective, required the cooperation of thousands. They were designed for employment against a foreign oppressor — the disruption of bus and air services, the sabotage of industrial projects by simple tricks, the holding up of essential work by deliberately losing files and mistyping instructions.

But it was expecting too much to ask the majority of citizens in a former colony to imperil their own fresh-won independence in this manner. And unless the PRRI's advisers could obtain the help of the bulk of the population, these acts of sabotage could never be more than a serious nuisance.

I asked Sjafruddin if the proposals for widespread sabotage were invented by Indonesians. No, he said, looking smaller and unhappier than ever. They were based on experience in Occupied Europe. Did he believe, then, that loyal Indonesians would deliberately hurt their own nation's economic development in this way — even if they *did* dislike President Sukarno? Again Sjafruddin shook his head.

On the day I left, Sjafruddin said, "You must remember several things about this country. We are not, by nature, a warlike people. We began our existence as an independent republic with a terrifying lack of trained men. Our inexperience in all things is very great, and we have had to rely on foreign friends to advise us in such matters as civil war and sabotage."

I was tempted to reply that, to me, his foreign advisers seemed more interested in pursuing a larger objective than Indonesia's welfare. Blowing up one's own backward economy seemed a curious way of moving forward.

My plans now were to continue northward to Medan, and from there to cross the strait to Malaya, where the prime minister, Tengku Abdul Rahman, was taking a keen if discreet interest in developments, and so return to Hong Kong. Later, if the rebellion still spluttered along, I wanted to see the big rebel operational command in Celebes — if such existed. The PRRI cabinet spoke of continuing the fight from Celebes, using friendly ports in British Borneo and remote islands of the Philippines for bases.

On the evening before I left a number of shadow plays were staged at dusk. Intricate shadows danced upon a screen, and judging by the swift tempo of the accompanying music the plots involved some bitter conflicts. Sultans died, armies clashed, the spirits prevailed. When the flares behind the screen expired and the music died away, we were left staring at a blank sheet surrounded by black jungle.

> *The tumult and the shouting dies;*
> *The Captains and the Kings depart:*

Murmuring those lines from Kipling, I stumbled off to bed, only to lie awake and wonder if my hosts were no better than the shadow boxers we had seen so quickly and easily dismissed.

14

"Black Colonialism"

THE SAME YOUNG MAJOR escorted me back to the motor
road. "The enemy will never drive us out of here," he said. "We
are too clever, I am telling you." I passed no comment. "We
will conceal ourselves and bleed the enemy," said the major.
"They are coming every day to bomb us but we are not afraid."

"They've bombed you?" I asked with awkward interest.

The major, marching ahead of me down the narrow track,
paused. "Well, they haven't bombed us *yet* but when they do,
we are ready. We are firing American antiaircraft guns." I
had seen some of the guns, poorly sited and buried too deep in
the hillside to be effective.

"Why haven't they actually bombed you yet?"

"Because," said the major, "we are not shooting at them. It
would be foolish to waste our ammunition." He explained some
theory of conserving firepower that seemed to have been lifted
from a conventional military textbook. His ideas had become
confused, however, between the need for what he called "fire
discipline" and the importance of sustaining a guerrilla army on
the broad foundations of a popular mass movement among the
peasants. To keep on good terms with the peasants, he seemed
to be saying, it was necessary not to shoot at the enemy too often.

We scrambled through jungle overhung with creepers, between trees strangled by thick lianas with huge twelve-inch
blossoms near their roots. The sweat poured off me and in a

sudden burst of irritation, I said, "Do you honestly believe you've got the support of the population?"

He stopped, looking back up at me, a worried frown on his chubby face. A bird screeched in the matted foliage, strung like seaweed in the branches above us. For a moment we hovered on the brink of truth and then his lips tightened, the schoolboy bewilderment went out of his eyes and he said, "Yes," very curtly, and crunched ahead again.

During the tedium of the days that followed, bumping over roads that had received little attention since the Pacific war, I grew increasingly doubtful about the major's claim. He took me by jeep to Muaratebo again, and from there I traveled once more on local country buses. If the rebellion represented a popular uprising against Java's rule, this wild and sparsely populated island would provide ideal conditions for a peasants' war. But back in the territory reclaimed by General Nasution's forces I found only calm resignation. The peasants had accepted a year of separatist rule because they trusted local leaders who carried out regional reforms in difficult conditions. The islanders of Sumatra, despite their fierce regional loyalties and their different racial and religious ties, still yearned for law and order. They were not prepared to fight a civil war and lose what little they had gained. Some tried to guarantee a secure future by keeping both rebel and republican flags hidden away for use when the appropriate occasions arose.

Before coming to Sumatra, I had talked with people in the Federation of Malaya who were concerned with the fate of their Islamic friends. The Sultan of Johore in particular was worried that the few survivors of Sumatran aristocracy would be wiped out, and had issued an invitation to the Sultan of Dele to come and live with him in his palace across the causeway from Singapore.

The Sultan of Dele lived near Medan, a peaceful little town

of pronounced European appearance on the northeast coast. To get there I had to return to Palembang and catch a local Garuda flight. Among the passengers was a stout Malay who carried a pair of hens under his arms — Rhode Island Reds with strings attached to their patrician legs. This casual use of local airlines by Asians of low and high degree was an unfailing delight. Just as the monsoon-driven junks stirred the racial pudding for many centuries, so Garuda, Malayan Airlines, Cathay Pacific and that unique and typically French service, the nonconformist Aigle Azure, in this century opened new opportunities for enterprising migrants. Their planes fly dependably from one remote marketplace to another, leaping the formidable barriers of jungle and mountain, anticipating the highways and railroads that have yet to be built. In those lands where military rule does not yet prevail, these cheap and efficient air services are valuable stimulants to the economy. In Indonesia, unfortunately, we had the unhappy spectacle of army officers and government officials taking priority over the more productive passengers. The flying farmer with his humble brood of hens was becoming an increasingly rare sight.

We descended across a harbor crowded with sailing craft and landed on the Medan airstrip to find it under central government command. In the town former loyalists were crumbling fast. Men who had supported rebel ideals now shouted Java's slogans of "Death to the Revolution" and "Long live Sukarno." One European consul told the story of a rebel pilot who machine-gunned the town in the morning and broadcast a public apology in the afternoon, having switched sides during lunch. It may have been an exaggerated tale but it perfectly illustrated the mood.

The Sultan of Dele's palace was on the outskirts, reached by way of tree-lined streets, and overlooking a verdant countryside on one side and the white mellowing Dutch-style villas and churches on the other. With aristocratic informality a drowsy old bailiff in mildewed robes led me through dim and dusty rooms crammed with souvenirs and potted palms. One room, illuminated only by the gloomy light filtering through hundreds of dirty panes of glass, seemed like an enormous greenhouse. Its contents revealed a jumbled mind and the tasteless acquisitive habits of wealth — a huge Victorian reading-chair with levers to adjust height and swing books into view; faded portraits of illustrious ancestors; tables piled with papers and models of the Taj Mahal and the Eiffel Tower; a photograph of Mistinguette signed "To Darling Jaja"; and a stuffed tiger oozing sawdust.

The owner of these poor relics pounced upon me with expressions of genteel delight. The sultan was a small man festooned with big pearls and precious stones. He wore bright green silk pajamas stitched with flashing diamonds, a golden turban with rubies, and golden sandals.

He sparkled in that roomful of cobwebs and memories, his pince-nez gleaming as he darted about the showcases recalling youthful adventures of long ago. His was still the world of playboy princes, and he yearned for the Europe of kings and vacationing rajahs. Geography, for him, was an almanac of royal playgrounds. Politics revolved around issues like how much of the Nizam of Hyderabad's wealth was really seized by the Indian government; or what new scandals had enveloped the Emperor Bao Dai of Vietnam.

He conducted me to the gardens at the rear of his glassy palace, to sunken courtyards among broken Greek columns, and clapped his hands to summon one of his two wives and their children. The lady dutifully appeared beneath us, at the foot of a wide and broken stairway, where she stood with head meekly bowed while three children stood in line with respectful smiles.

The sultan dismissed them with another clap of his small freckled hands and we retired to an enormous lunch of *nasi goreng*, garnished with fried bananas and pineapple and soaked in red-pepper sauce.

"How I love good curry," he said. "It is my Indian ancestry. Long ago my family conquered this region and extended its power into Malaya. I *do* think Malaya is now the right place. Sumatra must leave the republic and join the Malay Federation. It is the only way."

He accused President Sukarno of "black colonialism," calling him a Java-born upstart who denied equal rights to the other islands. He could express himself freely because the local people respected him and would resist any attempts by the authorities to interfere in his affairs. The fate of Indonesia's other sultans left no grounds for optimism, however. Eighty-three flourished in Java under the Dutch. Only one now remained.

When I left the old sultan, it was like stepping out of a nineteenth-century daguerreotype. His diamonds, the feudal routine of palace life, the broken urns and carved ebony elephants were pathetic souvenirs of another age. The sultan's ancestors had achieved a balanced relationship with the peasants, whose customary rights were too powerful to be ignored. But under Dutch patronage, the nobles dominated the peasants, whose political sense was dulled by economic exploitation and authoritarian rule. After independence, some Indonesian intellectuals tried to restore those ancient pastoral freedoms that once flourished before the Dutch arrived. Like the Sultan of Dele, they yearned for the days when the peasants exercised a strong instinct for individual rights. But unlike the sultan, no contemporary Indonesian commoner wanted to see the republic broken up. Even the rebels, though deeply opposed to President Sukarno's dictatorship, had no desire to destroy the unity for which they too had struggled.

It was possible to sympathize with the old man's wistful longing to rejoin his regal relatives and friends in Malaya. There, after a victorious twelve-year war against communist guerrillas, Malay leaders had embarked upon an economic and industrial revolution based upon traditional ways. Instead of destroying ancient feudal powers and uprooting the common people's deep affection and respect for the local aristocracy, an enlightened government had decided to work through these royal personages, using their authority and influence to popularize social and economic reforms.

I now flew to the Malayan capital of Kuala Lumpur, where the evidence of these peaceful and progressive changes gladdened the eye, from new and ultramodern industrial suburbs to the dazzling architecture of a swiftly expanding university. I make no apology for my prejudice in this respect. Malaya had shaken off the sociological theorists whose bleeding hearts so seldom matched their practical abilities. Instead of lazily seeking a major source of revenue by taxing foreign investors and penalizing its more enterprising businessmen at home, the country welcomed initiative and (in token of this) troubled the traveler with as few formalities as possible. It was astounding what a difference this generous political philosophy made to men of the same racial origins: the difference between official Indonesian scowls and universal Malayan smiles.

It was the difference too between my Sumatran sultan and another Muslim prince, the Malayan prime minister. Tengku (Prince) Abdul Rahman had anticipated the expansionist aims of President Sukarno's regime and he was trying to build a strong multiracial nation that might stand up to pressure from Indonesia as well as Red China.

The tengku was almost always available to foreign newsmen and he talked freely to me about his plans. It became clear, however, that he was uncomfortable about United States policy in

Asia, which he felt had so far failed to give due importance to popular peasant movements against all forms of oppression. He was disturbed by a dominant military influence in the United States assessment of Asian events, and he felt this led to the unrealistic optimism about the chances for a successful Indonesian rebellion against Sukarno. The British, in his view, had more wisely withdrawn support from the rebels when it became evident that the revolution was founded upon quicksands of vague promises and insubstantial hopes.

Malaya had become an eye of calm amid the storms of Southeast Asia. The tengku's ambition was to develop a civic pride among its citizens who, for too long, had been obliged to look abroad to China or Britain for inspiration and leadership. He wanted the Malays to play a larger role in national affairs, instead of remaining as the passive background figures to Chinese enterprises. He saw, in the island-state of Singapore, Chinese communist extremists threatening to topple the local government; and in the British-run territories of Sarawak, Brunei and North Borneo the danger of infiltration and invasion from the left-leaning Indonesian expansionists.

What the tengku proposed was a new independent nation of ten million people in an area somewhat smaller than Japan. This "Federation of Malaysia" would provide the necessary political stability and answer anticolonialist propaganda which had helped spread communism. Malaya would make use of Singapore's incomparable port facilities, instead of competing with them, and it would direct economic and technical aid into the Borneo territories with their oil and rubber resources. The inclusion of the Borneo territories would be opposed no doubt by President Sukarno, whose own two thirds of the enormous island lagged in technical development despite Soviet Russian offers to help.

But the tengku was determined to realize his ambitions. If the Borneo lands were included in the new federation, they would preserve the existing cultural balance and save the Malay-Muslim population from being swamped by an immediate influx of 1,250,000 Chinese from Singapore.

It may come as a surprise to Americans that the Malayan prime minister was publicly opposed to any United States participation in his plans. He felt that many of the defeats suffered by the democracies in Asia were directly attributable to a militant United States policy of backing extreme right-wing elements who professed anticommunist sentiments in order to win support. The end result was that United States aid went to unpopular and reactionary ruling families who had lost public confidence, thus adding fuel to the fires of communist propaganda.

This was why Malaya did not wish to give haven to Indonesian rebels. There was a good deal of sympathy for the dissident colonels, who were thought on the whole to be honest men. But in Malaya there was also distrust of the circumstances leading to partnership between rebels and the Chinese Nationalists.

The tengku's sensitivity was aroused by earlier interference in Malaya's affairs on the part of what he called "the United States satellites on Formosa." He recognized the value of Chinese talents but he did not want Malay-Chinese taking orders from abroad. He resented Peking's attempts to influence them. He was equally angry at attempts to enlist them in an anticommunist crusade directed from Formosa.

The tengku did not mind traditional Chinese enterprises. He recalled the old days when the British district officer was the highest local court of appeal. Then the Chinese entrepreneur had set the busy scene, trotting through the towns of Malaya in his horse-drawn gig, his plait decorated with long red ribbons and in his mind's eye the plantations of pepper and gambier that would help to launch new shops on the waterfronts and new ships in the harbors.

It was the other kind of clandestine activity that disturbed the prime minister. He said, "Formosa's Chinese are being used by Americans to interfere in other people's politics." He feared that they were using British Borneo as a base of operations against the legal government of Indonesia and might in consequence provoke Indonesian retaliation. He foresaw a day when Indonesian armed forces could threaten Malaysian security. His fears on this score were soon to be justified.

"We've had our baptism of fire," said the tengku. "We fought a communist terrorist campaign with every ounce of help that Britain could give us in men and money. We want to go forward from that point. We don't want to get entangled in military alliances."

He voiced his utmost admiration for American industrial enterprise. His only reservations were in regard to what he termed "American bellicosity."

Later, talking with other members of the Malayan government, I realized how deeply rooted was this fear that American impatience might provoke trouble. The Malays were not frightened of war. They had gone through a long and terrible conflict already. They just wanted time to get their house in order, to create a strong and independent economic unit to meet the later challenge with which they knew both China and Indonesia would confront them.

"What we need is another Raffles," said one cabinet minister. It was a striking tribute to an Englishman dead more than a hundred years, for it came from a man who wanted more than anything to be rid of the imperialist grip.

15

Rafflesia Parasitica

One ancient legend said the Indonesian kingdom
would be split into nine parts. But when 3,000
rainy seasons had passed the Eastern islands would
be reunited and the power of the White Man
would be at an end.

THE MAN WHO WROTE those words was Thomas Stamford
Bingley Raffles, born on board a British merchantman off Ja-
maica in the year 1781. He came to Malaya as a guinea-a-month
clerk in the East India Company when he was twenty-four years
old, and by the time he was thirty he governed Java. He founded
Singapore, for which his widow was later heavily fined, and he
was censured for "his precipitate and unauthorized emancipation
of slaves."

He was by the standards of any age a remarkable adventurer,
and his name is commemorated in the enormous flowers peculiar
to Malaya known as *Rafflesia*, pollinated by carrion flies, with a
smell like decaying flesh, and altogether parasitic. In an age of
revulsion against colonialism this may seem appropriate. But
Raffles achieved a great deal for which he is also remembered in
Singapore with such names as Raffles Place, Raffles Quay, Raffles
Museum, Raffles Hotel, the Raffles Institute. . . .

The Raffles Institute was inhabited by a notoriously crotchety
Englishman whom I had gone to see, largely at the tengku's

behest. The old man occupied a dark corner of the building. He was barricaded by books against intruders, sustained by sandwiches and beer; and he seldom emerged into the light of day except to check the cricket scores. Scott Leavitt, a resourceful writer on *Life* magazine, had been trying to communicate with this recluse for some time. "He won't answer our letters," said Scott. "What's more, I don't think he opens them."

The problem was solved when Scott discovered an open fanlight through which he glided paper darts at the old man. One eventually landed on the cluttered desk with enough precision that it could not be ignored. Its penciled message brought the recluse tottering and blinking out of his dusty hermitage.

He was not the usual Englishman of fantasy, building an empire on planter's punch, advancing through the natives in a fog of prejudice. He wore sandals and blue faded shorts and a loose khaki shirt with one sleeve ripped. He was like a bloodhound in a very moist oil painting, the pigments having run so that one great sad eye had slipped an inch or two. He looked at the history of European conquest not from the conventional western view but rather from the position that a Malay or Indonesian might adopt. He symbolized the British liberal conscience which had helped to convert British colonial policy from a political and economic imperialism to the concept of colonies as trusts to be administered only until the local population could administer themselves. During the nineteenth century, such Englishmen watched the overseas settlements with a vigilant eye, protesting against cases of injustice or the suppression of human rights. They were, and still are, frequently unattractive and narrow-minded in their own peculiar way, smug and ill informed on occasion; but heroically outspoken in their defense of the underdog. Nowadays they are mostly heard attacking western self-deception, insisting that we are neither superior to, nor wiser than, the Afro-Asians, pleading for patience, arguing against the recruitment of militant allies merely on the basis of anticommunist sentiment. They are the irritating but necessary voices of dissent, earnestly trying to put before the West the disagreeable argument that communism is a secondary threat in Afro-Asian minds to the dangers of prolonged colonialism.

In Raffles' day, the liberal conscience produced such well-meaning endeavors as the Aborigines Protection Society. It also launched unreasonable and venomous attacks on men like Raffles, who had founded Singapore, Temple of the Lion, by what they regarded as a combination of unauthorized bribery, the unsupported threat of force, and unscrupulous negotiation.

What British liberals overlooked, of course, were the hard realities with which Raffles had to cope. He made separate deals with rival rulers, exploited local discontent and frightened the natives with a display of naval power. He played a leading part in some of the most astonishing events in British history. But he was not quite the ruthless colonizer his enemies made out. He regarded the people with whom he was dealing as "highly polished, considerably advanced in science, highly inquisitive and full of penetration."

He saw the island of Java as "the center of an Eastern insular Empire." It was then in the hands of the French, who had won control of the Netherlands for Napoleon Bonaparte. Raffles persuaded Lord Minte, then the governor general in India, to conquer the island. In 1811 he was appointed lieutenant governor of Java. He increased the revenue by destroying the fetters imposed on trade and intercourse by the earlier Dutch rulers and established an administration aimed at being "not only without fear but without reproach." His five years in Java were followed by another five years as lieutenant governor of Sumatra, whose jungles he explored. By this time the Dutch had recovered Java and were trying to complete their control over the Eastern archipelago and to expel British traders. It was then that Raffles, now Sir Stamford, acquired Singapore and ended any Dutch hopes of creating a trade monopoly. When he died suddenly at the age of 45 in 1826, however, he had been brought home and was under bitter attack. Lady Raffles was fined £10,000, a huge sum in those days, including the cost of founding Singapore, for the alleged misdeeds of her late husband.

The liberal conscience had prevented Raffles from ending what he regarded as a destructive Dutch domination of the archipelago. When Sir James Brooke went there a few years later he wrote in support of Raffles' fiercely held view that "We are very certain that the policy of the Dutch has, at the present day, reduced this 'Eden of the Eastern Wave' to a state of anarchy and confusion, as repugnant to humanity as it is to commercial prosperity."

The case of Raffles seemed to be worth examining in the light of current developments in Southeast Asia. So often the so-called "liberal conscience" had been another name for indecision and a shrinking from unpleasant facts. In the middle of the twentieth century the conflict was essentially the same between powerful liberal voices and those on the spot who, while recognizing the faults of the past, saw no reason to make a blind withdrawal.

A positive Rafflesian demand for the action was to be heard from senior officers of the South East Asia Treaty Organization.* One of this alliance's chief handicaps, however, was that only three members were actually in Southeast Asia, and of these Pakistan was a self-avowed admirer of Red China, whose south-

---

* Thailand, the Philippines and remote Pakistan were the shaky grounds on which the five western partners (Britain, the United States, Australia, New Zealand and France) claimed the right to act together in the event of a military attack in Southeast Asia.

ward march this very organization was intended to halt. Furthermore another, the Philippines, was shaping up for a row with Britain about the future of Borneo. Above all, SEATO was suspected of "disguised imperialism." There were rumors that it provided haven for the rebels as well as aid, and these were fed by the embarrassing activities of a former British Commando, Raymond "Turk" Westerling, who had tried to overthrow the Sukarno government. Westerling, born in Istanbul of Dutch parents, styled himself Prince Justice and after a brief reign of terror in Indonesia fled to Singapore, where he announced he would be back to lead a popular revolt.

A strong if unofficial SEATO argument was that "if Red China and Russia can support guerrilla wars to establish totalitarian regimes in the name of anticolonialism, why can't we support honest patriots who want real independence?" But western liberals were not going to fall for this argument when they saw the kind of rebel that SEATO favored in Indonesia. Adventurers like Westerling, wrapping schoolboy romanticism in veils of anticommunism, blurred the image of Doctor Sumitro as an honest patriot.

There were western diplomats whose governments belonged to SEATO but who themselves deplored its activities. These believed that SEATO and western-inspired revolution only encouraged Indonesians to turn to the Soviet bloc for help. This division of opinion paralyzed SEATO and forced some of its more determined strategists — notably United States Seventh Fleet commanders — to act independently, demonstrating their strength at critical periods by carrier exercises, and secretly helping the rebels.

The hard and unpalatable facts, which were denied or wilfully ignored in London and Ottawa and Washington, were described to me by a SEATO commander in the following terms: "Indonesia is like a sagging hammock. If it collapses, the rest of Southeast Asia falls through. This is the justification for our interest in a country not technically covered by the pact.

"The republic curves under the SEATO region as if supporting the smaller nations there. It has a land area of 576,000 square miles — about 3000 islands of consequence.

"If we accepted Sukarno's claim (which the Soviet bloc does) to a twelve-mile belt of territorial sea and to all the waters around and between the islands, Indonesia would rank seventh among the world's largest nations. In population — 93 million — it ranks fifth.

"After Russia and China, it has the world's biggest communist party. After China and India, it has the world's largest number of peasants.

"Russia and China are in competition in Indonesia but this doesn't help anyone else. The *Moscow Literary Gazette* called the republic 'A highly strategic bridge between Australia and Asia. . . . Our beachhead in Central-South Asia.' The New China News Agency called it 'The next great Asian country to follow the Chinese path to socialism.' We simply cannot afford to let this happen."

This was the frankly military view. I think Raffles would have softened it considerably with more humane arguments. He would have said, perhaps, that the West was now leading the dismantling of empires; that it had a responsibility to perform this honorable task without exposing the formerly subject peoples to the ravenous appetites of the new imperialists. He might have recalled that the British were getting out of Malaya after a costly jungle war against communist Chinese intent upon reviving Peking's old empire. That war had cost, between 1945 and 1957, some $485 million and 11,000 lives. Britain did not mean to waste this sacrifice by abandoning Malaya; nor did she plan to stifle the genuinely liberal conscience that demanded full independence for Malaya.

All this a latter-day Raffles might have pointed out in support of those who, by no means imperialist in intent, wanted to protect Indonesia from sinister influences while her people won political and economic stability. Unfortunately he would have found few sympathetic listeners. Raffles, the Dutch, SEATO and Doctor Sumitro were synonymous with colonialism. Few troubled to look beyond this. Raffles, the man who made Singapore and destroyed piracy, was obscured by Raffles, the symbol of parasitical imperialism.

In the next chapter I have briefly surveyed the background to this dangerous self-deception.

16

Survival of the Fittest

"THERE SUDDENLY FLASHED upon me the *idea* of survival of the fittest," wrote the British naturalist Alfred Russell Wallace after a severe bout of fever delayed him in Indonesia for the month of February, 1855.

In the centuries preceding ours, those nations which survived were skilled in the arts of war. Today there is more room for civilizations which give priority to other matters, and this thought undoubtedly inspired many of the western liberals who prevented any decisive intervention in Indonesia during Sukarno's heyday. They regarded Indonesia as benefiting from the fact that neither the Sino-Soviet bloc nor the West would allow each other to dominate an area which had been fought over by rival powers during the past 400 years.

Wallace was fascinated by the fantastic variety of wildlife and vegetation he found throughout the Malay Archipelago. His name was given to the Wallace Line. It divides the Indonesian islands into a western group, which in its zoological affinities is oriental, and an eastern Australian group.

The people themselves divide ethnically into three groups: Negroid and Australoid aboriginals; Caucasoid stock planted during an early wave of migrants; and Mongoloid stock left by later immigrant waves. The impulse behind these movements of population was hunger to get at the immense natural wealth of the region which Moscow now calls Central-South Asia. Probably no other area on earth has such a long history of intensive colonization. Four hundred years ago it was part of the Malay Islamic Empire, which stretched from the eastern border of India across the Asian mainland to the Chinese frontiers and to the Philippines. Today it remains Asia's richest rice bowl, with a uniformly lush climate in which as many as four crops a year are possible. This is SEATO's *raison d'être*, of which Indonesia is an unwilling part. Within Central-South Asia, to use the Russian term, lie nine tenths of the world's natural rubber and two thirds of its tin. Here are the richest oil resources in the Far East.

To it came the Mongol armies of Kublai Khan and the Chinese invaders who put their word *viet* (to denote a conquered people) into the Vietnam of Indochina. From India came priests and traders, establishing colonies in Java and other coastal regions, bringing Hinduism and later two distinct forms of Buddhism. This intermingling of two great civilizations, Indian and Chinese, has sprinkled the region with racial types that vary from the Mongolian's straight black hair, small nose and peculiar fold of the upper eyelid to the more typically Indian characteristics of curly hair, bigger features, darker skins and the Caucasian eyelid.

The Indian colonies grew into Hindu kingdoms with a special cult of Sita which stunted the further growth of Buddhism. The kingdom of Sri-Vijaya on Sumatra became the dominant commercial power because it controlled the Malacca and Sundra straits. At its eighth-century peak it ruled all of Sumatra and Malaya and a good deal of Java. It began to wane in the shadow of new kingdoms on Java, whose sway by the fourteenth century extended over most of the islands. About this time came the Muslim traders who introduced Islam to the ports and who completed the collapse of Hindu power.

Europeans challenged the Islamic imperialists four hundred years ago, but they also wasted their energies by fighting among themselves. The Portuguese were involved in an exhausting struggle with the British, who, arriving late on the scene, moved swiftly eastward to capture Malaya and Burma, the Andamans and the Nicobars, and a large slice of Borneo. The French moved into Indochina, and the Americans fought the Spaniards for the Philippines.

Dutch domination of the Indonesian archipelago was achieved by advancing the interests of those local rulers who were willing to cooperate, while putting down the resistance of the more recalcitrant on the pretext of maintaining law and order. By 1602 the Dutch East India Company had been founded, and by 1650 it was supreme.

The Spaniards and the Portuguese had missionary ambitions. The Dutch were there to make money. They kept up the prices of the raw materials they extracted from Indonesia, by monopolizing trade between the islands and by destroying spices and other commodities they could not carry in their own ships. They excluded other European traders and restricted native and Chinese shipping, which for many centuries had moved freely through these waters.

The Dutch wiped out the Indonesian merchant class but promoted the role of the Chinese settlers as middlemen. They encouraged autocratic forms of government over which they kept supreme control. By 1800 they held all the Indonesian islands as far as west New Guinea, where they bought off one of Auntie Emiria's ancestors, the Sultan of Tidore, to forestall German and British encroachments.

An attempt was made by Sir Stamford Raffles, during his governorship of Java, to end the Dutch practices of forced labor and the monopoly of certain crops, and the pernicious "deliveries in kind" formula which forced the peasants to cultivate export crops at the expense of foodstuffs they badly needed to grow for themselves. The end of the Napoleonic Wars and Raffles' departure, however, meant a return to Dutch ways. The resistance to these repressive measures grew.

This resistance took the intellectual form with which the West has become unhappily familiar in China. Just as it took us many years to recognize that communism's history in China was a long one, so now we are awakening slowly to the deep historical roots of Indonesian communism. As early as 1926 the party, the PKI, had enough support from frustrated intellectuals and disgruntled workers to call a general strike. It provoked the Dutch into harsher measures of control while claiming they were working toward responsible self-government at the village level.

When the armies of Imperial Japan swept through the islands in 1942 there was little loyalty to the Dutch "protectors" who crumbled so ignominiously in the face of a real enemy. A Japanese campaign of "Asia for the Asians" was conducted with vigor. European officials were removed and the management of plantations and business enterprises placed in Indonesian hands, under Japanese control. The Japanese introduced press-gang methods of forced labor, the suppression of free speech and information, and a systematic brutality that betrayed a Japanese sense of superiority.

Underground movements against the Japanese all over Southeast Asia provided a training ground for communist fighters. In Malaya, for instance, the British made a hero of Chen Ping (alias Wong Ping, or "C. T. P."), who later became the brilliant leader of communist Chinese forces trying to wrest Malaya from British control. Such men were dedicated to one cause alone: "Asia for the Cominform."

In Indonesia, the Japanese collapse in 1945 left in its wake a militant combination of patriots and communists. Within ten days of the Japanese surrender, Sukarno proclaimed an independent Indonesian Republic with himself as president.

Somewhat belatedly, the Queen of the Netherlands had outlined proposals for a Commonwealth whose component territories could be self-governing in local affairs. The offer fell on deaf ears. Now the Dutch tried to negotiate a federal United States of Indonesia. This, too, was turned down. The Dutch tried to discredit Sukarno by speaking of his "made-in-Japan" government. They began landing troops in strength. An attempt at mediation by the British resulted in a draft agreement, signed early in 1947, for a Netherlands-Indonesian Union. But subsequent negotiations failed. In the summer of that same year, the Dutch tried again to win by force. They called their military occupation of key Javanese areas a "police action," and the United Nations Security Council was obliged to intervene.

The Dutch began an economic blockade. In areas under their administration, they sponsored the formation of separate states. They launched another military action in 1948, which was followed by the Round Table conference at The Hague. This ended in a ceremonial transfer of sovereignty on December 27, 1949. The Dutch were not able to prevent international intervention. The Indonesians had used guerrilla warfare and appeals to world opinion to win their case.

But the Dutch, unofficially, did not give up. Raymond "Turk" Westerling recruited troops from the Netherlands Indies army and began a private war of terror. Similar actions took place in other parts of Indonesia. A rebellion in South Moluccas is still, at least on paper, and at the time of writing, disturbing the peace; and a news bulletin is still published by the so-called "Republic of the South Moluccas" from Rotterdam.

These retrograde Dutch actions must be taken into consideration when judging Indonesian attitudes. Sukarno may not be an attractive proposition to western policy makers. His inadequacies, his maladministration and despotic tendencies have all been commented upon in the West. These criticisms, duly reproduced in Indonesia, did nothing to improve relations. Sukarno still exercised a powerful, personal influence over the entire chain of islands. Dutch bully-boys left a nasty taste. Sukarno was able to accuse the Dutch of trying to encourage separatist tendencies in the republic, and he could now claim that any genuine revolt was Dutch-inspired.

Belief in a permanent Dutch threat to Indonesian unity added urgency to the main bone of contention between the two countries: west New Guinea. By its possession of this territory, the Netherlands was able to maintain what Indonesians believed to be a hostile military and political apparatus on their doorstep.

The self-defeating nature of Dutch interference was illustrated by the overthrow of the federal principle in 1950. A provisional constitution had been drawn up for the United States of Indonesia. It provided for the union of seven autonomous states and nine other autonomous territories. Its bicameral parliament consisted of a senate and a house of representatives. There would be a federal prime minister and other cabinet ministers appointed on the advice of a committee of three selected by the federal president, Sukarno.

Two unsuccessful regional revolts, one led by Westerling and the other led by the East Indonesian minister of justice, Dr. Soumokil, convinced the public that the Dutch were instigating and abetting such uprisings. Elements of the KNIL (the former Netherlands Army in Indonesia, which was awaiting disbandment under terms of the Round Table conference) were active in both revolts. Federalism, regarded as a Dutch concept, was discredited. Sukarno issued emergency decrees for the immediate merger of the states of Central Java, East Java and Madura with the Jogjakarta republic; and later, other territories accepted incorporation in turn. On August 17, 1950, the Republic of the United States of Indonesia was formally replaced by a unitary republic.

From the start, the republican government had trouble asserting its authority. The Dutch had left an administrative vacuum which was dangerous for Sukarno, but they had also left a glowering suspicion of the West which was useful to him. Sukarno stoked up the fires of hatred against the colonialist past and excited a nascent nationalism by skillfully painting a picture of new western colonialist plotters. He had little else to work on; no civil service to cement the sprawling republic; and few other professionals (there were fifty graduate engineers when the Dutch left, and only a thousand doctors).

The Dutch, for the purposes of governing, had subdivided the Indies into residencies under Dutch governors whose aides were also Dutchmen. With all the senior administrators gone, Sukarno fell back on the Dutch dual system whereby native regents duplicated the work of the Dutch governors. Sukarno's action meant in effect doubling the number of administrators, because jobs previously held by Dutchmen were now given to Indonesians, and jobs held by Indonesians under the native regents were perpetuated.

It was easy at first to sympathize with Sukarno. The dual system had been used by the Dutch for political reasons, for it committed a significant part of the native ruling class to the preservation and promotion of the colonial power's interests. Sukarno kept the old system, however, because he could not tolerate a single body of professional civil servants who might oppose his will. He squandered what few qualified personnel he had at his disposal, preferring a muddle in which he could intrigue and keep power.

Six governments after the unitary republic was established, President Sukarno toured the communist countries in search of a new political concept that might bring stability. His view, outlined to the Constituent Assembly on November 10, 1956, was that:

> *We certainly cannot copy the liberal democracy of the West; neither can we import the conception of dictatorship from another range of ideas.*

He explained that Indonesia had neither the degree of literacy nor of prosperity required to practice liberal democracy, and he invoked instead the mystique of *gotong rojong*, the tradition of cooperative self-help which permeates life in Indonesian villages. Two years later he dissolved parliament and assumed vast executive powers.

Today there is a curious topicality in Wallace's theory of survival. He saw East and West colliding, zoologically speaking; but he also saw a parallel conflict of ideas. He saw Muslim audiences enthralled in shadow plays telling the great legends of Hindu mythology; he found volcano worshippers in Java and traces of Stone Age culture in the island of Nias, where religious rites are still conducted at huge stone altars.

Sukarno, in a later age of conflicting ideologies, hovered above a new battle of survival and himself borrowed heavily from the Chinese concept of "People's Democracy." In this new battle several factors favored the communist side. One was the western liberal conscience. Another was inadequate information on conditions within Indonesia, and insufficient knowledge about a grass-roots opposition to Sukarno's methods. Thirdly there were the embarrassing interventions of professional anticommunists whom Sukarno identified as coming from Formosa and South Korea with American help, and who only buttressed the walls of hostility to the West.

Finally there was the character of a people who, despite different origins and beliefs, had a special outlook on life. Indonesians call this easy flexibility, this good-humored love of life, *alus*. To many an impatient westerner, it seemed like a spineless evasion of issues; a chronic lack of decisiveness that could never resist the sharp edge of communist purpose. In such a psychological climate, matched by a tropical warmth where everything grew in abundance and you could always shake down a coconut to frustrate hunger, the military stand-off between rival power blocs did not mean in fact the growth of a great new civilization based upon mutual tolerance and irrigated by artistic tastes. It meant soft and tolerant conditions in which the single-minded agents and allies of Peking met with feeble and decreasing opposition.

17

The Sanctimonious Pirate

I FLEW DOWN to Singapore for the independence celebrations of June 1, 1959. By then, piracy and the barter trade around the eastern islands of Indonesia and Borneo had reached a very big scale. Sukarno's enemies were making use of this illegal traffic between the islands, but already it had become evident that the position might be reversed. Once Indonesian patrols had been sufficiently strengthened with Soviet-bloc ships and planes, it would be the British who must guard against the infiltration into their territory of agents and guerrillas. A small unofficial war was developing between the strictly unlicensed mariners of both sides.

The Royal Air Force flew antipiracy patrols in Sunderland flying boats, and the Royal Navy searched for pirate gunboats, empowered by a freshly signed Geneva Convention on the High Seas to arrest anyone guilty of "any illegal act of violence, detention or any act of depredation, committed for private ends by the crew on the passengers . . . and directed on the high seas against another ship . . . or against persons or property on board such a ship."

This was no novelty for the British. As long ago as 1579 Sir Francis Drake had described this as "one of the world's most lawless regions." His countrymen, coming out to trade, found they had to abolish slavery and put down piracy. They did this in the firm belief that prosperity and progress must naturally follow peace and order. They interfered very little in the internal politics of the lands with which they traded. But piracy, they agreed, was bad for business. It was this outlook that accounted for the survival of British interests. It explained the philosophy behind the bold experiment which began on that first day of Singapore's independence when seven hard-core communist leaders were released from custody.

Many observers condemned the release of communist conspirators as suicidal. Why endanger the long-term plan for a Malaysian federation by freeing men who would want to wreck it? The British replied that times were changing; and failure to make a timely accommodation would exacerbate the local political situation and play into communist hands. Communism, they argued, thrived on conflict. Many of its recruits were nationalists seeking a weapon with which to strike back at "colonialist oppressors." Self-government would teach true patriots the responsibilities and difficulties that could not be solved by doctrinaire theories.

The experiment was bound to arouse Red China's hostility. But having been defeated once already in a direct attempt to capture Singapore and Malaya, the communist Chinese decided to work through "neutral" Indonesia, which the British would be unable to engage in combat. In their favor was an undiscriminating Indonesian hatred for all forms of colonialism. Yet there were different degrees of it. The Portuguese had introduced the Inquisition, coming as conquistadors who sought converts. They were not the same kettle of fish as the shareholders of the British North Borneo Company, whose aim was dividends.

This British commercial interest had, however, left a legacy that the Chinese, working through the Indonesian communist party, were preparing to exploit. Britain's empire had grown out of Portuguese Asia more by accident than by design. Whereas the Portuguese were chasing their religious enemies when they tumbled into Asia, the British had no compelling moral doctrine to preach except the virtues of free trade. The Portuguese, "obeying the Decrees of Heaven," planted their fortresses from the Persian Gulf to the Strait of Malacca. The British, coming up behind, established trading posts which they were fully prepared to abandon if these failed to pay their way.

So when Raffles wrote that Borneo was "one of the most fertile countries in the world and most productive in gold and diamonds," the merchants came scurrying out, discovering too late how wrong he was. In a treaty signed between Britain and the Netherlands (which had by then recovered its eastern colonies) the latter got all the islands south of Borneo. The wording of the treaty was ambiguous. The British, it seemed, were free to colonize north Borneo. But nobody produced a legal definition, and the issue was left for the future to decide.

The time for that decision was drawing close on the day I sat watching the independence celebrations from the wooden verandah of Singapore's creaky old Cricket Club. The hidden drama seemed as exciting as anything that had happened before. Here the British sought to preserve their close relations and vital interests by adapting to the changes taking place, convinced that communist fervor could not survive genuine social progress and an alert, enlightened public. Among the crowds dancing at midnight through Raffles Place were a few gloomy westerners who were afraid that the floodgates of communism had been opened quite irresponsibly. And a few miles away in Indonesia were men determined to frustrate an experiment that would sap the revolutionary zeal of young communist recruits.

The view from the Cricket Club, as the militant youth wingers of the triumphant Peoples Action Party marched with portraits of their liberated heroes, was stimulating enough. Seen from the office of the Chinese prime minister, Lee Kuan-yew, it was a bit more alarming. Beyond the marchers he could distinguish the nearest islands of Indonesia and he knew it would be a race against time to stabilize the political and economic life of Singapore before Sukarno began to interfere.

Another cautious observer was Mr. Lee's erudite little friend, Mr. C. V. Devan Nair, who had spent five years in British jails for his communist sins. (Later he became widely respected as the general secretary of the powerful National Trade Union Congress.)

"I joined the communist party because it was the only way to hit the British at that time," he told me. "Now we've got independence and I want to build on a more enduring foundation than hatred."

We were talking at a time when the idea of a Greater Malaysia was in the minds of only a few. "They'll do everything to stop us," said Mr. Nair, nodding across the narrow strait. "That sanctimonious old pirate Sukarno will be a puppet in Chinese hands. They'll convince him this is a dirty British plot and they'll dig up arguments for him to claim all of Borneo."

Mr. Nair quoted Shakespeare's "sanctimonious pirate, that went to sea with the Ten Commandments." He smiled cheerlessly. "Sukarno can pluck out any one of the Commandments and find support in it for any action he wants to take." He thought the crunch would come when some attempt was made to link the British parts of Borneo with Malaya, setting the seal on the earlier marriage between Malaya and Singapore. The ingenuity with which this initial wedding was being planned was evident in a device to measure Singapore's political maturity.

This maturity was something which had to be demonstrated to Malaya before the more intimate liaison became possible. It would be done through an internal security committee, meeting monthly, with three British and three Singapore nominees sitting alongside a Malaya representative. Since the danger to internal security from the Chinese communists was at the bottom of everyone's misgivings, the committee provided a periodic means of checking Singapore's political health. The chances were that within five years the Malayan government could be convinced that it was not dealing with a communist Trojan horse.

In this probationary period, the British hoped that political extremists would discover the burdens of office. They were gambling on the probability that most youngsters attracted to communism were sincerely eager to improve the community, and that would they find other more useful outlets for serving a cause. This was important in Singapore's community of 1.6 million, of whom 1.4 million were Chinese tempted to look to Peking for guidance and instruction. The British, while discouraging contacts with Peking, were also opposed to American suggestions that the Chinese should look to Formosa instead, on the grounds that the development of democratic institutions and social progress could be accomplished only on a foundation of local patriotism, and because the British had grave doubts about the ultimate loyalties of Formosa's leaders, who were apt to make an overnight deal with Peking.

It was of course a risky experiment but, in the British view, better than blindly suppressing every unorthodox political idea. There were many who remembered with what bitterness the former Dutch governor of Indonesia, Hubertus J. Van Mook, condemned those who had fashioned postwar policy. "An excess of caution and deficiency of imagination stood in the way of a larger gesture that might have given the history of the conflict a turn for the better," he wrote in angry despair.

"At least the British have *tried*," said Doctor Sumitro a few days later. He had called me to ask if I could make the long-awaited journey to the rebel areas of Celebes, he having ear-marked a blockade-runner.

It was a tempting offer. I said it was high time I went home to Hong Kong, however. That was fine, said Doctor Sumitro. When the time came, the rebels would let me know and I could fly down to Labuan for further instructions.

I wangled a ride home in an Australian-owned Canso amphibian plane. As we sauntered over the scattered fleets of junks it was easy to see what immense possibilities still awaited an enterprising mariner with a couple of cannon stashed below the poop deck. For centuries there had been this slow procession of tall masts passing through the Strait of Malacca or the Strait of Sunda, west of Borneo, when the southwest monsoon blew from April to October. And in the northwest monsoon, taking the longer route south and east of Borneo, ships laden with Chinese cargoes had run the gauntlet of the pirates of the Sulu Sea.

Either way, the routes crossed near the northeast tip of Borneo. And it was here, near Sandakan, that pirate fleets assembled to pick off the heavy-laden vessels. By the eighteenth century, provoked by Dutch destruction of the native trade and greatly assisted by the spread of European weapons, the pirates multiplied and bred littler pirates until Raffles himself dryly observed that "the maritime enterprise of these people, though latterly too much devoted to piratical enterprise, could easily be directed into better channels."

But the only channels their energies had ever been directed into were the winding Borneo rivers. When European men-o'-war appeared, the pirates escaped upriver beyond the sandbars and shallow estuaries, which were impassable to fighting ships. Even the RAF's air patrols could do nothing to winkle them out. It was going to be even tougher when the tide turned and Sukarno used these slippery merchants to harass the coastal towns of North Borneo. Dictators might come and kings might go, but it looked as if these pirates were going on for ever.

We swept into Hong Kong at masthead level, the junks and sampans leaning aside for us — or so it seemed as their russet sails caught the slipstream. The little green ferries fussed across the oil-streaked harbor. We bellied onto a runway and waddled back to the hangars, where Glenys and the children waited in our old convertible, its roof folded back. Ah Mei, squashed in the back of the car, clutched a bag filled with bamboo shoots and smoked duck and dried seaweed for the rollicking Chinese dinner we'd have this night. She grinned, showing the gold teeth that represented most of her wealth, and spread on her fat thighs was the *China Mail* and the headline: SUKARNO WANTS MORE. Underneath was a report of Indonesia's renewed demands on New Guinea, based upon humanitarian grounds.

"The sanctimonious old —" I stopped myself and hopped into the car. One of the children asked where I had been. "Looking at pirates," I said.

"Gee, do they *really* still have pirates, Daddy?"

"All over the place," I answered and settled back for the inevitable barrage of questions.

Later Glenys dug out an Indonesian rebel press release. "Isn't it glorious?" she said, pointing to an announcement. They've appointed Doctor Sumitro as SPECIAL COORDINATOR OF SMUGGLING."

18

Skeptics' Isle

THE FLIGHT to Labuan was almost empty and we pulled off the runway into a tight turn across Hong Kong harbor. To the utter delight of my children, perched on their bedroom verandah, the airliner flew slowly along the upper slopes of The Peak. The house was a rambling old place near the top of the mountain. It had miraculously survived typhoons and Japanese shellings. Among its many snags was the damp cloud enshrouding its moldering battlements. But sometimes the cloud dissolved and revealed the teeming harbor far below, or a plane on the airport circuit flying beneath our windows. Today, for a change, I found myself peering back at the house and a row of four small blond heads bobbing up and down in excitement. It was rather strange, seeing my children in this way, unable to reach out and touch them, wondering when I might speak to them again, already separated from them physically by a thousand feet that could be just as easily a thousand miles. If a child toppled over the verandah this very second, I should be powerless to act. We inhabited different worlds.

A thin brown Malay steward balanced in the aisle, demonstrating the life-preserver, pointing out the shark repellent. The hearty Australian voice crackling over the loudspeakers said, "This is your Captain . . ." A Chinese stewardess, beaming from ear to ear, poured a generous helping of scotch into my glass, compliments of the company. Had European colonialists of earlier centuries been elevated thus, they might have considered it a multiracial heaven. Even including the shark repellent.

I sat back, thinking it was altogether too easy to ridicule those British blimps, the Dutch planters, the Portuguese and the French who had come here in vastly different circumstances. We were likely to forget that Europeans arrived a century ago without much hope of surviving more than a year of tropical fevers and primitive conditions. The Christian cemeteries of Asia were full of tombstones bearing names of men, women and children struck down prematurely by unknown pestilences. Now, when we traveled comfortably in air-conditioned shells high above the treacherous reefs and steaming jungles, we forgot that our predecessors' lives had been spent here in acute discomfort and danger.

But the anticolonial delirium being what it is, I had to listen to a pearly furry matron from Buffalo tell me how the European powers were responsible for making Asia turn communist. Their exploitation of cheap labor had created the conditions in which a philosophy of violence would thrive.

There was some truth in the charge. Then a young Californian perched himself on the furry matron's seat rest and pointed out that when the French had wanted to quit Indochina and the British talked of leaving Malaya, the first to oppose such dangerous notions had been the United States — unless its own troops could fill the vacuum. It was the sort of healthy argument from which I was glad to retire.

Nobody could argue about Labuan's position in the scheme of things. It was what it appeared to be: a sleepy British colony. A year had passed since I had been here. Much had happened to affect Labuan's future. But on the island all was calm. God was in his heaven and Raby was behind his desk at the runway's end.

Raby, burly redheaded representative of a diminishing empire, was, if you were unfamiliar with his type, a bit off-putting. He seemed pompous. He disguised his anxieties behind a mask of concern about petty matters such as the amount of his living allowance. He hardly seemed to be part of the modern world. Since I had last seen him he had become, in fact, a somewhat Gilbertian figure. His authority had been remarkably extended. He was not only chief of the fire brigade, and lord of customs and immigration, but he was chief of police as well.

But Raby in his extra-long gray socks and short-short khaki pants and his variety of official hats, Raby with his long pink eyelashes and florid cheeks, was no longer within himself Raby Esquire, a middle-aged party from one of the northern English provinces, more at home sitting on Blackpool beach in his suspenders and licking an ice-cream cone. He was, however much he secretly disliked it, White Raja Raby, without the palace or the servants but burdened with all the cares. Rather stuffy, typically inarticulate, balancing his ultra-conservative approach to each problem against a socialistic concern for those who lived on the island, he worked very hard to defend Labuan's 11,000 Chinese and native Kedayans against the rapacity of a few wily Indian merchants. Doubtless in some cold and damp street in a wet and windy Yorkshire town there were folk huddling over a pot of tea in a stone-terraced cottage who remembered him as a raw-faced boy and wondered what he'd been getting up to. But *his* people were no longer white. They were the islanders for whom he had got teachers and technical instructors, and for whom his cold manner was no measure of his deep affection. And in two years' time his salary, the equivalent of $65 a week, would end. He would be retired, at the difficult age of 48, on a pension of $12 a week, which might just cover living in a bed-sitter in Golders Green. Two years from now, he would be much worse off than many of his wards, and certainly he would never enjoy such affluence as might now be his, were he to accept a Chinese bribe to overlook an immigrant or two.

There was an aging rubber planter who, seeing me waiting around the airport, asked me to his home for a drink. I had little to do until the rebels contacted me. His house, reverse-gabled with a double roof in the Dyak fashion, was buried in thickets of pigeon-orchids and orange New Guinea ramblers. When he got out his old Morris Minor to show me the island, his alarmingly frail wife tugged open the wooden garage door. "She's badly beaten up, I fear," said the planter. Following my surprised stare, he added hastily, "No, no. The car."

We chugged down the drive. His wife wearily dragged shut the door. "Climate's been hard on her," said my host. "On my wife, that is. In prison camp all through the Jap war. I got away in time to keep my health but it almost destroyed the old girl."

His family had been in Borneo for many years. He took me to the grave of his brother, killed fighting pirates in the service of the British Borneo Chartered Company, which until 1946 ran the territories as a business enterprise.

Next to the grave was a memorial to Color Sergeant Adam Sutherland * "killed fighting Balanimi pirates 1847." I said the pirates seemed remarkably persistent. The planter fixed me with a rheumy eye. "You'll find 'em *much* more persistent in Sandakan," he said.

We drove to the *padang*, a park facing the harbor. A rusting

---

* By an odd coincidence, a British seaman named C. A. Sutherland was killed in similar circumstances 116 years later. Seaman Sutherland was one of a boarding party from HMS *Barossa*, a destroyer which intercepted a pirate ship at midnight on Sunday, February 12, 1963, near Sandakan. Ten of the pirates were killed.

tanker lay in the roads, nuzzled by sailing craft like piglets at an old sow's belly. It was so peaceful you could hear the screech of metal in the machine-shop a mile away among deserted sheds.

"Making this a free port hasn't done much for us," grumbled the old planter. "Sleepy Hollow of Asia, that's what we are. Still, ours was an honest attempt. Not like the blighters in Sandakan."

"What about Sandakan?" I asked quickly.

He removed his panama and scratched his polished skull. "Dog shouldn't eat dog," he muttered. "Borneo's a wild place. Only fit for independent men. The chaps in Sandakan are doing a good business in revolutions and up here we're just suffering from sour grapes."

He removed his glasses, and polishing them with the end of his tie, he said: "They look after their people their way, and we look after ours in the manner that suits us best. We've only got a few thousand people on the island, and the economic pressures are fewer." Which was all he would say until we returned to the airstrip. Then, before he got back into the battered car, he said, "Don't end up like Starr and Bruce, eh?" When I asked who they might be, he added, "American agents. They came here to contact Indonesian rebels. Only the Djakarta government heard about it first, sent some of their own men here disguised as businessmen, and kidnapped the silly blighters."

There was a Chinese hotel adjoining the traffic control tower (there always *is* a Chinese hotel, a Chinese bar, a Chinese bank and a Chinese grocery store). A message had been left in the manager's office. It was signed "Mister Willi," the rebel who had first launched me on this prolonged adventure. Arrangements were being made, said Mister Willi, to fly me to Sandakan the next day. Would I await further instructions?

I called for the manager. He creaked out of a back room lit by the macabre red glow of joss sticks burning at the feet of the family god. A Shanghai-made grandfather clock ticked away noisily at his back. I asked for a room and he nodded in slow time with the pendulum. "Your bags already put in room," he said, shuffling out of sight again. The Chinese may seem a timeless people but they are remarkably quick when you're not looking.

I decided to go off in search of Mister Willi, who, presumably, was somewhere on the island. The airstrip was deserted, and it seemed easier to walk back into town than search for some means of transport. The macadam road was longer and hotter than I bargained for, and when a small English car stopped and a voice offered me a lift I was glad to accept.

My new host was the district officer, Peter Edge. "Ah, yes," he said. "Been expecting you. Staying long?" I said perhaps a day or two, and wondered what grapevine had warned him of my pending arrival.

"Doing anything in particular?" asked Mr. Edge.

I couldn't very well say I was looking for Major Willi Pantouw, Rebel Agent. So I said: No.

"Jolly good," said Mr. Edge. "I'll take you on a tour of the island."

For the second time I was whirled around Labuan. Again I was taken to a cemetery. This time it was a manicured lawn with tiny stone markers set in the greensward. "Three thousand buried here," said Mr. Edge. "Australians. No names. Three thousand unknown Australian soldiers. All killed by Japs. Shocking bad show, eh."

I warmed to Mr. Edge a few minutes later when he pulled up at yet another cemetery, a shabby little one this time with a faded billboard announcing it to be "Christian Chinese Burial Place."

The D.O. said, "We've got a couple of hundred Chinese in there. All dead, of course." I said I supposed they must be.

"Mm," said Mr. Edge, looking put out. He uncurled his long

thin legs from under the dashboard and climbed into the road at a spot where the fence around the cemetery had come down. "I'm a bit of a tombstone fancier, y'know. Come and see this one."

A group of Chinese mourners stood at a freshly turned grave and glanced up at us with broad smiles. They were burning joss sticks and chanting a hymn. "Getting the best of both worlds, eh?" said the District Officer, chortling. "Now, look at this. Isn't it a collector's item?"

Next to the mourners was a time-worn stone bearing the following inscription:

> *To Joseph Yapp Yoon Chin: —*
> *A bitter grief, a shock severe,*
> *To part from one we love so dear.*
> *Our loss is great, we won't complain,*
> *But hope to Christ we'll meet again.*

I said, "People live in the past rather a good deal here, don't they?"

Mr. Edge tucked himself back inside the car. "No, I wouldn't say that really. We're proud of our past, I'll grant you. But we're awfully progressive. Faces turned toward the future and all that, you know."

He was a tall, spindly man who looked like an elderly Boy Scout in his blue shorts and stockings. His office was a rambling two-story building with a thatched roof and it sprawled across one side of the *padang*, next door to the Bank of Hong Kong and Shanghai. The bank was built of wood, and someone had prudently placed it on stilts above the flood level. Mr. Edge's office, it was apparent, spent a small but significant portion of the year under water.

"Frankly, we're autocratic in this town," said Mr. Edge, leading me upstairs to a room where the local municipal board held its weekly meetings. "I appoint the board, *and* the local Chamber of Commerce. Works very well, though."

There was a framed clipping on the paneled wall. It had been cut from *The Times* of London, dated December, 1848, and included a sketch map by a doctor "lately on cruise in search of pirates with the honorable East India Company's war steamer Phlegethon." With the sketch was a letter from a young lieutenant on the ship: "I fully expect we shall have another bombardment of Brunei. The sultan is dying and the villain Macota (the abettor of piracy) is again in power and carrying on his intrigues. I hear Sir James (Brooke) is drawing up a treaty which will be entered into by all the chiefs of the rivers acknowledging him as their chief and protector in a union for mutual assistance against piracy."

The past, despite Mr. Edge's denials, was never far away. He took me to the front of the *padang*, where, visible from his paper-strewn office, were three stone markers.

The first read:

THIS ISLAND

Was Taken Possession Of
December 24th 1846
In The Name Of Her Majesty

VICTORIA

Queen of Great Britain & Ireland
Under The Direction Of
His Excellency Rear Admiral
SIR THOMAS COCHRANE CB
Commander In Chief
By
CAPTAIN G. R. MUNDY
Commanding
HMS IRIS

The second commemorated

GENERAL MAIDA

Commander In Chief of the wartime
Japanese forces in British Borneo
who was killed in an aircrash at
Bintulu on 5th September 1942
when en route to Labuan
to open the airfield here.
On 9th December 1942 Labuan was named
MAIDA ISLAND
By Order Of
GENERAL TOJO

And the third said:

HERE ON THE 9TH SEPTEMBER 1945

THE COMMANDER OF THE 9TH DIVISION,
AUSTRALIAN IMPERIAL FORCES

RECEIVED THE UNCONDITIONAL SURRENDER
OF THE 32ND JAPANESE SOUTHERN ARMY
IN NORTH BORNEO AND SARAWAK

"You see," said Mr. Edge, and suddenly his pale blue eyes
were glinting behind the steel-rimmed spectacles, "we still have
a job to do."

"Which is — ?"

Mr. Edge clasped his hands behind his back and said, "Make
sure that when we go, no other bastard's going to walk in."

There were perhaps fifty Englishmen in the entire island, a
reticent lot. They were not deeply concerned with the growing
interest the Indonesian communist party took in their affairs.
What bothered them was the Mobile Marine Drilling Barge.

It stood out in the harbor, opposite the Recreation Club, a

pyramid of steel illuminated at night by fierce arclights. It was, as yet, unfinished. The American manufacturer had terminated a contract to have it built in Southampton, where he said British workers were demanding wages that were much too high. Instead he had hired Hong Kong welders to finish the job here. The Chinese worked all hours of the day and night, at a fraction of European wages.

"What bloody well gets me," said a Recreation Club denizen, "is the way the Yanks bleed for the poor oppressed underdogs in the colonies. Can't wait to free 'em. But they'll grab all the cheap labor they can get wherever they find it — a sort of jet age colonialism."

Over in the airport hotel dwelt the opposing faction. They were half a dozen American engineers and the same number of Britons imported from Southampton. The Britons were as fed up with residents of the Recreation Club as were their American colleagues.

"Stuck-up bluhdy lot," said an English foreman. "Scared, they are. Scared in case the Chinese turn aht as good workmen as the rest of us. Which they are."

The Chinese, 73 skilled men from Hong Kong shipyards, kept to themselves. They were building Asia's first oil-drill barge and their presence made the old hands vaguely uncomfortable. They and their strange vessel were omens of the future. It was this, really, that disturbed the Recreation Club. Not the welders' torches flaring and spluttering in the night but the fact that the men who held them represented, however indirectly, the new and unified forces of China.

The American technicians had no time to puzzle this out. They disliked the stuffy atmosphere of the club and the only alternative was their hotel, where they sat and told increasingly hilarious stories of British stupidity. "Every time I listen to this guy," one of them told me, "I think of the decline and fall of the British empire."

The funny thing was that if you talked separately to both sides, neither seemed terribly right or terribly wrong. The older men in the British community were afraid that 73 Chinese workers might precede a large flow of immigrant Chinese labor, upsetting the racial balance in British Borneo. "The local people need protection against such an invasion," said an elderly trader. "We've stayed immune from racial violence and political hot-heads all these years and given a bit more time, our people here'll stand on their own feet. We've got no crime, no vice, no wide-spread diseases and malnutrition. But if we start letting Chinese in from Singapore and Hong Kong slums, we'll be in trouble."

But there were others, and Peter Edge was one, who would say quietly and realistically, "We need Chinese capital, Chinese energy, Chinese skills. The real difficulty is to let them in here without upsetting the local people."

As to the Mobile Marine Drilling Barge, two years after its completion it still remained out of commission. Not because of local British opposition. It suffered from chronic "mechanical failure."

A much more successful Anglo-American relationship was in-dicated two nights after my arrival. My flight to Sandakan had been postponed and I had yet to find Mister Willi. Knowing by now some of the difficulties and the vagaries of rebel operations, I was quite resigned to a long wait. Most of it, I feared, would have to be spent in the small air-conditioned bar at the hotel. There I met the corporal, a short round man in RAF uniform with sad bloodhound eyes.

"Bet you're not popular round 'ere," he said, watching me sadly over the rim of his beer mug. I rose to the bait and he went on, "Don't like strangers 'ere, they don't. Especially near the air-strip."

I bought him the anticipated drink. An hour later he was saying: "These bombers fly in from Formosa, see. Night landings. Quick refuel job, then orf at first light. Mostly dropping supplies to these rebels, like. Sometimes they've bombed Indonesian ports. They 'it a British freighter the other day. Sunk it. The planes are painted black. No identification. Crews are Chinese and Yanks. Nice young fellers, in civvies. Well paid, too."

I supposed the money must be good, in view of what Indonesians might do if the fliers were shot down among them. I was thinking of a navy pilot who had machine-gunned President Sukarno from the air. A civilian pilot might expect shorter shrift from his intended victims.

"Arrrh," said the corporal. "Like this bloke Pope, a Yank 'e was. Said he'd got special leave from them Flying Tigers. You know, the freelance airmen wot flew for Shankers Jack." I asked if he meant Generalissimo Chiang Kai-shek on Formosa. "Arrrh," said the corporal, gargling his beer again. "That's wot I said. Shankers Jack. The Chinaman who got kicked out by Mousey-Tongue, the Commie feller. See, this bloke Pope bombed one of the Celebes ports and then got shot down."

I remembered the case very well. Alan Lawrence Pope of Homestead, Florida, had been sentenced to death by an Indonesian military court, but his easygoing captors were still holding him in jail. (He was released secretly on July 2, 1962, and flown back to the United States without publicity.)

Now that the bar was closing, the corporal eyed his empty glass uneasily. I suggested adjourning to my room for a final drink. He shook his head. "No, you come along o' me. I got something to show you. I'm a painter." He imparted this astonishing news with an embarrassed grin and led me, both of us gently weaving, to his austere quarters.

He was a man in middle years, an artist by instinct who knew he would never have enough financial independence in civilian life to develop his talents. So he remained an airman, painting in his spare time. He volunteered for hardship posts. This took him into exotic backwaters where duties were light and distractions few. His service record must have read like the dreams of a Paul Gauguin. In one exciting setting after another he painted with the verve of a man relieved from personal responsibility, knowing he had discovered in the RAF a generous if unwitting sponsor of the arts.

He had an impressive collection, mostly abstracts. But one canvas was starkly formal. It showed a black B-25 Mitchell bomber poised for flight into a tropical dawn, out of a purple sky pricked with the yellow dots of a flare path.

"You like it?"

"Indeed yes," I said. He scrambled under his metal cot and fished out another and another.

"I was trying to catch something," he said shyly, and his accent had graduated unexpectedly from the rough and commonplace almost to that of an educated man. "Death and destruction, born from the womb of night." He staggered slightly. "Man's machinery, raping an innocent world."

Looking at those paintings, you could almost hear the Mitchells shatter the morning calm; tails down, 120 knots on the clock, noses cocked and wings tilting to grip the agitated air; the engine cowls trembling to do violence to those lovely helpless dawns; the bomb bays bursting to spill seeds of western progress upon a backward country.

"Talk about one of Her Majesty's bloomin' sceptered islands," said the corporal. He laughed, leaning against the shabby whitewashed wall, legs crumbling, sliding visibly back into the Cockneyisms that protected him from inquisitive officers. "It's so bloody full of unexplained mysteries we've all become skeptics. — The only true thing in it . . . my painting."

He rallied briefly, wagging a solemn finger. "Thi'sh skeptics' isle . . . fortress built by Nature . . . against infection and the hand of war."

Suddenly he sat up straight. "I'm sloshed. Talkin' too much. This ain't no bleedin' art gallery. It'sh refuelling base with maximum security. So no more chit-chat, mate. No secrets, see?"

19

The Free Traders

MISTER WILLI aroused me early the next morning, coming to my room to avoid arousing anyone's curiosity.

"Well," I said, opening the door with one hand and clutching at the stringless bottoms of my pajamas with the other. There didn't seem much else to say.

"Good morning."

"Come in. It's a year — isn't it? A year since we met. I hope all goes well." I sat on the edge of my bed, head reeling. The corporal and I had really hung one on.

"The hair of the dog?" asked Mister Willi. He pulled a flask from his polished briefcase and poured me a medicinal measure. "I have booked you on a Borneo Airways plane to Sandakan this morning. And bought your ticket."

"Then I must pay you for it." The rebels had a habit of offering hospitality. I understood the purity of their motives but I was far from anxious to be obliged to them. Mister Willi, sensitive to these niceties, accepted my check without demur.

I said, "What's all this about rebel bombers using the airstrip here?"

"Please." He coughed. "One must be careful."

"All right, what about these characters Starr and Bruce?" I was feeling awkward this morning. "Is it true they were a couple of CIA men who got captured by central government forces?"

He coughed again. "You really *must* be careful."

"That's exactly what I've been told. Careful not to get dragged across the border by Sukarno's men."

"If you are thinking of the case of the American agents," said Mister Willi, "it was an unfortunate error." He split open a packet of Camels, hands trembling slightly. "This is why we asked you to stop here first. In case anyone follows you. It will confuse them."

He lit a cigarette. "As a matter of fact, I flew with you once or twice on the same airliner." He smiled at my surprise. "To make sure nobody followed."

Unless Mister Willi had been disguised as a Chinese merchant or a Malay dancing girl, however, I was reasonably sure he was not on board the De Havilland Rapide that bore me aloft later that day. As we climbed over the Borneo coast the damp equatorial heat, crouching in the jungle-robed mountains below, squirted thermals at us until we bounced like the lid on a percolating coffeepot. I regretted the late night and felt depressed. What business had I, poking into these matters? The corporal had talked about the South East Asia Treaty Organization. Its job was to cheat communist subversives. If SEATO meddled in the Indonesian rebellion, who was I to question the decision?

It was an old problem, common in Asia. You saw things that made you wonder where duty to a newspaper ended, and where broader loyalties intervened. Yet there had been too many times when a discreet press silence only permitted the continuation of tragic blunders committed in the name of an unknowing western public and arousing nothing but Asian hostility. If I could learn of these affairs while pottering around as a private citizen, it was certain that Asia's bamboo telegraph was carrying the message. Attempts at secrecy were so often, in these cases, self-defeating. Facts were suppressed on the pretext that the "enemy" might benefit by their publication. But often it was Peking and Moscow broadcasts that first revealed those facts. Who, then, did the West wish to fool? All too often, of course, the public back home, which might protest if it knew what disastrous policies were being pursued in its name.

We circled Sandakan. It looked vulnerable and innocent. But now I knew that under those humble wooden rooftops were Nationalist Chinese flogging guns and other war supplies sent by the United States to Formosa. Hidden in warehouses were rebels chartering and building blockade-runners, buying arms and selling Indonesian raw materials. Down there were transmitters in communication with Radio Permesta in the rebel hills 500 miles away; and a mixed bunch of thugs and idealists working for the revolutionaries or for President Sukarno, depending on how their pockets or their consciences might guide them.

Our plane was awaited by the usual knot of wistful European exiles. In customs, a Chinese inspector insisted upon opening the ruck-sack I carried for easy handling on the sea trip to Celebes. Out came jungle boots, a nylon hammock and bottles of cholera and smallpox vaccines for the rebels.

The customs man examined this strange loot. He fiddled with the Zenith Trans-Oceanic shortwave transistor I had agreed to deliver to a rebel colonel. Finally, with the ghost of a smile, he waved me through. "Have a pleasant journey," he added.

I walked into the cramped waiting room, aware that I could have attracted no more attention by parachuting in, and stopped dead in my tracks at the sight of eight Indonesians in army fatigues rising stiffly to attention.

It was no use pretending I had not seen them. Mindful of the fate of the kidnapped American agents, I advanced cautiously to the end of their table. *"Thai-hong,"* I said, feeling rather foolish at this use of our agreed code.

They frowned in puzzlement. I backed off hastily. They *could* be Djakarta's men. Or had they clean forgotten about passwords?

I was given no time to find out. A firm hand gripped my elbow and I looked up into the lean features of the local police chief. "I'm Fairfoul — Douglas Fairfoul." He had a warm Scots burr. "Go to my car. I'll take care o' these gentlemen." I gave the Indonesians a ghastly smile of apology and retreated to the waiting police car.

He joined me a moment later. "I explained ye were busy the noo. Ye'll be hearing from them again, nae doubt."

"Who were they?"

"Just a bunch of traders." He shrugged. "I do wish they wouldna' move around in platoons."

Chief Fairfoul was not disposed to pursue the subject. He had heard I was coming, he said with a grin. Thought I'd like to meet a few of the locals. By the way, Keith Wookey, The Resident,* would be grateful if I could find time to call on him at sundown. As we drove through the little town's peaceful streets, I reflected upon the discomfort of being in a goldfish bowl.

We stopped at the Sandakan Yacht Club, a wooden pavilion at the end of a rickety pier. Its glory had faded but not the atmosphere. Near the bar sat an attractive young woman, pouring tea for a silver-tailed gibbon. Chief Fairfoul introduced her as the wife of a local timber merchant. Then, having brought me an ice-cold lager, he withdrew with promises to see me again later. His expression was one of devilish glee.

"This is Wa-Wa," said the Englishwoman, indicating the beast in the chair beside her. "The name is taken from the native word

* The title was used originally to describe a diplomat or a representative of the governor general at the court of a native state.

for gibbon. Excuse me while I finish serving her tea. She goes berserk if she doesn't get priority. I made the mistake once of overlooking her when I had some guests home for a snack. Wa-Wa went wild. Threw the table over, yanked down all my drapes, piddled all over the settee and then jumped on the ceiling fan. I had to turn it on to get her down again. By that time all the guests had taken off."

While her mistress talked Wa-Wa slurped tea and consumed a plate of cream cakes at breakneck speed. I sat mesmerized.

"I've brought her up from a baby," said my hostess, casting an affectionate eye on the beast. "Before that, I had a proboscis monkey. Awful things, don't you think?"

I said I wasn't sure what a proboscis monkey looked like. "My dear," she said, "simply revolting. It's nothing but a big purpley-red nose. All nose and arms and legs." She shuddered with a tiny thrill of pleasurable disgust. "Just this immense nose, do you see? The kind you see on old roués afflicted with gout."

The gibbon fastened upon me a pair of button eyes. It was a stare of peculiar and ominous intensity. I pushed my own chair back as unobtrusively as possible, with some vague notion that any sudden move on my part would trigger the gibbon's tensed limbs.

"Please don't go yet," said the owner of this disconcerting creature. "Do you know what the local people call the proboscis monkey?" She rattled on. "They call it *orang blunda*. It means Dutchman. Isn't that just too — extraordinary?"

She stopped, her lips slightly parted, watching me with eyes that had widened a trifle too innocently.

"Yes. Odd. Poetic justice, perhaps?"

She laughed. "I have a great many good friends in Holland," she said. "They're a lovely people. But something *happens* to them when they get east of Suez. Like the English. We have all been intolerable colonizers at times. It seems such a mistake," she said, "clinging to bits of territory the way we do. Except that we seem to have adjusted to changing times better than most. The British, I mean.

"I must say," she added, "it hasn't been easy. Here in Sandakan. The slump in timber. The changes in shipping routes. Before the war, you know, we commanded the main trade routes from China to India by holding Hong Kong, Singapore and — this place. Now we're no longer the world's biggest naval power. But we still have responsibilities."

Wa-Wa slipped down from her chair and I saw that a short chain linked her collar to the chair leg. It struck me that her mistress was not as featherbrained as I first thought.

"That remark you made just now — about the Dutch. Did you have anything particularly in mind?" I asked her.

She glanced across the room at the bar boy. "Bandira!" she called. "Fetch me a *stengah*, please." The boy disappeared into a small back room.

"I wondered if you were one of these people who want to put the Dutch back into Indonesia," she said with unexpected frankness. "Doctor Sumitro acquires such *odd* friends."

She studied me for a moment. "I can see you're not. But why *are* you here?"

I explained my journalistic interest. "Well, at least you look an honest man," she said finally. "What I think — what *we* think you should know is that here in Sandakan nobody takes sides. Our business is to provide the people here with a living. When the Japs came, the local inhabitants risked their lives for the British, who were first to be executed or jailed. We've never forgotten that loyalty. Because a lot of Chinese and Malays died in consequence. Now we're buying time. Literally buying it. Time to train the Dyaks and the other people whose home is

North Borneo. Time to get industries going. Time for us to
withdraw gracefully, and not merely leave a vacuum for the
communists to fill."

"Do you think President Sukarno's a communist?"

"I was thinking of Red China. No, I don't think Indonesia's
going communist under Sukarno. The rebels, like Sumitro, hammer at this anticommunist line to get money out of the Americans."

She had finished her *stengah* and was preparing to go. I said,
"What are you buying this time with?"

"Copra." She stood up. One of those unnaturally thin English-
women you find in colonial outposts; high cheekbones, freckled
complexion, tired eyes, and irritatingly efficient. She slipped the
gibbon's chain from the chair leg. "Let me drive you to the
hotel. We've put you in the Sabah Hotel."

I could only submit, like Wa-Wa on her lead.

In the car, she handed me a government guidebook. "Copra,"
it said blandly, "plays an important part in economic activities
. . . and maintains the livelihood of the citizens. Most comes
through barter trade with nearby islands."

I chuckled. She gave me a brief glance. "Lovely, isn't it?"
she said. "No wonder people say the English are such lousy
hypocrites. We all know where the copra comes from. We'd
all be sunk without it." She took one hand from the wheel and
reaching behind her in an automatic gesture, gave the gibbon a
sharp rap on the skull. It whimpered and dropped to the car
floor, where it shortly fell asleep.

"I expect you think we're lacking in political morals. But can
you honestly say who is right about Indonesia? The Dutch are
furious at being tossed out, but they may be perfectly correct
in saying Sukarno is leading the republic into bankruptcy. Sumitro says it is hopeless to try and change the situation without

violence. Yet maybe the situation would change if the West would leave Sukarno alone, and if your Doctor Sumitro would try to change conditions through a policy of collaboration. The Americans say Indonesia is the target of Sino-Soviet ambitions and they may be right — but what workable alternative can they offer? Uncontrolled free enterprise doesn't work in an under-developed economy. It only widens the gap between millions of poor peasants and a rich minority.

"Well, these are questions for statesmen to decide. Here in Sandakan, we're only concerned with survival. And the rebellion helps us survive."

The question of how and when I could leave Sandakan rested with the rebel shipping agents. My intermediary was a British customs official who took me first to a Chinese merchant. He said a motor vessel was expected from Celebes in the next day or two, carrying nutmeg from one of the islands between Celebes and the Philippines. Then it would return to Inobonto, a rebel village on the north coast of Celebes. There would be no diffi-culty in finding me a berth.

I had a drink with the police chief in his club that evening. How was it, I cautiously inquired, that Sandakan could be used so openly by the rebels?

Chief Fairfoul peered at me speculatively over the top of his beer glass. "It's a wee bit too open, if ye ask me. Mind now, I'm no' saying we've anything tae hide. It's none of our business where the cargoes come or go."

He did recall, now that he came to think of it, that others had been here before me. They'd waited to sail, and the longer they waited, the more closely their movements were being reported across the border in Indonesian Borneo. Well, that was the penalty of keeping open house. He drained his glass and re-minded me to call on the resident.

Back in my hotel I bumped into a young police inspector working with the Inshore Flotilla on antipiracy patrols. He asked me if I knew anything about the American pilots in the rebel capital of Manado, in northeast Celebes. I said No. He sat for a bit, twirling the ice in his glass. "Can the American State Department put pressure on you?" I said it would be highly unlikely.

"Still," he said, "they might try. Maybe you know Jim Mossman? Works for an Australian paper. Yes, well his government was asked to have him removed from this area. The Central Intelligence Agency said he was embarrassing the situation."

"How could he do that?"

"He reported some Indonesian sailors here who said there were American pilots flying for the rebels. They'd seen them at Manado."

I said: "Everyone seems to know that." And I told him about the use of Labuan for refueling.

"You don't have to convince me," he said. "Although I know that corporal up there, and he's got a pretty strong imagination. No, Mossman was dead right. All I'm saying is: everyone'll deny whatever you report. They'll try and make you out a liar."

It seemed to be the normal hazard of reporting any form of conspiracy. The authorities could always deny the story, since the very nature of these clandestine activities required that nothing be documented. On the other hand, one could also sympathize with the authorities when a conspiracy was reported that did not, in fact, exist. It would be very difficult for the Central Intelligence Agency to *prove* that it was not involved in the Indonesian rebellion. Especially when Djakarta had in its possession such evidence as the arms parachuted to rebel forces, and the American pilot shot down after bombing Makasar.

British Borneo was an ideal base from which to help the Indonesian rebellion. Supplies, agents and instructions could be funneled through any number of private Chinese firms. And if Formosa were the source of logistical support, then the Nationalist Chinese were the perfect medium. If anything went wrong, they could always be blamed.

What puzzled me was the official tolerance of these activities. Sandakan's prewar role had been that of a trading post, as well as the capital of a colony run by a chartered company. The war destroyed the town and its traditional trade. But new opportunities were created by the surrounding chaos. The people of the volcanic islands in and around the Sulu Sea wanted to sell their spices and other raw materials, which had been piling up for want of customers. They badly needed the food and commodities for which they had been starved for four years. Rather than wait for the inefficient and corrupt trade agents of the central Indonesian and Philippine governments, they sold directly to Sandakan.

A new Sandakan rose from the ashes. By the time the Indonesian rebellion was in full swing, the town was mentally adapted to the kind of illicit trade necessary to the rebels. In one year, 200,000 tons of copra and other illicit cargoes were smuggled from the Permesta rebel area. Customs men levied a generous tax before the stuff was re-exported as "Produce of British Borneo." Among the overseas clients were western Europe and Japan, and an additional and hungry customer, Red China.

The philosophy of the open marketplace prevailed. It was best expounded by The Resident, Keith Wookey. He believed that British motives and actions had always differed from those of earlier colonizers. This explained, in his view, why Sandakan could conduct its business without regard to ideological conflicts or the international political situation — except as it affected trade.

The first trading depot was opened in Sandakan Bay by William Cowie after successful campaigns had been launched against pirates harassing the native cargo routes. Cowie got the excited interest of Baron Overbeck, who was the Austrian consul general in Hong Kong at the time.

Those were the days when a diplomat in such a post could parlay his small influence into more tangible assets, and the baron used his position to wring concessions out of the sultans of Sulu and Brunei. This peculiar passage in history would occupy a disproportionate part of this narrative, but it will be apparent that the baron must have been quick on his feet, because by 1881 a royal charter had been granted to the baron's business partners — all of them old Far East hands — who founded the British Borneo (Chartered) Company. The charter provided that the company should be at all times British, should undertake the abolition of slavery, administer justice with due regard to native customs and laws, and refrain from any interference in local religious activities.

The tradition of freedom of movement was established, and the company's posts provided facilities for "native craft" to the extent that thousands of small communities (as the British governor of North Borneo pointed out 80 years later) lived by this unrestricted trade.

The company territories were run as a commercial enterprise right up until the Japanese invasion. Sandakan was then the permanent seat of government, and the company governor was seconded by the British government. Even after North Borneo became a crown colony in 1946, the company issued its own currency for another seven years, and these BBCC dollars are still redeemable.

This was why Sandakan, for so long the base for aggressive political trading, was still open to all comers. The postwar government embarked on plans to rebuild and develop the economy, and it extended social services and trained the local people for eventual self-administration. A new constitution in 1950 heralded local self-government at the level of native chiefs and village headmen. But the ruling business community was not yet deeply concerned with the political forces blowing around Borneo, and warnings or guidance from Whitehall were looked upon as unwarranted interference from bumbling bureaucrats.

The Indonesian rebellion was a source of prosperity. If the rebels skirmished with Java's agents on British territory, they must expect trouble. But if they behaved themselves, nobody would interfere. Smuggled copra was a major source of income. Little of it was grown in Borneo. The smuggled cargoes were brought to the Sandakan quayside, where handsome duties were levied under the general euphemism of the barter trade. It yielded one half of North Borneo's total revenue in customs duties alone.

Little wonder that the colonial government's annual report commented: "The Barter Trade has been considerably harassed by pirates. Action intended to liquidate them continues."

20

Chinese Quarterbacks

JIM ROBINSON of the National Broadcasting Company had joined me. He felt, as I did, that a quiet sail across the Sulu Sea might prove a pleasant way of passing a few days of this unusually hot summer.

Jim brought a touch of melodrama with him; a telegram from "Harris," the pseudonym for Doctor Sumitro, who was now back in Singapore. It read: REGRET STRONGLY ADVISE POSTPONE VACATION. This was the prearranged code that meant Sumitro feared trouble. His agents in Djakarta, we discovered later, had obtained details of an Indonesian naval operation by which the central government hoped to catch us hotfooting it across Celebes soil.

The telegram was sent first to Chief Fairfoul, who gave it to Jim at the airport. Neither of us pressed the police chief for an explanation. It seemed to be a situation where the law and the citizen might observe a discreet silence to their mutual profit.

But then a telegram was delivered to me at the hotel. This one, from Mister Willi in Labuan, conveyed the rather ominous message: PLEASE TAKE CARE OF TWO GENTLEMEN.

I bustled into Jim's room. "What's this mean?"

Jim peered up at me. Both his ears were plugged into a Ficord, the transistorized tape recorder. He looked at the telegram and bellowed: "IT LOOKS LIKE AN ORDER TO BUMP US OFF, HA! HA!"

I flapped my arms, shouting to him to lower his voice. Finally I had to pull the plugs from his ears. "It's not addressed to you," he said, voice suddenly diminished, totally unaware of how loudly he had roared above the recorder — which, of course, I couldn't hear.

I examined the telegram again. It was for Mr. Thai-hong of birds' nest fame.

So back to the warehouse we went. Mr. Thai-hong Hang was at his desk, a plump Chinese merchant with an air of quiet competence. "Ah, yes," he murmured. "You are the two gentlemen." He bobbed his head gravely. "I am sorry. It was sent to you by mistake."

"And how — er, do you expect to take care of us?" asked Jim.

"A ship." He stood up abruptly. "A ship to Celebes, of course." He gave us a brief unceremonious nod and scuttled from the room. It was a small office, and apparently in a state of fantastic muddle, with books and files stacked on chairs and in corners. It was typical, however, of the successful Chinese entrepreneur. What seemed to be an untidy mess to the untutored eye was in fact an efficient business operation of which the details were carried in Mr. Thai-hong's high-domed head. The ledgers and files were only the outward manifestations, the inescapable tokens, of respect for British law. No income tax inspector could expect to discover in these dusty papers any incriminating evidence. Mr. Thai-hong had decorated the pages with symbols which meant one thing to British officialdom and another to himself.

The office was on a mezzanine above the warehouse, and we could hear Mr. Thai-hong rummaging around below. One almost imagined him searching for the promised ship, down among the cooking pots and birds' nests and Japanese soup cans.

"Which telegram do we ignore?" I asked Jim. It seemed an

occasion to defer to his superior knowledge. His charming and
very attractive Chinese wife, Barbara, had inspired him with an
unusual understanding of these oriental situations.

"Doctor Sumitro's telegram was sent before Mister Willi's,"
said Jim. "So I guess whatever danger there was, must have
passed." I nodded, chiding myself for my stupidity. "On the
other hand," said Jim, "if Mister Willi is in Labuan, he might
not know what Doctor Sumitro knows in Singapore."

I blessed Barbara, doubtless at this very moment sharing a
beach in Hong Kong with my wife and our combined families.
She had taught Jim the valuable habit of examining both sides of
a question. Now it only remained to decide upon the proper
course of action.

"So what do we do?"

"Well," said Jim, lighting a cigarette, "I guess we leave it to
Mr. Thai-hong. If he finds a ship, we go. If he doesn't, we
don't." So much, I thought sadly, for consulting an expert.

Mr. Thai-hong now returned and sat at the desk. We waited.
He smiled vaguely. We beamed back. He picked up the telephone and began a long, laborious conversation in Cantonese
with some distant partner. Finally he put the phone down. "The
nutmeg ship," said Mr. Thai-hong, "leaves in two days and will
take you wherever you want to go."

A group of four or five Indonesian rebels had moved into the
hotel when we returned. We shared a meal with them. The
dishes were set out on a big table instead of coming in one by
one, as in the Chinese fashion. There was a faint air of reserve
about these men, a slight hostility. They spoke little. All were
Christians from Celebes and I sympathized with their off-hand
attitude. It was not easy, if you were an Indonesian patriot, to
appreciate the skylarking mood of two foreigners.

I carried a letter for Kawilarang, the rebel commander in

Celebes. After dinner that night one of the newcomers sought me out. Could he take delivery of the letter?

"It's from Kawilarang's wife in Hong Kong," I said. "I promised to hand it over personally."

"As a security precaution I should see it." The rebel officer's smooth features hardened.

Still I could not relinquish the letter. Playing for time, I asked how my interlocutor had discovered that the letter existed.

"It was reported to me. I must examine it to be sure there is nothing in it of value to our enemies. You will understand what difficulties it could make for us if you were caught by government forces and the letter taken."

"I can always burn it," I replied.

The rebel officer hesitated. "Also there is another question . . ." His face resumed its original mask of amiability. "Perhaps we might talk this over in my room?"

There he poured us both a drink and introduced himself as Jojo, a senior member of the rebels grouping around Jim and myself.

"The other difficulty is this," said Jojo, resting his feet on the bed. "General Nasution has been writing letters to Kawilarang. They have to be delivered of course by hand, and we know you have been recently in Djakarta."

It seemed that, in this most incredible of revolutions, the Indonesian army chief of staff had been wooing rebel "Major-General" Kawilarang. In searching for the means to redeem good men who had gone astray, Nasution found cause for hope in the background of Alex Kawilarang.

First, there was the fact that Kawilarang had defected in the belief that this might save Indonesia from disaster. This proved at least his patriotism. His father had been an officer in the Dutch East Indies Army and probably set the boy on the wrong path.

Later the young Kawilarang went to Washington as a military attaché. This (or so General Nasution seems to have reasoned) further accounted for a promising officer's mental abberation. The future rebel leader had been brainwashed by the West into believing Indonesia was falling into communist control.

Jojo, explaining all this, showed a broadminded readiness to see both sides. "You see, Kawilarang was caught in the same quandary we all were — even General Nasution.

"If the communist PKI did seek power by parliamentary means, we knew — Kawilarang in Washington, he knew — the PKI might very well win. Look at the kind of voters we had in Indonesia. They were spellbound by this egomaniac Sukarno. They were uneducated in the responsibilities of parliamentary democracy."

I thought this sounded like a good argument for Sukarno's own philosophy of guided democracy but Jojo hurried on. Kawilarang had resigned from his post in Washington to join the rebels. His attempts to patch up the quarrels plaguing the revolutionary government were unsuccessful. By 1959 he was committed entirely to the rebellion in his native Celebes, having been badly disappointed by the lack of resistance to General Nasution's invasion of Sumatra.

This disappointment was shared by the young military commander in north Celebes, Colonel Sumual. He controlled the region to which Jim and I hoped to proceed on the nutmeg ship; a lovely mountainous area called Minahasa of which Manado was the chief port. Sumual had been one of the first colonels to run an independent administration, and it was during this period that President Sukarno had sent him a guileful invitation to take tea in Merdeka Palace. The colonel refused to fly into this web and finally formed an alliance with the rebels 1500 miles to the west in Sumatra. His was the movement called Permesta.

I told Jojo how astonishing it seemed to an outsider that General Nasution would be still corresponding with rebel military chieftains. "Well," said Jojo, swallowing his disappointment about the letter, "it seems Nasution remains confident he can appeal to Kawilarang's sense of patriotism. He tells him that if he is wanting to fight communists, or other traitors, he must be going back to Djakarta."

I sensed Jojo's own torn loyalties. He came from the Minahasa too, and had attended a theological college at one time. He had the round, cheerful face and lighter skin of the Polynesian, but there were depths of foreboding in his sad brown eyes. I questioned him about American and Chinese Nationalist involvement in the rebellion. Yes, he could confirm the existence at one time of rebel bombers which had operated until recently from airstrips near his home in Manado and also from the island of Morotai. The planes were Skymasters and Mitchells, he believed. The pilots were American civilians. The planes were said to come from Formosa.

Jojo would be sailing with us, and he proposed that I meet the Chinese director of operations. This turned out to be another voluble trader named Mr. Kan, a partner of Thai-hong. Both had been seamen before the Pacific war, and later smuggled food through Japanese patrols to the beleaguered coastal communities of Borneo. Thus enriched, they had capitalized on the postwar turmoil by placing their maritime knowledge at the service of the highest bidder.

Mr. Kan was a different person altogether from Jojo. It was easy to see in him how the lean hard-working Chinese, with their intensely practical natures, had dominated Jojo's dreamy ancestors. What was alarming about Mr. Kan was the unabashed way he sold the anti-communist line. He turned up in the hotel lobby clutching military maps which he spread over coffee tables and on the floor so that nobody could be in the slightest doubt about his interests.

"You gotta understand this is not just an Indonesian war," he said with the slightest flavor of an American accent. "This is a world conflict between us and communism — right? If we don't stop it here, we're never gonna stop it."

As he talked, jabbing here and there across the charts, painting his awesome vision of the final struggle, I searched my memory. The voice, the American-Chinese accent, the technique were all so familiar. The West was doing nothing to thwart Red China, he said petulantly. Take those fellow travelers in the State Department, for instance. *They* were the guys to watch. They'd talked Washington into cutting off military aid for the rebels. They'd stepped in just when it seemed Americans at long last were going to draw the line here in Indonesia and fight for freedom, honor and justice.

Suddenly I recognized his type: the military guides who took visiting American senators around Formosa and the offshore islands. The burden of their message was always the same: Give us more money and guns and we'll destroy the communist menace for you.

I said: "Do you still bring in arms from Formosa?"

He squinted up at me, unsuspecting. "It is very difficult, getting supply ships through the Indonesian patrols. The Indonesian Navy has got all these communist warships. We have nothing to protect our ships."

"What about the rebel bombers?"

"They have been flying from — the Philippines." He hesitated for the slightest fraction of a second. "After we lost the rebel airfields in Celebes."

"American pilots?"

"No. That's all lies. Indonesians are good pilots. What's the need for foreigners? You got to watch these communist spies spreading lies. In the war against communism there should be more sense of responsibility by the newspapers. Take this Australian journalist —"

For the second time I heard about James Mossman, whose inquiries had led the CIA to request his withdrawal from this area. I said that Mossman had been vindicated when Pope, the American pilot who claimed to be "on leave" from CAT's Formosa headquarters, was shot down over Makasar and captured. Mr. Kan brushed aside the case of Mr. Pope, saying: "Lies. All lies."

Mr. Kan's biggest line of business now was the building of boats. One in seven rebel blockade-runners was being sunk by the growing Indonesian Navy; a satisfactory enough rate of attrition in Mr. Kan's view to justify his new enterprise.

The amateur boat builder, Jim and myself drove down to look at the shipyards. It meant going out of town to the fringe of the rain forest. Here, partly hidden by casuarina trees, keels were being laid under thatched roofs supported on tall wooden stilts. Beyond them, on the mud flats, new vessels lay on their sides awaiting the sluggish tide.

"Can we make photographs? Shoot film?"

"Of course," said Mr. Kan with pride. "Why not?"

"Well, it *is* a rebel boatyard. Aren't you afraid the Djakarta government might take some action?"

Mr. Kan laughed, displaying his three gold teeth. "We got to show you boys we mean business."

I supposed that was the purpose of Mr. Kan's frankness. The rebellion was now lacking foreign support to such an extent that everything must be done to get favorable public attention. I half suspected that Sandakan itself did not mind a little publicity either, if this would help to boost business. For one thing, it was quite impossible to camouflage the purpose of the new shipyards producing with sausage-machine precision the warlike *kumpits.* These were long and narrow, and shallow in beam. Powered by twin 50-horsepower outboards, they were supposedly too fast for Indonesian patrols and carried up to 24 armed guerrillas balanced in pairs as in a war canoe.

Back in the decorous atmosphere of downtown Sandakan we were told that another ship had been found for us. Not the nutmeg-runner. Something bigger. It would sail tomorrow. This was an agreeable surprise. I had wandered back and forth between Singapore and British Borneo, tasting the frustration of rebel ineptitude, for so long that I had almost lost hope.

A small celebration had been arranged in a Chinese restaurant, doubtless the property of either Mr. Thai-hong or Mr. Kan. The two partners were there to receive with deprecating smiles our suggestions that they join the voyage, patiently awaiting the moment when they might slip away to balance their accounts. A great deal of warm rice wine was drunk, many toasts were offered, and a solid foundation of fried shrimps, spareribs, sea slugs, chopped eels and beggar's chicken laid for the coming voyage.

Outside, the stars shone coldly bright above the band of faint green light separating sky from sea.

"May I walk with you?" It was Mr. Kan, catching up as I strolled back to the hotel. Knowing that he did little without a purpose, I welcomed his company. "It will be a calm sea tomorrow," he said, rubbing his hands.

"How long do you estimate it will take us?"

"To reach Celebes?" He pondered. "Perhaps five days. Maybe six. You may have to wait three weeks though for another boat to bring you back."

I digested this news in heavy silence. Three weeks? More like two months, to judge by earlier experience.

"You figured it would be so long?" asked Mr. Kan, bobbing along beside me.

"Well, I hadn't thought much about it. I'm not sure if I can justify wasting all this time."

"Wasting it?" Mr. Kan sounded slightly offended.

"I mean, I've spent a lot of my paper's money and time. And really, I haven't much to show for it."

"Then why — ?"

"I was wondering that myself. Professionally, every correspondent in the Far East knows there's a lot going on here that isn't aboveboard. But very few have the time or resources to investigate. It's one of the mad things about the press and radio, or television, for that matter. They all compete with each other to tell the same stories. We never get time to look beneath the surface."

Mr. Kan received this with a dubious nod. "What do you expect to find here?"

I could not answer him if I tried. Why *did* one expend all one's energies on an assignment of this kind? The same amount of effort, properly directed in a safe little office at home, would carry one to dizzy heights. Why rack your brains to get at the truth, about which nobody would feel any great concern, when you could be exercising the same ingenuity to greater personal advantage? You could exhaust yourself mentally and physically ferreting out the facts that an editor was free to toss into the wastebasket.

I said, "I don't expect to find anything much at all. But you know how it is. Some people are just born curious."

Mr. Kan nodded happily. He was getting onto his own ground now. "Yes. You'll be wanting to see if the rebellion adds up to more than a coupla puffs of smoke in a dark alley. People like you have to see for themselves . . . People like me — we Chinese — we have one obsession too."

"What's that?"

"We have to keep working. We're practical people. That's

why the Chinese are in so much trouble in countries like Indonesia."

We had come to the heart of the matter. Mr. Kan's involvement with the rebels was not so much a crusade against communism as a racial mission. He wanted President Sukarno cast down as the man who was victimizing the Chinese. For centuries they had drifted down in junks with the northeast monsoon, equally ready to burn charcoal in the fever-ridden mangrove swamps or to work veins of gold. Known to the commercial agents as "pigs," they swarmed so eagerly that their lives came cheap. "The natives here think no more of killing a Chinese than does a tiger," a British governor had once written.

But the immigrants had a powerful urge to win economic independence. It was, said Mr. Kan, an urge as strong as mine. "We all have these peculiarities," he said. "Yours is to explore new ideas and places, and satisfy your inquisitive nature. Ours is to be independent."

"And make money? And hold power? After all," I added, "I like making money too."

He winced. "We are not afraid to lose money either. You know that."

It was perfectly true. The Chinese coolie would save until the opportunity came to launch into private business. If they had started, in the old days, as common laborers selected for their frugality and endurance to build railways and roads, they ended up running small transport systems. Others grew crops like pepper, gambier, rubber and copra. Still others became shoemakers, tailors, blacksmiths, welders, smelters, engineers. "Their power," Raffles reckoned, "is ten times that of the Europeans." And when they lost it, when they gambled once too often, they were never afraid to start all over again from the bottom.

The present grudge against Chinese businessmen was often simply sour grapes. "They are foreigners," said one of President

Sukarno's financial advisers, "and yet two million of them control the economy. They must choose to be Indonesians or get out."

It had been a traditional Chinese policy that these migrants could keep their Chinese nationality even if born in Indonesia. This was such a potential source of conflict between Red China and Indonesia that Premier Chou En-lai had suggested in 1955 a treaty compelling all Chinese to make a choice of nationality. This was duly signed, but both Peking and the Nationalist Chinese government had advised their followers to keep their national identity. It was unnecessary advice. No race on earth resists integration so stubbornly.

To try and squeeze them out, the Indonesian government coddled its own traders and industrialists. The Chinese only fattened and thrived, against all known economic laws. When the teaching of Chinese was banned in schools, hundreds of impromptu classrooms sprang up. When President Sukarno issued regulations to drive 300,000 Chinese village storekeepers out of business, a breakdown in the rural economy and civilian communications followed.

Sharp diplomatic notes were exchanged between Peking and Djakarta. The Indonesian PKI communist party was put in an embarrassing position. Pursuing the Chinese ideological line, it had to announce its belief in "nationalism first." Chou En-lai, disregarding the effect on international communism, denounced Djakarta's actions as smacking of racial discrimination.

I asked Mr. Kan if his people had not brought some of these disasters upon themselves.

"Why?" He was a picture of outraged, genuine innocence. "We brought our skills. We developed the country. We did not, like the Europeans, exploit anybody or turn these territories into colonies."

"I'm thinking of right now. You help the rebels."

Mr. Kan said: "We're not openly helping. President Sukarno blames us because he hates to admit the truth, which is that his administration is hopelessly inefficient."

This was only partly true. Sukarno did need scapegoats, and when the Dutch were gone he blamed the Chinese for his economic woes. Unfortunately, he also seemed to have the evidence to support his accusations of Nationalist participation in the rebellion. Kicking out the Chinese, however, was not going to help solve some Indonesian problems. On the contrary, the economy was far worse off without their energies and skills.

Here in British Borneo you could measure their stimulating effect. In 1938, when they numbered little more than 50,000, exports were worth the equivalent of only 3 million United States dollars and there was a favorable balance of trade amounting to a modest $1.2 million. Many of the Chinese were miners, and their solidarity took the form of *kongsis* in which each member profited in proportion to his contribution of capital. They lived in dormitories with group canteens, kitchen gardens, piggeries and arrack distilleries. (The *kongsis*, incidentally, came long before the mainland People's Communes.) They multiplied so that by 1960 they were 104,855, or almost one quarter of the total population. Of more significance, they dominated commerce, agriculture and industry, and in the same period when their numbers multiplied British Borneo's exports jumped to 70 million United States dollars a year, and its favorable trade balance to $9 million.

If only Indonesia had harnessed such talents (not needing to go to extremes as the Dutch had done, promoting the Chinese until they drove out the native tradesmen) the republic might have been in better economic shape now. The penalty, however, would have been very great; in fact, far too great for any self-respecting "new" nation. For the Chinese, eager enough to work for Dutch masters, were not willing to serve an "inferior" race.

When President Sukarno's campaign against Chinese residents got into full swing, a battle for their loyalties was being fought between Red China and the exiled Nationalist government on Formosa. It was an intolerable situation, made worse by the refusal of Chinese residents to cooperate with the Djakarta regime. It seemed to President Sukarno that he faced an influential community serving the interests of lingering Dutch colonialists and their new allies in the United States; and that Washington, to conceal its direct interest in toppling the Sukarno regime, was working through Formosa to recruit this community's help. Furthermore, as the president himself was obliged to say, the future offered the even less rosy prospect of this same Chinese community becoming won over to Peking's side.

I asked Mr. Kan if his activities on behalf of the rebels might prove self-defeating.

"How?"

"Well, the Djakarta government gets mad and takes it out on the local Chinese."

"That's the price we pay in fighting the war against communism," said Mr. Kan piously.

This was a bit thick. I could not resist pointing out that *he* was making a profit. His compatriots in Indonesia paid the price.

"I sacrifice time and money organizing anti-communist forces," he protested indignantly. "I've been recruiting radio technicians in Korea, for example."

"All the same, getting back to Indonesia . . . when the Chinese there suffer because of your people in Formosa, won't that turn them against you? Won't it make them look to Peking for help?"

Mr. Kan refused to consider this possibility. He had protected his conscience with a thick padding of anticommunist sentiment. If he made a profit from the cause, this was the reward of virtue.

An Indonesian journalist had told me once: "There are no secrets in our country." This I could well believe. It meant that Mr. Kan's existence was almost certainly known to Djakarta, and I wondered what disastrous effects this knowledge might have.

His American accent, for one thing. He told me it was picked up during a period of the Pacific war when he worked for an American in China, a Mr. Willauer, "the head of United States defense supplies." This turned out to be the late Whiting W. Willauer, a wartime director of the quasi-military China Defense Supplies Inc., which sent fuel and arms to General Chennault's Flying Tigers, now familiar to the reader as Formosa's versatile CAT — "the world's most shot-at civilian airline."

You could hardly blame President Sukarno for feeling alarm when he encountered such strange people on his doorstep. Especially if he noted that Mr. Kan's former boss was publicly described as having been the American ambassador to Honduras who "helped quarterback the 1954 revolution that overthrew the procommunist regime in neighboring Guatemala." *

* *Time* magazine, August 17, 1962.

21

MF 275

JOJO, a black stubble of beard darkening his plump cheeks, awaited us next day at the warehouse. "I am sailing ahead. There are coming two boats, and for myself will be the faster." He stumbled over his English.

"You had a late session?" Jim was grinning from ear to ear. One or two of the onlooking Indonesians tittered.

"We were in conference all night," said Jojo, stiffening. He spread a chart on a packing crate. "Here is Inobonto. I will be reaching it perhaps a day before you." He passed a limp hand across his moist copper forehead and faintly closed his eyes. "We are having news of a Yugoslav frigate pulling a barge for the central government forces. There is a 36-barrel communist rocket launcher called *Unita* on the barge. It is being the same as what Russians are called 'Stalin's organ.'" He turned and shouted to the coolies toiling in the cavernous depths of the warehouse. "Now." He turned back. "You will be watching for the barge. It has destroyed two towns in central Celebes."

We said indeed we would be looking out for Stalin's barrel organ. Jojo grunted. "It is necessary to be watching for pirates also." He pressed a stubby finger in the middle of the Celebes Sea. "There." His warning seemed incongruous, after the rockets.

He left about the time that respectable citizens were arriving at their air-conditioned offices behind the warehouse. Fierce sunshine splashed the blazing white concrete beyond the warehouse door. Looking out, I could see stores being piled into small launches. In the distance, the green arms of the bay descended into a sparkling sea. The men worked quietly, shifting the rebel cargo. Jojo's vessel blew a solitary smoke ring. The boat was scarcely larger than a *kumpit* and lay low in the water like a black coffin. Almost imperceptibly, it drifted toward Sim Sim and the harbor mouth.

The morning wore on. Trucks came and went. Men paused in their labors, clustering in small groups, gossiping and then dissolving again. Bowls of rice were brought. We squatted with the men, dipping our chopsticks in the communal stew. The temperature rose into the nineties, the humidity climbed, and our shirts clung to our sweating skins. But there was no sign of our boat.

By midafternoon the tempo of work had increased. The men were mostly Chinese, lean and intelligent, with tremendous reserves of energy. They required little direction. It was not inspiring work. It required ingenuity, though, to shift bulky crates without benefit of pulleys and tackle, or to load a small boat to the gunwales without actually tipping it.

There is all the difference in the world between the reluctant performance of manual labor, and the tireless driving enthusiasm with which the Chinese exert physical strength. They are not a muscular people. The ratio of production output to calorie intake must be the world's highest. They work doggedly from early morning to late at night, seemingly able to exist on a few hours' sleep. In China itself, watching this enormous expenditure of effort on a national scale, I had wondered what fantastic feats they might achieve if they were not already exhausted by the routine of daily living.

Growing impatient with the delay, Jim and I walked up to the

Recreation Club. The change of mood was remarkable. Outside, the heavy sweet scent of the mango flowers mingled with the dockside smells of sawdust and cement. Once across the club portals, we were in another world of crackling leather upholstery and stale newspapers.

Chief Fairfoul, who could mingle equably in both worlds, was chatting with the bar boy. "Ye're not awa'?" He looked surprised. "What was yon boat I seen, then, leaving harbor this forenoon?" We told him about Jojo. He nodded. "Aye, he'll be scoutin' ahaid for ye."

He, too, had a warning to deliver. The pirates were active just now along the coast. One group of raiders had attacked a nearby village, leaving it in flames. The RAF flying boats, patrolling from Singapore, were unable to spot more than a small percentage.

Who were these pirates?

Well, said the police chief, they came from the Philippines and the small volcanic islands hereabouts. Some were Indonesians who lost their businesses when the Dutch left. Mostly they preyed on the smugglers, who could make large profits with cargoes of duty-free tobacco, bicycles and radios. Their techniques varied. The favorite method of attack was to use an innocent-looking junk and sail alongside the unsuspecting victim. The pirates were more inclined to slit throats than take prisoners. It was for this reason, and not to supply arms to the rebels, that the British provided guns for crews of small vessels.

At 4:30 a messenger came up from the warehouse. Mr. Kan wished to see us urgently at the pier.

"Tha'll be your summons to be off," said the chief. "Well, best o' luck."

Mr. Kan was pacing up and down the pier. "Your kit's aboard. Good luck." He clasped our hands briefly.

A villainous-looking crew had assembled on a sailing vessel

moored alongside. They were Bugis, described by the Encyclo-
paedia Britannica as "semi-civilized Moslems from south Celebes,
particularly liable to a homicidal mania known as 'running amok'
and noted for their enterprise as pirates." These were to be our
companions.

Their vessel was a *prahu:* blunt-bowed, flush-decked with a
high poop and a long blade lashed to either side of the stern as a
rudder. Long before the caravels of Portugal and Holland invaded these waters, the Bugi *prahus* were sailing along the coast
of Cathay and west to Madagascar.

I felt a twinge of doubt, dispelled at once by the cheerful
face of Mister Willi emerging from a palm-thatched hut amid-
ships. He had sailed around the Borneo coast from Labuan.
"We're going to take the *prahu* out of harbor, to avoid detection,
and then transfer to another boat," he said.

The precaution was necessary. Chief Fairfoul had even suggested, the previous night, that we "borrow" a police launch to
make a similar rendezvous at sea. This would cheat any Indonesian government spies.

Our harbor pilot now appeared: Stephen Garry Bowers, a
lean leather-cheeked Australian in a soiled white linen suit. He
carried a banjo.

We hoisted sail in a freshening breeze. A few of the rebel
boat builders straightened up to wave us farewell. Mr. Kan's
chubby Chinese face was wreathed in smiles of what looked
suspiciously like relief. The ship scarcely had time to heel under
the wind's pressure before Mr. Bowers let out a great shout of
"Oi! Turn about!" This we did, coming smack up alongside the
pier again. Mr. Bowers leaped ashore and sprinted away like a
minute-miler. He came back immediately, but this time mounted
on a white bicycle. "I keep forgetting the bleedin' thing," he
wheezed, and hoisted it aboard.

He had a neat turn of phrase. "This blankety bicycle is like an 'orse to me," he said. "When I leave you, these boogie-woogies" — nodding in the direction of the slack-jawed Bugis — "will drop me bloomin' miles up the coast and I'll have to pedal all the perishin' way 'ome."

His home was a converted oil tanker. From it, Mr. Bowers sold water to any ocean steamer passing by. Business was slack. In his best month, he'd sold a thousand tons of water for $640. His fuel costs were low: resinous logs hauled out of the nearby mangrove swamps. But the tanker, and the cost of towing it from its Hong Kong scrap heap, had set him back $30,000. It represented all his savings after many years of taking freighters through the Nationalist Chinese blockade into Red Chinese ports. This had entailed creeping past the guns of Nationalist offshore islands. The communist charter agents paid him $400 a trip in danger money.

"How did the danger compare with the Indonesian blockade?" I asked.

Mr. Bowers began tuning his banjo. "You've got about as much chance of getting through as I 'ave of riding across this 'arbor on my bike," he said.

We transferred to the dirtiest, saddest old hulk I had ever set eyes upon. Tattered awnings made of flour bags covered the foredeck, and black tarpaulins concealed the stern. She was sixty foot long, with a square stern and a stubby black funnel poking out of the wheelhouse — or so it seemed. What looked like a canvas-sided armchair, without legs, stuck out over the rudder; this was the toilet. There was an overpowering stench of diesel fumes.

Blockade-runner MF 275 was under the command of Captain Ling, a makeshift replacement for the previous skipper, who had wisely left while the ship still floated. Captain Ling had never navigated beyond the Gulf of Siam, but what he lacked in experience he made up for in ingenuity. He relied upon an old school atlas and ruler for information, and on opium for inspiration.

"Welcome," said Mister Willi, avoiding my eye, "aboard the Happy Dragon."

"Good luck," shouted Mr. Bowers from the departing *prahu,* one hand firmly gripping the white bicycle and with the other waving his banjo. "You'll need it."

22

The Diesel Develops a Cough

WE SAILED AWAY from Sandakan to the strains of Harry Belafonte singing "Cordelia Browne." The sea bubbled beneath our black hull, the awnings flapped wildly in the mild evening breeze, and Mister Willi changed the record. As the sun slipped into the purpling ocean, Frank Sinatra voiced some fashionable lament. I've forgotten the title now but I can never listen to Mr. Sinatra without feeling again that breathless sense of freedom from responsibility that comes with voyaging into a strange sea. MF 275 lacked the more usual conveniences but her captain had loaded up with goods that were certain to fetch a small fortune in the volcanic islands that sprinkle the waters around Celebes. And the most popular items in his illicit cargo were battery-driven Japanese record players and the latest American song hits. Even Radio Permesta had been infected, and the rebel broadcasting station in Celebes arranged to give us the all-clear to land at Inobonto with a mouth-organ rendition of "I Got Plenty o' Nuttin'" — without, unfortunately, Mr. Sinatra. For the purpose of receiving that signal, Mister Willi now erected the telescopic aerial of the Zenith Trans-Oceanic that I had nursed so carefully all the way from Hong Kong.

It is at this point that truth does not become stranger than fiction. The perfect narrative should lead us now to a climactic description of dramatic events in the beleaguered garrisons of the

Permesta rebels. The dull reality is that right up until the very end, my brief experience with the rebels was to be one of teeth-gnashing frustration.

We were unable to receive "I Got Plenty o' Nuttin'" on our first night out. We were not able to get Radio Permesta at all. Instead the crew of seven men gathered under the swinging kerosene lamp slung forward of the "bridge" — a wooden hut rather like an old-fashioned bathing cabin. They seemed to be arguing with Captain Ling about navigational matters. "Some of them want to stop at one of the islands to sell a few articles," Mister Willi explained. It seemed a casual approach to war.

It seemed even more casual when Mister Willi, wearing a falsely bright expression, said the crew was worried about the dangers of "crossing with foreigners."

"You mean, *we're* dangerous?" Jim sounded incredulous, as well he might. Nobody could have seemed less sinister that evening than the NBC's Far East correspondent in bathing trunks and an old shirt, a sweatband tied around his forehead, his bare feet so dirt-ingrained that already they were turning the same mahogany color as the splintered deck.

"They mean, it's dangerous if they're caught with you on board," Mister Willi said hastily. "They say the Djakarta government will know about you and will try to sink this ship."

"If it doesn't sink first," said Jim. "Jeeze, did we have to come all the way out here to find this out?"

But we sailed on, the vessel shuddering now as it hit the heavy swells of open sea. An old German diesel drove us forward at a speed charitably estimated at four knots. Each time the stern lifted out of the water, the propeller shaft rattled as if it would tear the hull apart. Yet it was a quiet night on a quiet ocean. We could hear the slap of porpoises playing around us and the occasional thud of a flying fish as it struck the mizzensail, a torn piece of canvas that flapped forlornly in the stern to steady our course.

Whatever private fears haunted the crew, the men were hospitable to a fault. Under the patched awning on the foredeck they erected two army cots for Jim and myself. Cans of beer were served, fresh from the slabs of ice we had seen dumped earlier into the holds. From the galley, where the Bugi cook was trapped in hot diesel fumes from below, rice arrived by the bowlful. We squatted crosslegged in a circle, a mixture of races, each with our separate thoughts, caught in an amiable communion. Before us lay 400 miles of water, an unpredictable sea veiled in the legends of sudden disaster, and the strange tentacled island of violent volcanoes where we had every reason to suppose we should be shortly welcomed by bands of guerrillas.

Before turning in, Jim and I dangled our feet over the bows, watching the phosphorescence twinkle under the shuddering hull. We recalled similar voyages and agreed that a millionaire's life was nothing compared with this. "And to think we get paid for it," said Jim.

By four in the morning, we were less sure about the pleasures and privileges of the nomadic life. The trouble was the cots, so generously donated. They were made in Hong Kong and designed for the slender, light frames of the Chinese. Mine was first to cave in. I awoke, aware of a sinking feeling and an ominous ripping of fabric. A moment later Jim, on the other side of the hatch cover, turned in his cot and subsided through it with even greater force. Mine had ripped just enough to place me a little below the plimsoll line. I could still see around me. Jim had vanished into the folds of his sleeping bag, his rear end resting on the abrasive deck. We spent the rest of the voyage creased between the wooden frames of the cots, assuring the anxious crew that all was bliss indeed. They had provided the cots at no little cost to themselves and we hated to hurt their feelings.

Scarves of mist covered the morning horizon. The diesel had developed a cough. Our forward motion was perceptible, but only just. I spent a large part of the day on my stomach, head protruding over the side, watching the jungles of coral passing far below. Once — and how very long ago it all seemed now — I had swum down among such corals. Remembering that other expedition, and the Japanese seaweed collectors who had dived with us to the sea's bottom, I wondered about Jana. She had known this underwater world too.

"What happened to her?" I asked Mister Willi during our *al fresco* lunch. He grinned. "She has been in Celebes for two months. You will be seeing her there."

The whole day passed in a strange mood of reminiscence. The sun blazed down. The ocean rose and fell beneath us. Nothing broke its calm surface. Once a plane passed high overhead and Captain Ling broke out the red and white flag of the Indonesian Republic. We played cards in sleepy slow motion, or trailed lines over the stern in the hope of snaring a mackerel.

Another night passed. Mister Willi tried again to tune in Radio Permesta. There were fresh consultations over the school atlas. The engineer came up from the inferno of the ailing diesel, with what I thought was a shifty look in his eye. But during the night we picked up a little speed. Shortly before dawn, wrestling with our cots, we heard what seemed to be the distant rumble of thunder. A light winked on the horizon ahead.

At noon on the second day Captain Ling lowered the Indonesian flag. We still had the sea to ourselves. Junior, the cook, caught a steel-blue mackerel — at least, we identified it as such, although he called it by the local name: *tenggeri*. Three more were caught in quick succession. Junior gutted them and cut the flesh into strips, which he handed round. Feeling a little heroic, like mariners adrift on a raft, Jim and I chewed on the succulent fish. It was raw, but fresh and juicy, and the strips vanished down our parched and grateful throats. Once again, we congratulated each other. What Wall Street tycoon, we asked, could hope to command a more satisfying meal?

We were in the middle of a game of *vingt-et-un* when Captain Ling called us into his chartroom (if that is not too elegant a word). Could either one of us use a sextant? I had a vague memory of learning to shoot the sun as a very green sub-lieutenant. Jim had spent long months on a troop transport in the Pacific. Neither of us felt qualified to help Captain Ling in his obvious extremity. Mister Willi joined us, and we bent our heads over the little atlas.

"Where does he think we are?" Jim shot me a glance of utter incredulity.

Mister Willi cleared his throat. "Here." He put a finger delicately on a point somewhat to the south of the Philippines.

"That's impossible." Jim frowned at the greasy page. "We'd have to travel backwards to get there."

Junior rapped urgently at the door. With a look of unexpected relief, the captain abandoned us. Later, looking up from our deliberations, we glimpsed him in agitated conversation with the cook.

"I don't think anybody knows where we're going," said Jim, after a lengthy pause. We both turned accusing stares on Mister Willi.

"Well." He fumbled for a cigarette. "You see, it was hard to find a boat that would take you."

Captain Ling returned to our little circle of lamplight and ignorance. MF 275 plodded sturdily onward, to God-knew-where. He spoke gruffly to Mister Willi.

"There is an island near here called Siau," he said. "That is the opinion of the engineer. We could —" He paused, looking at us hopefully. "We could stop there and — er, ask directions."

"Whose side are the islanders on?" demanded Jim Robinson, looking stern for the first time in this long and trying voyage.

"Ours." Mister Willi dragged forth a large flag, yellow with a big black P in the middle, as proof. "This is the Permesta flag. We will fly it."

"Hang on a moment." Jim and I withdrew for a hurried consultation. Siau was one of the islands that belonged to the Indonesian Republic. Probably the crew had all along planned to go there. Its inhabitants would pay well for the cargo we carried. We came back, resolution shining in our faces. "No," we said. "We must not stop at Siau."

Captain Ling nodded his head morosely, without waiting for the translation. Mister Willi said: "I am thinking in any case the engines are not working properly."

It had been an indeterminate but ominous discussion. We dispersed, Captain Ling to his ruminations at the wheel, Junior to his galley, Mister Willi to brood in the boxlike arrangement overhanging the stern.

The sun had baked all our brains that day, and a cloud of indecision veiled our little vessel. The evening meal was conducted in an atmosphere of resolute comradeship. There was no question, however, that we had frustrated some deeper Bugi design.

There was still a bottle of Johnny Walker's Red Label in the stores. Under the mellowing influence of good scotch, tossed back raw, the Bugis unfolded a little. They were not, in the ordinary course of business, merely couriers for the rebels. Nor were they, in any way at all, friendly with the Indonesian central government. They were, they said with embarrassed smiles, in business for themselves. And it was a necessary part of this business that they should call at the island of Siau.

Jim and I were in full agreement that Siau should not be on the itinerary. It was more than likely that Djakarta's troops were in occupation. The Bugis denied this. They had relatives on the tiny island. To this we replied that they could always call there on the way home from Inobonto. The argument went on, interminable, mangled in translation.

At about two in the morning, the engines stopped.

The engineer joined us on deck, wiping his hands with a rag, a bent and forbidding figure in the shallow moonlight. The diesel had broken down, irrevocably, beyond doubt, perhaps forever. He crouched facing us and contemplated his bony knees, squatting with feet tucked under his buttocks, hands dangling. MF 275 rocked gently in a silence profound.

Mister Willi joined our doleful group. "We will have to go back."

"Can't. The engines have quit."

Mister Willi stole a nervous glance in our direction. "Perhaps, if we are turning around, they will work again."

Anything was better than lying here waiting, for all we knew, to be picked up by an Indonesian patrol. "What's a Wall Street tycoon got that we haven't?" Jim jeered.

By first light we were chugging gently home.

It may be that Bugis have second sight. Their determination not to continue with the voyage, despite all the diverting palaver about Siau, stemmed chiefly from a real fear of approaching the Celebes coast. Days later, we discovered how right they were.

"Indonesian warships appeared off Inobonto on the night you were due to arrive," Doctor Sumitro told us. "They bombarded the coast. In the morning, Indonesian fighter-bombers attacked from the air. Great damage was caused. Three rebel boats were sunk. You were lucky."

We were talking once again on neutral soil. Doctor Sumitro listed the defeats suffered at the hands of the central government forces. Jim Robinson listened impatiently. "But you can't go on like this," he finally broke in. "This is causing havoc to the economy. You're giving President Sukarno every excuse to build up his armed forces. And you're not getting anywhere."

"We shall outlive Sukarno," said the rebel leader. "We must continue to fight; to stick to our principles."

"What principles? You've got fanatics for allies — the Darul Islam — the Chinese Nationalists. What great cause do they represent?"

Doctor Sumitro folded his hands, his eyes sunk deeper, the hollows under the cheekbones more pronounced. "I know. I know. We cannot pretend to pick and choose, however. Some day the democracies will wake up and understand what it was we tried to do. It will be too late then. There *cannot* be any compromise with principles, so far as Sukarno's regime is concerned. And so we must fight with any weapons we can find.

"There was a time when we had the support of the United States Seventh Fleet. But then the United States opposed us, and said we were not much better than bandits. It became a struggle between Pearl Harbor and the Pentagon." He turned the phrase over on his tongue, relishing the sound of it. "Yes. It was Pearl Harbor against the Pentagon."

Jana arrived a month later in Hong Kong. She looked very fit, very lean — and very dirty. Her hair had been cropped short, like the glossy feathers on a raven's head.

She had been at Inobonto when the central government raided the coastal village.

"It was over very quickly. They landed Djakarta troops after the bombardment. All the villagers had gone into the hills. The troops wore the arm flash of the Suliwangi — the most famous regiment. I was caught and put on a troop transport for Java."

How had she escaped?

She shrugged. "We are not a bitter people. The soldiers took away many citizens suspected of helping the rebels. The local magistrate. Many Chinese shopkeepers." She lifted her shoulders. "It was a long voyage. Everyone was very bored. The colonel was lonely. When we reached Djakarta I was no longer a prisoner." She smiled defiantly.

I asked Jana if she thought the rebellion had a chance still. "Yes," she said. "In some places. But you see, many people were becoming angry with the rebels. We had little money. We lived off the land, and became a burden on the peasants. A few months ago, for instance, you would have had no difficulty in sailing to Celebes. Now, many of the seamen have turned against us, or they've become frightened to help us, because they say we bring them only trouble."

I mentioned Mr. Kan and his boat-building endeavors. She wrinkled her nose. "He works for the Asian Anti-Communist League. It's one of those movements that creates opposition without meaning to. The league is based in Formosa and tries to recruit people in Korea and south Vietnam. But it won't work. We ought not to be mixed up with such people."

Jana had come to Hong Kong to meet rebel agents who were organizing the shipment of arms from Formosa. She telephoned the house one evening. Could my wife and I have dinner? We went to an address near the university. It was a small, austerely furnished apartment. There, his chubby face wreathed in smiles, was the same Jojo who had sailed ahead of us with such confidence from Sandakan.

Once again we were plunged into the rebel world of intrigue. A Nationalist ship would be arriving off Hong Kong waters shortly. Jojo and the girl were boarding her, to return to the Permesta region. Did I wish to go? Firmly, a little reluctantly, I declined.

We invited them, the following Sunday, to sail with us. We kept a small motorized junk in the Chinese fishing port of Aberdeen, and they met us at the mooring. It was a lovely autumn day. We picnicked on Lantau Island, and talked about Indonesia.

"We are too poetic. There is our fault. As a people, we are too poetic," said Jojo, sprawled in the sand.

"How do you mean — too poetic? Can any of us afford not to be poetic?"

"I am thinking poetry is what makes men civilized. But poetry may also make men too gentle or perhaps kind to a point of silliness."

Jana interrupted. "Are we a silly people, then?"

Jojo shook his head doubtfully. "No, we are not silly by ourselves. We sing. We laugh. We are being blessed with a rich country. We are not having to struggle and fight. To be happy is not silliness.

"It is that we are silly before others. The Dutch have come to our islands. Not the Dutch I have known in Amsterdam who are sometimes poets too. The other Dutch. Practical men. Builders, explorers, sailors. They were making things, and always looking for more and more money. They did not stop to dream or dance with us. We were not able to fight them or resist their greediness. Now, is it more civilized to be a man who is making money and building things? Or to be a poet?"

I said perhaps the ideal combination was to be both.

Jana let a handful of sand run between her fingers. "I under-

stand you, Jojo. It is not only the Dutch who were the strong
knife cutting through the soft flesh of the Indonesian mango.
This is the story of all men." She glanced up at me, speaking
carefully, not wishing to hurt any of our feelings. "The white
man thinks he is superior to us because he confuses civilized
living with the endless construction of material things. He must
keep on building and he thinks anyone who spends time in simply
enjoying life is backward.

"The white man has an unfair advantage in the argument.
Being practical, he builds guns and swords better than ours. And
beating us with these weapons, he persuades himself that his
civilization is better than ours." She gave Jojo an encouraging
smile. "The white man will keep on building and destroying until
he smashes everything he has."

Jojo looked even more gloomy. "You are forgetting that
white men have used their most destructive weapons against
Asians. If one day the white men must blow everything up, we
shall be included."

I sat back. "Would you say the Japanese were poets and
dreamers?"

"No," said Jana sharply. "They also are infected with this
desire to create large material achievements. They conquered
us and they were brutal beyond anything the white man did.
But do not forget they were once an artistic race and respected
the creative imagination above all. Then they learned, earlier
than we did, that they could not survive western technology
unless they learned to compete with it. This is the same with
China. The Chinese have placed their scholars, their artists and
writers and musicians, above all other professions. And what
happened? The West sent its men of action to destroy their
civilization. Now they are hurrying to catch up."

There were flaws in the argument. Yet it had become a popular Asian view that in the struggle for survival between different branches of the human family, the men of action pushed everyone else to the wall.

Jojo said, nodding in my direction: "You have nothing in your heart to answer us." Before I could interrupt, he said, "We Indonesians are not good fighters. It is not our way. But you are seeing what is happening to us? We are losing *our* civilization. We must become brutal, like you."

I said, "Well, if you mean all of us in the West, we're not being brutal enough right now, are we? Your own rebel leaders complain that we don't take the conflict in Asia seriously enough. We seem to be condemned, whatever we do."

We sailed back across the channel as dusk fell. The sky above Hong Kong was bright with the reflected lights of the city. Ahead, against the bulk of Mount Davis, a string of lights bobbed gently on the water. The Chinese shrimpboats were out.

Jana, curled up in the stern, said, "Perhaps the pendulum is swinging the other way. You have had your revolutions in the West. Now it's our turn. You are the ones who have become soft and poetic."

My wife, sensing the new line of argument, said, "No. I don't think we're soft. We've just become guilt-ridden. The colonial past weighs on our conscience."

Jana sighed. "It's time you forgot your consciences then. In a few more years, Indonesia will be a powerful nation in Asia, with her own colonialist ambitions."

We sailed through the shrimpboats, their bobbing lights hung out on bamboo poles. There were dozens of the small craft strung out like glowworms, constellating the darkness with hissing pressure lamps. We passed close to one of the sampans, its brilliant lights illuminating a young girl pushing and pulling at the *yulah* sculling oar to keep the boat pointed up into the whispering waves. The waves crested under the tossing lanterns and turned bright green in the pools of light, then expired in a sigh of foam. The wildly swinging lanterns made grotesque shadows and the girl at the oar rose high above them and then shrank from sight behind the next wave. We were surrounded by the tossing boats, black figures swaying in their sterns like dancers in a ritual festival.

Now the land smells came drifting on the wind; drying seaweed and gasoline and fishnets and charcoal fires. I lay with an arm stretched along the tiller, guiding the junk into the Aberdeen fairway. The big junks ahead prodded the sky with their tall masts, solid ranks of ocean-going vessels hanging a lattice of masts and rigging against the town's glow. A diesel-powered deep-sea trawler thundered past, a dog barking in the bows, its wash rocking our lighter craft.

Jana stood in the after well, staring ahead, one hand on the old-fashioned bulb horn we kept lashed above the small cabin. She began sounding the horn, frightening the eggboat girls out of our path. The girls fishtailed their cockleshells between the immense rudders of the high Fukien junks crowding the middle channel. The horn made a noise like an angry bull elephant.

Jana began to laugh, squeezing the huge horn and waving to the Chinese families crowded in the gaping holds of the big junks. The old women shouted loud vulgarities back at her, cheerful obscenities which in Chinese were not meant offensively. I suppose we all caught the same carnival atmosphere, loving these people and the noise they made, relishing their energy and good spirits and love of activity in conditions of hardship and danger.

"What will you do now?" I asked Jojo. "After you return to Permesta?"

He squatted beside me, studying his cigarette glowing in the darkness. "I am not sure," he said. "But even if our leaders surrender, I cannot. I will stay, and see what can be done."

I throttled back the motor, dodging the stern of a junk, turning into one of the channels between the big moored vessels, letting the flood tide carry us across the narrow entrance so that we missed the jutting spars and rudders. We came alongside a wharf and I cut the outboard. In the sudden silence Jana's voice was very clear. "Doctor Sumitro is right," she said. "The weak ones will surrender. The rest of us will have to hide in the hills for a long long time, nursing our strength."

The Indonesians always did have a great sense of theater.

23

"Design of Darkness . . ."

IT IS HARD to exaggerate the lengths to which the Sukarno government now went to suppress voices of dissent at home and to prevent the publication abroad of reports on the rebellion.

Inside Indonesia the brave young intellectuals who contributed to a lively and independent press had all gone. Their leader was Mochtar Lubis, the editor of *Indonesia Raya*, whose arrest for alleged treason I have already mentioned. He was removed from jail and placed under house arrest, where he remained incommunicado. (He was released in April, 1961, when he reaffirmed his devotion to the principles of press freedom; whereupon he was thrown back into a military prison.) Lubis and the bright young men around him launched their newspapers in the early years of the republic, with the help of a government that respected and valued their patriotic desires to expose misrule and corruption before these evils established a pattern. One by one they were forced out of journalism.

Our own aborted expedition had repercussions out of all proportion to its signifiance. In New York the National Broadcasting Company heard with characteristic calm an Indonesian protest against Jim Robinson's interest in the rebellion. The Indonesian ambassador to Canada, Dr. L. N. Palar, who often doubled as leader of his country's delegation at the United Nations, flew to Toronto to deliver a personal denunciation of me. He accused me of playing a propaganda role for the rebels. When the editor and publisher of the *Globe & Mail*, Oakley Dalgleish, suggested that I be allowed to restate the other side's case from Djakarta, he was told that the Indonesian government could not be responsible for protecting me "from the fury of the people."

I had always believed that the western press had a special responsibility in reporting the difficult early stages of nationhood among the new states. There had been a time when Indonesian government newspapers reprinted my reports on that country's progress. But those were days when, as a foreigner, you were careful of local sensitivities. You acknowledged the fact that the new countries were emerging with only a handful of educated men and women equipped to share between them the burdens of leadership; and you saw some of these young people undertaking the vital job of establishing a vigilant domestic press. You trod carefully, knowing that the local journalists would suffer for your own indiscretions.

But when, as in some other Afro-Asian states, what started as a fight against poverty and ignorance deteriorated into a damaging power struggle among leaders, and when the local editors and writers began to disappear and the voices of dissent to be suppressed, then the western press became the only outlet for rebellious spirits to air their views. This, anyway, was how one justified the frank reporting of conditions in Indonesia after men like Lubis had gone to jail.

It was not long before I was withdrawn from the Far East. When I caught up with first-hand news on Indonesia again, it was in the most unlikely circumstances. Meanwhile, the statement of 81 Communist Parties meeting in Moscow in December, 1960, drew attention to a new region of political conflict: Oceania. This was the region dominated by the Indonesian Republic and it included Australia and much of the south Pacific.

It was hard to convince anybody in 1960 that Sukarno's Indonesia would be the means of Moscow's penetration of Oceania. Yet within two more years Sukarno's forces were the most powerful in Oceania, and they were controlled by Moscow. Sukarno's troops were in west New Guinea and suddenly there was alarm in Australia. Much if not all of Indonesia's foreign policy was dictated by Aidit of the Partei Kommunist Indonesie, which suddenly campaigned to prevent the formation of a free and prosperous alliance: Malaysia. The rebel network had been infiltrated, and by the end of 1962 it was supplying military intelligence to the communists from the rebel bases in British-administered areas, including Sandakan.

How could all this happen, so quickly and unexpectedly that by 1963 the Australians were worrying about an Indonesian grab for territory under their control, and the British prepared to defend parts of Borneo against Indonesian attack? How were the British caught napping by a revolt at the end of 1962 in their protectorate of Brunei, when the rebels had been training in Indonesian military camps for months ahead, wearing the uniform of the self-styled North Borneo National Army?

Where, above all, was the evidence of conflict between Moscow and Peking? This split was caused by a difference of ideological approach to world revolution. The Russians thought priority should be given to disarmament, so that money could be released for economic aid and the peaceful encouragement toward communism of the underdeveloped countries. China said publicly this was a foolish proposition; the military strength of the communist camp came first. Yet when it came to practical decisions in an area clearly regarded as highly strategic, the Sino-Soviet alliance seemed to work effectively. What had happened to all those pious Russian arguments while the Indonesian air force was acquiring its ten TU-16 jet bombers, its twenty Il-28's and forty MIG-15's and MIG-17's? All the doctrinal differences in the world failed to stop the supply to the Indonesian Navy of eight destroyers, fourteen motor torpedo-boats, thirty gunboats and six submarines — all made in communist states. The unified Indonesian services command had $600 million of Soviet credits on which to draw by the end of 1962; it was taking delivery of the first of several battle cruisers; ground-to-air missiles were being acquired; and half the Indonesian budget was committed to defense expenditures at a time of economic difficulty.

The economic picture was so bad that Sukarno relied on foreign aid to keep solvent — and here the communist pretense of disinterested assistance played its part. The Indonesian communists urged more and bigger military expenditures — to crush the rebels, to "liberate" neighboring territories — until the country could avert bankruptcy only by going more heavily into debt abroad. Both sides in the cold war lent him more than enough to spark the economy. But only one side, the Russian, was ruthless enough to prop up Sukarno in return for Sukarno's obedience. He knew the West dared not threaten his destruction because there were too many fair-minded westerners who would rush to his defense.

And this was where the West had come unstuck. The liberal conscience that was largely responsible for the peaceful transfer of authority to many colonies was also inhibiting action against the dark forces gathering around Sukarno. It was blind to the practical benefits of enlightened colonial rule. It neglected the new imperialism of China in Tibet, of India in the Naga hills, of Indonesia in — for example — west New Guinea.

The last was a classic. In the 1950's, a new breed of dedicated young Dutch administrators went to west New Guinea. They saw a chance to redeem Dutch prestige. They went with little hope of commercial gain. The island was an impenetrable tropical land, desperately poor in natural resources, populated by people who sometimes hunted for human heads and seldom knew the use of the wheel or of iron. To educate these people and provide the foundation of public welfare, the Dutch began to spend $30 million a year in a long-term program of development.

By 1962 the Dutch were about to be driven from west New Guinea, victims of a combined military and diplomatic operation conducted by Sukarno's skillful advisers. This began in January, when another attempt was made to kill Sukarno with a grenade. The incident occurred in Celebes. The rebels were blamed. The extensive rural organization of the communist PKI stirred up renewed outcries against the rebels as pawns of Dutch and neo-colonialist forces. A New Guinea invasion force, then assembling in Celebes under the code name Operation Mandala, made threatening moves against the Dutch bases in New Guinea. By this time the West was so alarmed by the prospect of conflict ending in a communist-backed Indonesian victory that pressure was put upon the Dutch to withdraw. Yet only eight years earlier, the Australian minister for external affairs, Sir Percy Spender, had said, "Indonesia has no claim on New Guinea, which is the very key to Australian defense."

But let us be fair. For if at times an excess of fair-mindedness has benefited the enemies of independent thought, it would be a disabling and grotesque consequence of emotional anticommunism if the West — pioneers of tolerance — came to appear intolerant of unpalatable truths.

Sukarno's claim was based on the 1946 agreement that gave sovereignty over "the whole territory of the Netherlands Indies." The Dutch took advantage of a treaty loophole providing for "special arrangements" in regions unwilling to join the Indonesian union; and they retained their New Guinea holdings on the basis that Papuans were ethnically, linguistically and religiously different from the Indonesians.* They also argued that New Guinea would provide haven for 200,000 Eurasians whose lives under Sukarno were being made miserable.

Indonesia won overwhelming Asian support in the United Nations for the rejection of Dutch pleas for Papuan self-determination. The Dutch offered to transfer their own powers to an international authority under the United Nations, but this was also defeated by the Asian United Nations vote. At this stage, Dutch businessmen began to bemoan the cost of the dispute: the loss of some $1.6 billion in Indonesia itself through confiscated industries, plus public humiliations and the expense of the New Guinea garrisons. Under pressures at home and from abroad, the Netherlands government offered to negotiate for a peaceful settlement without preconditions and in the presence of a third party.

This gave Sukarno the opportunity to wave a big stick that he knew it was unlikely he would use. He issued the command for the "liberation" of west New Guinea, crying, "We were born in flames of revolution. . . . We are not a nation of beggars but a nation of fighters."

Nobody called his bluff. He had an invasion force that would face grave difficulties in crossing some 200 miles of open sea, but he never had to risk it. His battle was being won in the United Nations, whose charter (Article 24) places primary responsibility for peace on the Security Council. An Indonesian military attack therefore would be followed by an appeal to the Security Council. There, any proposal unacceptable to Indonesia would be vetoed by the Soviet Union, which had already

---

* The Indonesian claim was put forward in the 1949 Round Table negotiations. In Article 2 of the Transfer of Sovereignty it was declared that the *status quo* of the Residency of New Guinea would be maintained with the stipulation that within a year the question of political status would be determined through negotiation. But it subsequently appeared to the Indonesians that the Dutch were stalling.

given Sukarno military and moral support. If the issue were transferred to the General Assembly, Indonesia had command of a third of the votes — enough to block a Dutch appeal. With such diplomatic advantages on his side, Sukarno could afford his bombast. He whipped up nationwide excitement. Every civic and military organization proclaimed its readiness to fight. Lightning raids were made against Dutch territory, in the first of which Commodore Jos Sudarso, who was Indonesian deputy naval chief, lost his life.

The United States was in the unenviable position of attempting to tranquilize a situation which, if it developed into a Pacific war, would become (in Afro-Asian eyes) a "colonial" struggle, with the Sino-Soviet bloc on the side of the underdogs. A secret conference, which the United States had arranged after long and patient effort, collapsed in March, 1962, when the Indonesians insisted that the Dutch agree in advance to handing over the administration of west New Guinea. The Dutch refused. It was their only remaining bargaining point. The Indonesians walked out.

The Dutch inevitably had to agree, months later, to a formula allowing them a withdrawal that was not too hasty or humiliating. Indonesia would take control of the territory in May, 1963, and there would be a plebiscite in 1969. Recalling a similar "agreement" by which India promised a plebiscite in Kashmir that was never granted, it seemed clear that 700,000 Papuans were being abandoned to their fate.

The pity was that the Dutch, however belatedly, had drawn up a program utilizing the best available expertise to carry the Papuans through to self-government. That program went by the board. And within three months of the agreement awarded to Indonesia, Sukarno started a vigorous campaign for the Papuan right to self-determination to be withdrawn.

Now Australia had real cause for alarm. The postwar idea

of colonizing its eastern end of New Guinea and Papua became an embarrassment; Australia found itself one of the last colonial powers, offering Sukarno the temptation to step across the land frontier with the cry again of "Freedom!" Indonesian troops had gained entry into what was, geographically, a part of the Australian continent. For New Guinea, like an enormous kangaroo leap along the Australian northern seaboard, is part of the Sahul Shelf — a submarine extension of that continent.

Indonesian troops were "neutrals," but they represented the arrival of Sino-Soviet influence in Oceania, and within 100 miles of Australia. If these forces, armed and trained with the help of the Sino-Soviet bloc, had arrived on Australia's doorstep in their true communist colors, there would have been the most vigorous reaction. They did not. They came behind a man with a desperate appetite for power; a man like Fidel Castro of Cuba, whose egotistical demands made him putty in communist hands.

But unlike Castro, the Indonesian president did not alarm the West too much. Sukarno's chief value was that he commanded a large following in the Afro-Asian world and he could still talk in a manner that reassured western liberals. He was nevertheless a political and economic prisoner of Aidit and the PKI communists.

With Aidit's control over the trade unions, his influence behind seemingly nonpolitical pressure groups, his hold over sections of the armed forces and with two million dedicated members of the Party, it was possible to ease the country into large commitments with the Sino-Soviet bloc. Already Sukarno had been convinced of the need for a strong, centralized, authoritarian government to undertake economic planning. This required a powerful defense structure.

The cost of the antirebel and "liberate west New Guinea"

campaigns was crippling. As I write, the latest confirmable figures were those for 1961, when foreign exchange reserves had fallen from $300 million to about $10 million and external debt had risen from $200 million to $800 million. Foreign trade had fallen from the previous year's *surplus* of $350 million to a *deficit* of more than $400 million. The demand for troop transports for a possible invasion of New Guinea badly hurt inter-island sea traffic, although by this time the Indonesian National Shipping Line had more tonnage than its Dutch predecessor. The United States dollar, officially worth 44 rupiahs, was buying 350 rupiahs in the black market.

Sino-Soviet bloc aid became vital. And between 1956 and 1961, it totaled $1,250,000,000. Almost half of this was in the military credits. A bad trade picture was quickly exploited by China, which by 1961 was pumping goods on credit into Indonesia at the rate of six million dollars' worth a month and buying less than two million dollars' worth of Indonesian goods in return.

The speed with which Indonesia was being cut down to satellite status was not in any way reduced by western aid. We had put into Sukarno's bottomless pit very much larger amounts: out of a total of $2 billion received by Indonesia in external aid between 1950 and 1962, only 30 per cent came from the Sino-Soviet bloc. The United States alone had supplied $538 million in credits, technical assistance, grants and so on.

If there was any doubt about which side in the cold war now spoke through Sukarno, it should have been cleared up by early 1963, when, against the declarations of his own foreign minister that Indonesia "wished Malaya well" in its efforts to bring about a federation, Sukarno began to exert every effort to prevent such a development.

The communist motive was simple. The three million Malays

who lived in the state of Malaya enjoyed a per capita yearly income of $113. More than 70 million of their fellow Malays in Indonesia received only $40 per capita. Any intelligent Indonesian did not need to look far for the explanation, nor could he fail to draw other significant conclusions. The Malayan government, after independence, did not nationalize its rubber industries. Instead it combined realism with business flexibility. By so doing, it won the cooperation of men like Sir John Hay, who was perhaps the last of the *tusan besars* (the Big Sirs) and who was certainly one of the first western businessmen to make the transition from privileged colonialism to competitive free enterprise under the new welfare-minded government. Sir John developed new techniques to increase rubber yield. His research cost him a great deal of money, but he shared his knowledge with the official Malayan rubber research agency. As a result Malaya was, by 1961, supplying one third of the world's natural rubber. Twenty-five per cent of the nation's income came from this single source.

Indonesia, which had been the world's biggest supplier of natural rubber, nationalized its rubber plantations. It was displaced as the prime producer by Malaya.

This Malayan prosperity, the product of intelligent partnership between a socialist-minded new state and sensible western enterprise, made it possible to expand so that the last four parcels of the British Empire in Southeast Asia could be linked in the far-flung Federation of Malaysia. On the doorsteps of China and Indonesia, colonialism was dying in a way that frustrated communist plans. Without violence. Without ideological propaganda. Nobody had beaten drums for capitalism. The results would speak for themselves.

I was in Africa when I saw the evidence — for me final — that Sukarno's Indonesia was a formidable example of the way "neutrals" could be turned into effective weapons of Sino-Soviet strategy. Malaysia had by then become the main target of Radio Peking's vituperation. It was an experiment which could seriously undermine the Chinese crusade for militant communism in the underdeveloped countries. In December, 1962, a revolt was staged in Brunei by guerrillas armed and trained in Indonesian military camps, by jungle warfare experts including communist political agents. The Indonesian communist party held a congress to which Sukarno sent greetings. He acknowledged the large communist contribution in "smashing imperialism" and ended, "Go ahead! Go ahead! Let us go forward together to complete the Indonesian revolution!"

Then the campaign against Malaysia was carried into the diplomatic field. Ready and waiting as the propaganda vehicle was the Afro-Asian People's Solidarity Organization, with its headquarters in Cairo but with two thirds of its funds derived from Moscow and Peking. In the second week of February, 1963, the organization held its third conference in the newest of Africa's independent republics, Tanganyika.

There were some 400 delegates from more than sixty countries in Africa and Asia — the Soviet Union's white-faced representatives blandly declaring that they were Asian. The vast majority of these delegates came from communist states or represented communist parties. Many flew to Nairobi, the capital of Kenya, which was still a British colony. They planned to drive from there over 200 miles of rough road to the conference site in a school on the slopes of Mount Kilimanjaro.

The names of the delegates began appearing in the local papers as they arrived. Many were familiar. Some I had known. I chuckled to discover that Bintang Suradi, the deputy secretary general of the Indonesian communist party, far from calling himself Aidit's chief lieutenant, had claimed to be nothing more sinister than "the editor of an Indonesian literary magazine."

But I was a trifle less amused to find Mr. Abdullah Salim Mohammed describing himself as the minister of state in the "exile government of Brunei," because it was not so long ago that the same gentleman was carrying an Indonesian passport and pretending to be a rebel in Sandakan. His task now seemed to be to marshal Afro-Asian support for an attack (military, diplomatic and propaganda) against Malaysia to be led by Sukarno, whose "neutrality" would mask the true instigators — the communist leaders of Asia.

It was a pretty obvious maneuver. The self-styled Brunei leader would get the conferees to support a resolution condemning British occupation of territory in Borneo; and this would carry great weight if the issue came up in the United Nations through an outbreak of hostilities. Then, exactly the same politico-military defeat would be inflicted on the enemies of communism in Malaysia as had been inflicted upon the Dutch in New Guinea.

Driving myself down to the conference, I wondered how on earth the genuine African nationalists going to it would ever perceive this exploitation of their anticolonialist fervor. I was reminded of a verse by Robert Frost which offers a miniature example of active malevolence stalking the earth. The American poet had found a moth killed by a white spider. The white spider had captured its victim by hiding behind a white flower. But normally the flower's color was blue.

> *What had the flower to do with being white,*
> *The wayside blue and innocent heal-all?*
> *What brought the kindred spider to that height*
> *Then steered the white moth thither in the night?*
> *What but design of darkness to appall? —*
> *If design govern in a thing so small.**

* *Complete Poems of Robert Frost,* copyrighted by Robert Frost and Holt, Rinehart & Winston, Inc.

24

'Bye 'Bye Blackbirds

THE ROAD WAS MOSTLY red dirt, skirting the Nyiri Desert, winding through broad plains dotted with wild game. Soon after I had driven past the former detention camp for hard-core Mau Mau terrorists, the familiar scene appeared of figures attempting to repair a broken car.

"Better stop." My companion, the late Doug Willis of the BBC, stuck his head out through a window and waved encouragingly to a disconsolate group of Japanese standing beside an African chauffeur who quite clearly knew nothing about replacing a burst tire.

We stopped, helped the driver, and introduced ourselves. The Japanese were on their way to the Afro-Asian solidarity conference and looked hot, tired and bewildered. "Have some imperialist beer," we said to revive their spirits. An hour later we were all bowling happily to Tanganyika when the hired Japanese car broke down again. Again we helped change tires. Again we toasted each other in imperialist beer.

The road from Kenya to Tanganyika is littered with its victims and it was not surprising that the hired car suffered yet another flat. This time there was no spare. We finished the beer and took the Japanese delegation aboard my station wagon.

The leader was Toshio Tanaka, a member of the Japanese Diet, who carried in his little airline bag a large quantity of silk scarves imprinted with maps of the Far East displaying "aggressive imperialist American military bases." He planned to hand them round among the African delegates. I examined one of the scarves. It showed an aggressive American base in Borneo, where, to my certain knowledge, there was none.

"You don't believe this?" I asked Mr. Tanaka.

He nodded vigorously. "Yes, yes. It is needful to mobilize opinion of peoples everywhere to stop neo-colonialist schemes." His face a trifle red from beer and sun, glasses glinting, he wagged an indignant finger at me. Suddenly I remembered the gravestones in Labuan, the lingering hatred in Sandakan, and I was struck by the thought that Mr. Tanaka must find that his political beliefs conveniently coincided with Japan's reviving nationalism. I wondered if the commander of the Ninth Division, Australian Imperial Forces, on accepting the unconditional surrender of the Thirty-second Japanese Southern Army in Borneo, had foreseen this novel method of re-entry by a communist back door.

Mr. Tanaka turned out to be well informed about Borneo and Indonesia. He remembered very well how Sukarno had worked with Japanese forces there. He clucked his tongue regretfully upon recalling that Sutan Sjahrir ("not a very good prime minister and not tough enough as a socialist") had been jailed again for conspiring with the rebels.

My ears pricked up. Did Mr. Tanaka know much about the rebellion in Indonesia? He gave me a careful stare. Well, he said, it was well known that Doctor Sumitro was now working with that notorious warmongering alliance led by American imperialists — SEATO.

We deposited the Japanese at their hotel in Moshi, the site of the conference. It was a small prosperous township on the lower slopes of Kilimanjaro, once a week-end meeting place for German coffee growers, and now filled with the colorful robes and headdresses of visitors from other equally exotic lands. Among them were two delegations from Singapore and Malaya, come to express left-wing support for the new concept of a Malaysian federation. They were a bit worried. Somehow their reserved accommodation in Moshi had been taken over, and they were billeted fifty miles away at Arusha. That would hamper them in participating in the conference, wouldn't it? I said yes, indeed it would. Furthermore, they said, their names did not appear on the official revised list of delegates. Funnily enough, now they came to think about it, only one of their names had appeared on the very first list; that was Othman Wok from Kuala Lumpur, and inexplicably his name had now vanished too.

I had an uncomfortable feeling that many more inexplicable things would happen to Mr. Wok and his companions before the week was out.

Moshi is a Swahili word for fog, or smoke, and it soon became apparent that most delegates had little idea of the mechanics of such a conference. The operators were clearly the Russians and Chinese who, coming in large numbers directly from Moscow and Peking, overwhelmed the permanent secretariat of the organization, whose members were mostly from Cairo. The theme of the conference was the solidarity of the masses living in Africa and Asia and confronted with the wicked plots of western imperialism. Dozens of resolutions had been prepared, all paying tribute to the enlightened and peaceful significance of African and Asian ambitions, and flailing the West in the most violent language.

It seemed faintly comical at first. The head of the Russian delegation, in his opening speech, spoke of the white colonialists "in their pith helmets and cracking their whips." The Chinese hammered away at American imperialism, which, they said, had embarked on such a warmongering course that it was folly to speak of disarming now.

But was it really so funny? This performance was being

staged in Tanganyika, which had just won independence from British rule. The president, Julius Nyerere, had opened the conference with a speech setting forth his political philosophy. It boiled down to very much the same line of argument pursued by Sukarno. The one-party system was more efficient in bringing about rapid development; democracy was somehow unnatural — too sophisticated, in fact — for Africans for whom tribalism was the real basis of society.

The Chinese delegates nodded their heads approvingly, as well they might. A few years ago they had persuaded Sukarno that guided democracy was the right form of single-party government based upon that old Indonesian tradition of amicable village discussion. Now they had Nyerere convinced that such a system was suited to Africa because it was based on that old tribal tradition of amicable family discussion — or as Nyerere put it, familyhood.

However, the little president of Tanganyika went on to warn Africans against the colonialist ambitions of the richer countries on both sides of the cold war. There were, he said, socialist states capable of practicing the worst excesses of western imperialism. This was the one feeble attempt made to draw attention to the rapidly growing empires of Russia and China. By and large it was ignored. Only the head of the Chinese delegation referred to it. He agreed, he said, with Mr. Nyerere, who had given such a convincing description of western imperialism.

I was still inclined to find the show more comical than sinister. One of the three Russian ladies who had come to practice their fluent Swahili got locked in a toilet of the Livingston Hotel and was lucky that her cries for help (in Swahili) were understood by the Greek proprietor, because none of her neighbors spoke either Russian or Swahili. When the Russians found their translation headphones had been swiped one morning, they were told by a technician that the Chinese had taken them, whereupon the Chinese next day found all their headphone jacks were spiked. An African delegate presented himself at the hotel reception desk one morning holding a bedroom key.

"What number does this say?" he inquired.

"Forty-two," said the reception clerk.

"And who is in forty-two?" asked the African.

"Er —" running a finger down the register — "*you*, sir!"

"Exactly. And what color is my skin?"

"Er — black, sir."

"Exactly," said the African delegate, with triumph rising in his voice. "Now, can you tell me why I have just been to room number forty-two to find a pair of white feet sticking out from the bottom of my bed?"

Well, it was that kind of a conference. Confused. Overcrowded. Delegates getting into the wrong rooms, resolutions getting into the wrong hands, and only the Chinese looking as if they knew what they were about, as indeed they did. They took over the geography room of the school where the conference was held and filled it with duplicating machines. They moved into the biology room for their strategy meetings. They produced neat little signs to hang over the doors of the classrooms they had requisitioned — signs that said TECHNICAL COMMITTEE — PRIVATE — KEEP OUT.

On the second day I ran into Devan Nair, the former Malay communist mentioned earlier. As general secretary of the Singapore Afro-Asian Solidarity Committee he naturally expected to be heard. But somehow he could never gain admittance to the open sessions, nor could any of the Singapore and Malay delegates. Much of their time was spent being driven in ancient taxis over the bumpy roads between Moshi and their hotel in Arusha.

Mr. Nair said on the fifth day, "I'm going to have to issue a statement on behalf of our two delegations. The Chinese are preventing us from talking at all."

"How?"

"They've got the Japanese and the Indonesians to sponsor a resolution attacking Malaysia, and they've manipulated all the sessions of the credentials committee so that our application to be heard never gets considered."

On the sixth day Mr. Nair addressed a press conference. It was obvious, he said, that the communist Chinese were working through the Japanese and Indonesians to outmaneuver anyone opposing Peking's views. This was particularly the case where Malaysia was concerned. He and the other Singapore and Malay delegates had flown here to present the case for the Malaysia federation, but this was opposed by the Chinese, who had exploited the inexperience of other delegations to get their own way.

"I'm an anticolonialist who has suffered for it," said Mr. Nair. "I was five years in British jails in Singapore. I joined the communist party because it was the only way to defeat the British. And I assure you that the Malaysia concept is not a British neo-colonialist trick. It is an attempt to utilize all the good things left behind by the British — common public services, communications, developed resources, for the good of the people in all these adjoining territories."

He introduced some of the other delegates, for example Jek Yeun Thong, close confidant of the Singapore prime minister and treasurer of the ruling People's Action Party, "a man," said Mr. Nair, "who has also spent terms of imprisonment as a political detainee of the British."

None of this made the slightest difference to the conference. On the seventh day I found Jek Yeun Thong in the hotel lobby being verbally lashed by an African nationalist. "Nobody asked you to come here," said the African. "Why are you trying to break up the solidarity of this conference?"

Jek retreated, his black Chinese eyes hard with anger.

"What started that rumpus?" I asked Jek.

"I was handing these sheets out to the heads of delegations." He gave me one.

It was an appeal to be heard. "We represent a majority will," it said. "We have fought against British imperialism and have suffered for it. . . . We stand for socialism. . . . We came to call for non-interference in the internal affairs of the territories of the projected Federation of Malaysia . . . to show that the Federation would mean the liquidation of the last outposts of British colonialism in Southeast Asia.

"We came to show that foreign opponents of Malaysia are more interested in the oil of Brunei than in the eighty thousand people of that tiny Sultanate; and to prove that the so-called rebellion in Brunei was foreign-inspired. We came to warn that peace in Southeast Asia was seriously menaced, not because Malaysia was a neo-colonialist venture but because our neighbors of China and Indonesia who publicly profess their belief in peaceful coexistence are in fact entertaining neo-colonialist ambitions in Borneo."

It ended: "COMRADES, IF YOU WANT TO SAFEGUARD PEACE AND AFRO-ASIAN SOLIDARITY DO NOT RATIFY THE ANTI-MALAYSIAN RESOLUTION PUSHED THROUGH BY FORCES OUTSIDE MALAYSIA UNLESS YOU DESIRE THE BLOOD OF THE PEOPLE OF MALAYSIA ON YOUR CONSCIENCE."

None of this, of course, altered the course of events.

The anti-Malaysian revolution was submitted by the gentleman calling himself Brunei's exiled minister of state. It "fervently greeted the fighting Kalimantan [Borneo] people" and gave full support for the rebels. It appealed to Afro-Asian governments to support "the struggle of the people of North Kalimantan against any federation being intensively imposed by imperialists in cooperation with their agents and to recognize the newly proclaimed full independent state of North Kalimantan." It called for worldwide measures to prevent British troops from suppressing the new rebellion.

I drove back from Moshi a little staggered by the effontery of it all, and a little more astonished that so much nonsense could be swallowed by noncommunist delegates. Indonesia had become the "front" for communist ambitions and Indonesia had won the support of the conference, which approved the resolution, so that it could now justify on "moral" grounds a military attack and guerrilla warfare in British Borneo.

None of it made any sense. But then, these conferences seldom did. I remembered another Afro-Asian conference — one that attracted to it the representatives of Afro-Asian governments — the Bandung conference of 1955. We had giggled a bit at that one too. Few of us from the West took seriously the danger that this was the beginning of Indonesia's involvement with the communist bloc. But it was.

At that conference, Sukarno had said: "The voiceless ones have recovered their voices. Man gasps for morality and safety in a world of fear. . . . Do not be guided by these fears, because fear is an acid which etches men's actions into curious patterns. Be guided by hopes and determination, be guided by ideals and, yes, be guided by dreams."

There was a faithful echo of those sentiments in the speech by Tanganyika's president seven years later. Nyerere too had called for boldness and freedom from fear. He too had appealed to his countrymen to be guided by dreams. Would he, like Sukarno and like so many other great Afro-Asian leaders, then fall into the same trap of buying the cynical communist dream and forcibly "guide" his people into chasing it?

Behind the scenes at Moshi, while delegates passed their pious resolutions, there had been a great deal of unpublicized activity. There were uprisings to be supported in the remaining European colonies; saboteurs to be trained for the approaching guerrilla wars in South Africa, Portuguese Angola and Mozambique. These were the material foundations on which Russia and China could build; foundations of guns and violence directed against western stupidity.

Was it not, after all, rather stupid of the West to give only halfhearted support for Doctor Sumitro's rebellion? I knew now its fate. Most of the rebel leaders had returned meekly to Sukarno's fold. Even that Iron Man of revolution, Colonel Zulkifli Lubis, was back in Djakarta. On communist initiative, the Indonesian government had jailed forty opposition leaders, including the Masjumi party chief Mohammed Roem, on the grounds that they conspired to help the anti-Sukarno rebels.

The rebellion itself had been turned inside out. It had been infiltrated by Sukarno's men and members of the communist party, and its defectors had been persuaded to provide the fullest information about the rebel bases on British territory. Thus Sukarno and his foreign backers were made a present of invaluable details — discovered by experts in conspiracy — about British security methods, lines of communication and ability to patrol the pirate-infested sea lanes and the long jungle-choked frontier between British Borneo and Indonesia. This had made possible the uprising in Brunei, and it was sure to be followed by more guerrilla activity as the anti-Malaysia campaign continued along the well-tried path of military and diplomatic pressures.

It was tempting to argue that the West should have exerted its strength to make Doctor Sumitro's revolution a success. But

I remembered the advice of the socialist leader Sjahrir, before he was jailed. Yes, he had said. Communist techniques *are* dangerous. They *are* hard to counter. But unless Russia or China exerts direct military influence, communism can only succeed in certain conditions. These were poverty, industrial backwardness and feudalism. It was in our own interests to change those conditions quickly.

What about Indonesia today, however? Western aid seemed to be supporting a communist puppet. Certainly, it took strong nerves to stand by while a country was threatened by communist subversion; and we all knew now the danger of letting impatience and frustration provoke our direct intervention into would-be neutralist parts of the world. Nevertheless, you had to take note of what President Kennedy had called "the relentless struggle in every corner of the globe that goes far beyond the clash of armies or even nuclear armaments." Kennedy had described perfectly the conditions with which I had become familiar: "Subversion, infiltration, and a host of other tactics steadily advance, picking off vulnerable areas one by one in situations which do not permit our own armed intervention."

What was the answer? Surely not the kind of clumsy conspiratorial activities which marked Doctor Sumitro's rebellion. Yet some of the rebels had been worthy of help — a great number of them, when you came to think of it.

Perhaps it was necessary to remind ourselves that dismantling the old empires was not enough. The British, for instance, had done more than any other nation to end colonial rule. They had emancipated nine tenths of their former empire. Seldom had power been more gracefully conceded. Yet the ensuing good will had been quickly dissipated. Instead of following an American lead in an open-handed and frank approach to the new independent states, the British often tended to cling to past attitudes of superiority. Some of their policies, notably in Suez and Africa generally, had created a universal suspicion.

Some of this suspicion was unjustified. There were, for example, Americans who could hardly wait to ease Britain out of her colonies but who panicked when it seemed that communism would fill the vacuum. There were Americans who feared that Britain would find other means of pursuing an essentially imperialist role or who suspected the progressively minded anticolonialist Englishman of being a disguised communist. There were Britons who believed the United States was trying to take over their empire.

This mutual distrust seemed to paralyze the western nations, so that communists and their "fronts" marched breezily forward, gathering recruits among the underprivileged nations by directing their hostility against us "colonialists."

The damage we inflicted upon ourselves was illustrated by the fatal misunderstanding that arose between the Allies at the end of the Pacific war. General MacArthur had captured Dutch New Guinea but the territory was transferred from his command into that of Lord Louis Mountbatten, who wanted jurisdiction over all Indonesia in order to mount a major offensive that would retake Singapore and Malaya. MacArthur opposed this and repeatedly voiced the suspicion to President Roosevelt that the British had political and economic motives in wanting to break into the Indies.

Mountbatten has described how he asked for, and was promised, those intelligence files gathered by MacArthur's command. None materialized. MacArthur could not bring himself to pass on the vital information. For lack of it, although they finally did go into Java, the British misjudged completely the extent and quality of the Indonesian national movement. As we have seen, that little example of Anglo-American jealousy cost us dear.

There was no doubt in my mind that these bumbling rivalries were behind the messy disorganization that dogged the original rebellion. Long after the rebels had been taken over, as it were, by Sukarno, a well-known American gun-runner was still supplying weapons and ammunition to what he supposed were anticommunists. They were in fact the communist-sponsored North Borneo Nationalist Army.

The same confusion seemed to becloud the mind of the oldest and closest of American friends in the Far East, the government of the Philippines. It attacked the project for a Malaysian Federation on the grounds that this might open the floodgates to communism in the area. To make matters even worse, the Philippines laid claim to British North Borneo, which was to be a vital part of the federation, and refused — for a time at least — to accept the indignant cries from Malaya that these were actions most calculated to encourage and not to defeat communism.

Discussing this as we crossed the Tanganyika-Kenya border again, Willis and I began to chuckle. The rather hostile-looking African sentry grinned in sympathy and his face broadened into a toothy laugh so that soon we were all giggling together without much notion of why. I got out of the car and signed the frontier register and the African and I continued to smile and nod at one another, wrapped in a warm if uncomprehending bond of amiability.

Here was part of the answer, perhaps. Maybe we were all taking each other a bit too seriously. I thought of Jana and Auntie Emiria, neither of whom approached any enterprise — no matter how deadly its intent — without a generous smile in the direction of their enemies. But you couldn't lubricate international frictions with laughter all the time. I remembered the jailed editors, the humorless communists intent upon suppressing all the voices of dissent, and the men who had suffered and died in an ill-supported revolution against the dark suffocating forces symbolized by Sukarno.

If the West had neglected its greatest saving grace, a sense of humor, it had also ignored its two most important assets — freedom of speech and a sense of justice. This, surely, was one way in which western differences might be sunk in a common enterprise. Our concern should be with the denial of human rights everywhere; with the suppression of opposition parties and newspapers, preventive detention acts and the misuse of emergency powers. Already two organizations had sprung into being, each interested in just such matters, each supported by jurists and journalists in North America, Britain and western Europe; the movements known as Justice and Amnesty, both devoted to helping the oppressed in lands on both sides of the cold war. These were endeavors in the best tradition of nineteenth-century Britain, when opinion was constantly mobilized in favor of the oppressed peoples abroad.

At this late stage in Indonesia's reduction to the role of a communist stooge, it might seem ludicrous to speak of mobilizing western opinion against Sukarno's perilous adventures. Yet it was not entirely too late. Much more could have been done, for example, to inform the Afro-Asian peoples of the nature of the Malaysian experiment, which offered a new constructive partnership between economic planning and private western enterprise.

And far, far more might have been done to inform our public of the events that led to Indonesia emerging as an unfriendly world power. Few western newspapers bothered to take an abiding interest in that country's affairs. As a result, much was done and many promises were made in the name of Washington, London and The Hague that none of us knew about until it was too late. The rebels, let's face it, were an intolerable provocation with their obvious western connections.

Justice William O. Douglas had said: "The press with few exceptions gives no true account of forces at work in the world." He blamed this upon conservative newspaper owners and the fact that "money-makers have taken over the press." He added, "The people of the United States — the ones who could, if awakened, take up the challenge — are largely immobilized. Fears of communism are subtly transformed into fears of the unorthodox."

It would take some pretty unorthodox measures to frustrate Sukarno now, I reflected when I got home that night. The whole Malaysia concept had been an example of unorthodox, imaginative thinking in which the British had recruited the help of former communists.

I glanced at that day's *Tanganyika Standard*, a newspaper already anticipating President Nyerere's whims and fancies. The front page carried a report of the singular misfortune that befell the Kilimanjaro Blackbirds at Moshi.

The Blackbirds — the name was of their own choosing, and all of them were black as the ace of spades — had played in the Kilimanjaro Hotel throughout the conference. On the last night, in the middle of a Caribbean limbo dance, in walked the Kenya minister of communications, who took one look at the band and said, "Arrest them!" The minister, it turned out, owned all the instruments. He had bought them, drums and saxophones and trumpets and all, so that the impoverished Blackbirds could play at a political rally in his home town 500 miles away. The band had been known as the Mombasa Blackbirds. Then they ran away and became the Kilimanjaro Blackbirds of Moshi. The local jail, reported the *Tanganyika Standard*, now bulged with the runaway players and their silent instruments.

The headline on top said 'BYE 'BYE BLACKBIRDS. Elsewhere, a brief sardonic comment appeared. "All those words of vituperation against western colonialism, uttered at the Moshi conference, were cabled to Moscow and Peking and a score of other capitals," it noted. "The telecommunications carrying these denunciations were operated by Englishmen. The headmaster of the school where the conference took place was an Englishman. So was the Tanganyika government official who made reproductions of every speech to give the press. Who knows? Perhaps the conference itself was a neo-colonialist plot?"

There seemed some hope left, after all. I could think of no totalitarian state where a sense of humor had ever survived. Laughter seemed suddenly to be a very precious thing. I blessed the black African who had written the headline and his colleague, scarcely freed from the British yoke, who penned the comment.

And I wondered if the course of Indonesian history might have been altered by the eruption of an irreverent giggle or two.

Laughter was no less infectious than anger, or hatred, or the desire for revenge. All the Asian religions made some reference to the Buddhist theory of a moral chain of evil, which maintains that human nature makes us pass on to other people the evil which has been done to us. It seemed about time someone invented a moral chain of laughter that would roll and thunder through the darkest corners of men's minds, blowing away the dull doctrinaire suspicions and the malevolence, disintegrating the armor of national pride, tickling the solemn crusaders and maybe even tumbling a bird's nest or two from the beard of some forgotten rebel. The notion would have certainly raised a chuckle in Sandakan.

Bibliography

Asian Relations. Report of the Proceedings and Documentation of the First Asian Relations Conference, New Delhi, March–April, 1947 (New Delhi: Asian Relations Organization, 1948)

AZIZ, M. A. *Japan's Colonialism and Indonesia* (The Hague: Martinus Nijhoff, 1955)

BEEKMAN, D. A. *A Voyage to and from the Island of Borneo* (London: 1718)

BLUMBERGER, J. TH. Petrus *De Communistische Beweging in Neder-landsch-Indie* (Haarlem: 1935)

BONE, ROBERT C., JR. *The Dynamics of the Western New Guinea (Irian Barat) Problem* (Ithaca: Cornell University, 1958)

BOT, TH. H. *New Relations Between the Netherlands and Indonesia* (The Hague: 1951)

BRIERLEY, J. L. *The Law of Nations* (Oxford: Oxford University Press, 1949)

BROOKE, V. (RAJAH OF SARAWAK) *Expedition to Borneo* (J. R. Geographical Society, 1838)

——— *A Vindication of His Character & Proceedings* (London: 1853)

CHAUDRY, L. *The Indonesian Struggle* (Lahore: Feroz, 1950)

COAST, JOHN *Recruit to Revolution: Adventure and Politics in Indonesia* (London: Christophers, 1952)

COLIJN, H. *Koloniale Vraagstukken van Heden en Morgen* (Amsterdam: 1928)

DJAJADININGRAT, IDRUS NASIR *The Beginnings of the Indonesian-Dutch Negotiations and the Hoge Veluwe Talks* (Ithaca: Cornell University, Modern Indonesian Project, 1958)

DOBBY, E. H. G. *Southeast Asia* (London: University of London Press, 1950)

Eastern Archipelago Pilot, Vol. II (Hydrographic Department, British Admiralty, 1949)

ELSBREE, WILLARD H. *Japan's Role in South East Asian Nationalist Movements, 1940–45* (Cambridge: Harvard University Press, 1953)

EMERSON, RUPERT *Reflections on the Indonesian Case* (*World Politics*, Vol. 1 [1948])

—— *Representative Government in South East Asia* (Cambridge, Harvard University Press, 1955)

ENGERS, J. F. *Het Indonesische Vraagstuk en de Amerikanse Pres* (Leiden: 1946)

FURNIVALL, J. S. *Colonial Policy and Practice. A Comparative Study of Burma and Netherlands India* (London: Cambridge University Press, 1948)

GERBRANDY, P. S. *Indonesia* (London: Hutchinson, 1951)

HATTA, MOHAMMED *Legende en Realiteit rondom de Proclamatie van 17 Augustus. Verspeide Geschriften* (Djakarta: C. P. J. van der Peet, 1952)

HUNGER, F. W. T. *Federatieve Staatsbouw, een Vraagstuk Nederlandsch-Indie* (Amsterdam: 1928)

ISAACS, HAROLD R. *News from Indonesia* (New York: Republican Information Center, 1949)

JACOBY, ERICH H. *Agrarian Unrest In Southeast Asia* (New York: Columbia University Press, 1949)

KAHIN, GEORGE McT. *Indonesia, Major Government of Asia* (Ithaca: Cornell University Press, 1952)

—— *Nationalism and Revolution in Indonesia* (Ithaca: Cornell University Press, 1952)

LEIMENA, J. *The Dutch-Indonesian Conflict* (Djakarta: 1949)

LOGE AMM, J. H. A. *Het Straatsrecht Van Indonesie. Het Formele Systeem* (Bandung: 1954)

MOUNTBATTEN, VICE-ADMIRAL, FIRST EARL LOUIS OF BURMA *Report to the Combined Chiefs of Staff* (New York: Philosophical Library, 1951)

McVEY, RUTH T. *The Soviet View of the Indonesian Revolution* (Ithaca: Cornell University, Modern Indonesia Project, 1957)

MAO TSE-TUNG *Selected Writings*, Vols. I–IV (Peking, 1956)

MOSSMAN, JAMES *Rebels in Paradise: Indonesia's Civil War* (Oxford: Alden Press, 1961)

PREGER, W. *Dutch Administration in the Netherlands Indies* (Melbourne: Cheshire, 1944)

ROBEQUAIN, CHARLES *Malaya, Indonesia, Borneo and the Philippines* (London: Longmans, Green, 1954)

SASTROAMIDJOJO, USMAN *The Indonesian Struggle for Freedom* (Perth: 1948)

Schiller, A. Arthur *The Formation of Federal Indonesia 1945–49* (The Hague: W. Van Hoeve, 1955)

Sjahrir, Soetan *Out of Exile* (New York: John Day, 1949)

Talbot, Phillips (ed.) *South Asia in the World Today* (Chicago: University of Chicago Press, 1950)

Taylor, Alistair M. *Indonesian Independence and the U.N.* (Ithaca: Cornell University Press, 1960)

Tervooren, E. P. M. *Statenopvolging en de Financiele Verplichtingen van Indonesie* (The Hague: Martinus Nijhoff, 1957)

Thayer, Philip W. (ed.) *Southeast Asia in the Coming World* (Baltimore: Johns Hopkins Press, 1953)

Ubani, B. A., Durrano, O., and Moein, M. *The Indonesian Struggle for Independence* (Bombay: 1946)

Vandenbosch, Amry *The Dutch East Indies* (Berkeley: University of California Press, 1941)

—— *Dutch Foreign Policy since 1815* (The Hague: Martinus Nijhoff, 1959)

Van Helsdingen, W. H. (ed.) *De Plaats van Nederlandsch-Indie in het Koninkrijk, Stemmen van Overzee* (Leiden: 1946)

——, with Hoogenberk, H. (eds.) *Mission Interrupted, the Dutch in the East Indies and Their Work in the Twentieth Century* (Amsterdam: 1945)

Westerling, Raymond "Turk" *Challenge to Terror* (London: William Kimber, 1952)

Index